To Don Revie
who changed the direction
of my life

ACKNOWLEDGEMENTS

I should like to thank my wife Pat, whose encouragement in the preparation of this book reflects thirty-eight years of happy married life.

I should also like to thank all the players who've played with me and for me, for making my career in football such a rewarding one.

Finally, I should like to acknowledge the co-operation of Peter Byrne, with whom I've enjoyed a good working relationship over the years and who supped with me in recording many happy and some not-so-happy moments.

CONTENTS

1

CHALK AND CHEESE

There's a saying in our part of the world that if you shout down a pit, up will pop a footballer.

The North-East of England has certainly produced its fair share of footballers. And our family has produced more than its fair share – not only me and my brother Bobby, but also my uncles Jack, George, Jimmy and Stan Milburn, and the most famous of all, my mother's cousin, Jackie Milburn.

I was born on 8 May 1935, in the Northumberland village of Ashington, about eighteen miles due north of Newcastle and two or three miles west of the sea at Newbiggin. Local people used to say that it was the largest coalmining village in the world. If you stood at the top of the main street, you were within easy walking distance of five or six pits. The mines were the only source of jobs in the area. You either worked in the pit or, if you were lucky, you went away to play football. My father worked six days a week down a mine all his life. So, later, did my two younger brothers – and so, nearly, did I.

Ashington stood at the top of the coalfield that stretched south into Durham as far as Middlesbrough. Once you left the pit heaps of Ashington, you were in open countryside and among tiny farming communities which stretched up to the Scottish border to the north, and across to the Cumbrian border to the west. Even as a small boy, I loved to roam this unspoilt country, bird-nesting, ratting, poaching, or just walking in the fields. Often I'd be gone for hours.

Charltons have been around here a long time. There were people of that name here back in the Middle Ages, when the area was wild border country dominated by brigands known as 'reivers'. I like to think that some of their fierce independent spirit has passed down to me.

The eldest boys in our family have always been called John, though just like the eldest Milburn, I'm invariably known as Jack. The only person who ever called me John was my headmaster. Two years after me my brother Robert was born, who became the man the world knows as Bobby Charlton but I knew as Our Kid. That's just a common Geordie expression for a younger brother; I always called him Robert or Bob at home, never Bobby. After a break of seven years came another brother, Gordon; and then finally, two years later, the babe of the family, our Tommy. We all look alike, though I am the exception in being much taller than the rest. Being tall in a mining area like ours was fairly unique, and the family thought I must have been a throwback to my great-great-grandfather, who was six foot two.

As I've said, this part of the world produced its fair share of footballers, and nobody was particularly impressed if a lad went away to play professional football. In fact we never used to say going away to play football, we just used to say 'going away'. The great shame and the great fear for any lad who went away was if you didn't make it in the game, you got sent home.

People in the North-East have a passionate interest in and a great knowledge of football – and my mother Cissie was no exception, coming as she did from a famous footballing family. Strangely enough, my father Bob had no interest in football, but my mother used to take us to football matches from the time when we were nippers. Our Robert, still in his pram when we first started going, would jump with fright at the roar from the crowd whenever a goal was scored.

As I've said, Cissie Charlton knew her football, and, what's more, she practised it. Many's the summer evening she came out on the street and joined in our games. Football, for her, wasn't just something to be endured by a parent. She genuinely loved the game, and later in life, when we'd all left home, she coached the local school's team.

My mother wasn't an excitable person. Other parents might shriek and shout while watching their boys play, but she just stood there, watching and analysing. And we didn't have to tell her whether we played well. She knew her football, and what she had to say about our performances was reasoned and constructive.

As a family, we were never blessed with large amounts of money, but somehow my mother managed to find enough to buy me my first pair of football boots. I was seven at the time, and the war was still on. Cissie read in the local paper that there was a pair of second-hand boots for sale, priced at ten shillings, only fifty pence in today's money but a substantial sum in those days. It must have been near the end of the year, for she said she'd buy me the boots as a Christmas present. Armed with a ten-bob note, I set off for the address given in the paper. The woman let me in, and showed me the boots – and when I saw them, my heart nearly stopped. They were Mansfield Hotspurs, the top boot of the time, almost brand new. I remember they had big, hard toes. In my eyes, they were absolutely beautiful – but intuition told me not to let on. I was only seven, but already I knew the way to bargain. I offered her seven shillings. That threw her a bit, but eventually she let me have them for eight. So I strutted back home with the boots under my arm and a grin as wide as the Tyne. I'd taken the first step to being a footballer – and what's more, I was able to give my mother back two shillings' change.

It isn't easy for kids to appreciate it now, but during the war it was impossible to buy clothes without a coupon, even if you had the money. The school provided you with a football shirt, but the rest was up to you. Many youngsters went without – but not the Charltons. My mother wanted her children to look like footballers, so she knitted us stockings, red and white ones. And shorts? Well, that was a bit of a problem, until Cissie typically came up with the answer. As I mentioned, there was a great big war going on outside, and every household in the country covered the windows with blackout curtains to make life difficult for Hitler's bombers. My mother used some of this curtain material to make shorts for our Robert and me. Equipped with Mansfield Hotspur boots and black shorts that went down to my knees, I felt ready to take on anybody or anything.

You had to improvise in those days. One of the biggest problems for us kids was laying hands on a football. They just weren't made at the time, and they couldn't be bought for love nor money. If you were lucky enough to have one from before the war, you were the envy of the neighbourhood, someone who could call the shots when it came to playing and organizing games down in Hirst Park.

For some reason or other, I ended up with the leather case of a ball – how I got it, I don't know – but, unfortunately, I didn't have an inner tube to go with it. A man told me that if I could find a pig's bladder, it would do the job fine – but the butchers of Ashington looked at me as if I'd two heads when I told them what I wanted. So instead we learned our trade with tennis balls, like so many others did at the time. We played with tennis balls going to school, in the schoolyard, played with them on the way home, headed them against walls, had competitions in the street, five against five, ten against ten, twenty against twenty, depending on how many wanted to play. I used to play with my brother Bob across the front yard at home, between the two brick walls, using the doors where the coal got delivered as our goalposts. When we used to play in the air I used to win because I was so much taller, but when we used to play on the ground he always used to win.

And all the time my mother encouraged us. My father might keep life and limb together by grafting in the mines, but essentially she was the one who ran the show, making all the decisions about the children, managing the family budget, taking us on expeditions. We could never afford to go on holiday to any great degree, but we used to roam up and down the river, and sometimes we'd all traipse the two miles to Newbiggin-by-the-Sea. I remember too her dragging us all to see a bomb crater near my Auntie Esther's house at the bottom end of the village. The whole of Ashington had come to see it, and there were kids clambering all over the place looking for pieces of shrapnel. I remember thinking, why have we come all this way just to see a hole?

The war didn't really touch us in Ashington, though at night we could hear the bombs dropping and see the flashes of the guns to the south around Newcastle. For the first two years of the war I remember we used to hide under the stairs when the air-raid sirens went off. After that they built a proper air-raid shelter across the street, but we never used to go in there because it was such an evil-smelling place. I don't think any other bombs dropped on Ashington, except one night when a plane dropped its load on Woodhorn Colliery. My father was out duck-shooting, and he told me the plane flew so low over him that he could have shot at it.

We had a big family, and they were all near by. It meant that if I was up at one end of town and I wanted something to eat and drink, there was always an aunt I could call in on who would give me a bit of bread and jam or a piece of cake, which was very acceptable to us lads.

There was no running hot water at home, no bathroom, and of course no central heating. Everything had to be cooked on an open coal fire. The coal was kept across the street, next to the toilet. We legged it down to Granny Bailey's for our weekly bath. Every Friday night or Saturday morning, depending on when my father finished his shift, my parents would have their weekly bath before going to one of the local working men's clubs or a film, the highlight of their social week. By the time they got home, I'd have cooked what they called their panhageldie special for them. It consisted of corned beef – about the only beef you could buy at the time – and potatoes, layered on each other. Heaven knows, it wasn't gourmet eating, but my mother always

14

thanked me. And I felt a bit special about that.

My father Bob was a quiet, conscientious man with a good sense of humour, whose main aim in life was to put enough food on the table for his family. All he ever wanted for himself was to meet his pals now and then for a couple of pints. At the time, wages for men working in the mines amounted to no more than about five pounds a week. By the time I was into my teens, it had reached the princely sum of six pounds ten – and we needed every penny of it.

Money, of course, was not the only thing in short supply when I was a lad. Britain was at war, and food rationing was part of the price we paid for stopping Adolf Hitler. Ordinary people who didn't have much money in their pockets had to improvise – and when it came to improvisation, Bob Charlton was right up there with the best of them. One of the earliest impressions I got of my father was that he wasted nothing – absolutely nothing. Everything, no matter how small or insignificant, was put away for the day when it might just come in useful. If he was burning wood which he brought home from the colliery, he'd sift through the ashes meticulously to save any nails or screws which might be in it. And then he'd take out a hammer, place the nails on a stone, and carefully straighten them out.

I think that's one thing I've inherited from my father. I've always hated waste, and I've always tried to get the players I've been responsible for to understand that. Some people think I'm mean, but that's not correct. I've worked hard to get where I am, and now I'd be the first to admit I'm not hard up. But I like to think I've never forgotten the value of what I've got, and I remember what it was like when we didn't have much money. That's why I hate waste.

15

My father and I used to argue now and again in later life, but he never laid a hand on me as a boy, even though I was forever getting into scrapes. 'Give that Jack a whack, he's cheeking me,' my mother used to say – but my father would just clap his hands together and reproach us, 'Now then, lads.'

Allotments were an essential part of every household during the war, for if you couldn't buy food in the shops, you had to grow your own. In my spare time, I tended potato drills and weeded cabbage patches – and I hated every minute of it.

I was much more at ease with the chickens and the pigs which my father kept to keep our stomachs filled. Three days a week, I'd put a barrel in my wheelbarrow and set out through the streets of Ashington to collect pigswill. Competition for the stuff was pretty sharp, but we'd enough relatives in the place to just about fill it, and in time I charmed a few extra customers into giving me their leftovers. One way or another, I usually had that barrel full by the time I got back. Then I'd take it down to the back of the garden, mix it with a pig feed called 'crowdie', and boil the bloody lot. And when it was all finished I used to go and feed the pigs. It was mucky work, but I knew that my parents' decision to keep three or four pigs was what stopped us going hungry.

I was perhaps seven or eight when my father said, 'Go on down the garden, Jack, and kill a chicken for the Sunday dinner.' What? I'd grown up with the things, but wring a chicken's neck, and it alive? Honour demanded that I do as I was told, however. I must have chased the bloody thing at least a hundred times around the garden before I caught it – and then failed, undeniably failed, to present a dead chicken on the kitchen table. While I was trying unsuccessfully to despatch the wretched bird, my shame was being witnessed by our next-door neighbour looking over the garden wall. Old Witton – we never knew him by any other name – eventually offered to rescue me from my predicament. 'Here, Jack,' he said. 'Gimme that and I'll show you how it's done.' Then, with the practised skill of a man who knew what he was about, he stuck two fingers under its neck, moved the head one way, twisted in the other direction – and in three seconds flat, he handed me back a lifeless chicken. I knew in that moment that I still had a lot of growing up to do.

Slaughtering pigs, on the other hand, was definitely a job for men. It invariably took place in our allotment on a Sunday morning. The animal always seemed to have a premonition of what was about to happen, and it usually required three or four pairs of strong miners' arms to get it out of the stye. Once the pig had been manoeuvred into the garden, the local butcher went to work. Not for us the sophistication of the abattoir: instead, the man relied on cruder methods – but the end-product was just the same, as the carcase was jointed, salted and then stored away in the kitchen. Looking back, there always seemed to be a side of bacon hanging in our house. I never grew tired of eating it, but I have to admit that our bacon always seemed to me more fatty than the stuff I saw in the butcher's shop.

We also kept pigeons. And any pigeons we wanted rid of, we just wrung their necks and had them for dinner the next day. I'm still partial to a pigeon or two to this day.

When the talk turned to football three or four hundred feet underground – and football was always the great topic of conversation among miners – Bob Charlton, I'm sure, had his two pennies' worth to say. But, essentially, boxing was his sport. His most treasured sporting possession by far was a penny piece which an American heavyweight named, I think, Black 'Butcher' Johnson, had given him while on tour in England many years earlier. He carried that coin in his pocket as if his life depended on it; and if truth be known, he probably valued it more than any of the football trophies which would later come into our possession.

In fact, if my father'd had his way, I'd have been a boxer rather than a footballer. As a kid, I remember him taking me to the boxing club on the other side of the village and hanging about to see how I made out in training sessions.

He never did that when we played football. In his spare time, he'd take out his whippets, or look after his garden, or at weekends walk to the local club for a drink. But he never came to watch us play football, and I found that strange.

The reason I didn't stay in the boxing club was interesting. Even in a small place like Ashington, there were divisions. We lived in what they called the Hirst end, around Hirst Park, whereas the boxing club was in the other part, up near the Regal Cinema in the main street – and whenever I went there, I never felt particularly welcome. Now whether it was that, or whether it was because I was tougher or stronger than they were, I don't know, but the other kids in the club would never spar with me. Very soon I got the message and left.

I boxed for my school. They had tournaments there a couple of times a year, the parents of the boys would come and watch – and, as I recall it, I usually won my bouts. But for me, boxing was merely a thing I fitted in between other, more important interests.

One of the disadvantages of being the eldest in a widely spread-out family is that you have little contact with those at the bottom of the pecking order. That's what it was like for me when I was growing up. I didn't have much to do with our Tommy, who was thirteen years my junior. Gordon, too, was out of my age group – but while I saw little of them during the day, we were very much a family at night. All four of us slept in the same bed, and if there were frequent arguments as to who got to be in the middle during the summer, the reverse was the case when the days grew short and you needed to be cosy in wintertime.

We found nothing strange in that, except that right under us, my mother had what we called the laying-out room. It had the best furniture, the best carpet, and the best pictures, and it was intended for use when visitors came to stay with us. The problem was that we didn't have that many visitors, and it went unused for most of the year – though during the war my father would often bring home soldiers for the night. My mother would feed them in the morning, and then they would be away.

My parents had another room, and then there was my father's sister Aunt Kitty, a kindly woman who lived with us and who could always be relied on to come up with a penny or two when my mother's benevolence ran out.

As the eldest, it was my job to look after Robert, and later Gordon as well. Sometimes I'd have to take Our Kid with me to the flicks on Saturday mornings. I remember the day my mother was expecting Gordon, she gave me half a crown to take Robert to the flicks.

When we got back she announced, 'You've got another little brother.'

Whenever I went out, Ma would say, 'Take Robert with you.' That was common practice in the area. Mothers generally looked after the house, but when it came to playing outside, big brother was the one who acted as guardian.

To be honest, I didn't much fancy the idea of having to watch out for Bob. I didn't want to be responsible for him while I was out with my mates. When you're six and your little brother's only three, there's a huge difference, much bigger than it seems later on.

But there was another reason why I didn't like looking after Robert, which was that his interests were totally different to mine. I liked to be out and about doing things in the countryside or messing about by the sea or in the Wansbeck River. He, on the other hand, always seemed to prefer to hang about the house. He wanted to be close to my mother at all times, straying only to kick a ball, either out on the street or down in Hirst Park. Robert was always her favourite – and correspondingly, he was a bit of a mother's boy.

As the boss, I normally insisted that if I was specifically charged to look after him, he did most of the things I wanted to do. And it has to be said that he did most of them only reluctantly. He didn't like the countryside, he didn't like sliding down pit heaps on corrugated iron sheets, he didn't like bird-nesting, and, most serious of all, he didn't like fishing.

Now that, as far as I was concerned, was a serious flaw in his character. Football was fine, but I soon found out that there was just as much fun – and a lot more profit – to be had from fishing. In the summer I'd go fishing in the sea, which was only a couple of miles from our house. I remember that my first investment was a split-cane salmon rod which I bought from a lad called Ronnie Goldsworthy. It must have been fifteen-feet long, and deciding that it was too big for sea fishing, I cut it down to two-thirds of its original size. In the process, unknowingly, I ruined a fine rod.

But it served me well when I first went fishing at Newbiggin. We'd go off the rocks there, maybe three or four evenings a week after school in the summer. There might be anything up to a hundred people stood waiting for the mackerel to show when they chased the sprats inshore. Suddenly the water would start to boil, and a hundred voices would yell excitedly, 'They're in, they're in!' That was the signal for frenzied activity along the shore as hundreds of lines hit the water.

We used a fly made up of silver paper and a piece of goose feather, and what was known then as a Scarborough reel. It was a long way removed from the modern gear which can throw a bait for miles. But once you got the hang of it, you could cast out fifty yards or more, reel in, and if you got lucky, you might have three or four mackerel every time.

In the autumn we would go and fish the storm beaches. This was a pursuit for only the most hardy. We'd set off after school, and providing it didn't rain, we'd stay there until the dawn broke and then walk the three or four miles back home to be ready for school. God, we must have looked a motley crew. I mean, we'd have two or three pairs of socks on, two pairs of trousers and a couple of jumpers – anything to keep you warm against the chill of the night.

There would always be a brazier full of hot sea coal on the beach. The problem was that if you stood with your back to it, you froze in front. So we had this practice of rotating around the fire, all the time keeping an eye on your rod tip to make sure you could see the bites. There might be fifty or sixty of us there of a night, young and old, searching out the cod which came in on the surf. I never got anything enormous, once or twice a six- or seven-pounder, but I could never wait to get home to show my catch to my mother.

Parents in those days never thought anything about their kids staying out all night to fish. It was accepted, and so long as you stayed well wrapped up and it didn't rain – remember, there was no rainproof gear in those days – all was well.

Later, when I was perhaps twelve or thirteen, I discovered there were trout in the Wansbeck River at Bothal, about a couple of miles upstream from Ashington. I'd been to the place before for minnows, but one day I saw this huge trout. We weren't allowed to fish for them, of course, but I said to myself, hell, I'm going to have one of those before long.

I soon figured how I'd do it. I'd take a ball of string, attach a piece of wood, and then tie on a dropper with a worm on the end. Then I'd retreat around the corner, so nobody could see me, and wait. I'd sometimes catch as many as ten trout a night. It was all totally illegal, but I was growing up fast in a hard world, and I never got caught.

Now, you'd never find our kid doing things like that. When I went river fishing, he'd sit on the bank. Eventually, with a lot of persuasion, I got him to wet a line. And then one day when we were fishing in the river, he caught a fish – or so he thought! I can still hear him shouting, 'I've got one, I've got one.' I ran a couple of hundred yards down the bank, only to see him lose a large trout at the last second. And he goes,

'But it still counts, doesn't it?' And being the mean devil I am, I said, 'No, it doesn't, get one on the bloody bank and then we'll start counting.'

But the little bugger still had the last say. I'm gone back up the bank when he starts hollering at me to come back. And when I get there, he says, 'Hey, Jack, will you put a worm on for me?' That was our Robert, never liked handling things such as worms. And I could never understand why not.

If I could handle worms, there were many, many things which he handled better. Take school. On the academic side of things, I'm afraid I was a bit of a non-starter. Even if I say so myself, I was good at the lessons which interested me. I liked subjects like History and Geography, I could rattle off most of the capital cities of Europe, and when they totted up the marks, I was top or pretty close to the top of the class in Geography. But I just wasn't interested in subjects like English and Maths. Many's the cuff I got from the teacher for allowing my eyes to stray towards something out in the schoolyard when I should have been watching the blackboard. So when the time came to take the eleven-plus, I failed and was sent to Hirst Park Secondary Modern School.

Robert was different. Not for him the wayward glances at what was happening outside the classroom. He was attentive and he was bright. And his handwriting was the envy of the whole class.

That part of his make-up he inherited from his mother. For a woman who received only elementary education, she could compose and write a letter better than anybody I knew. Years later, I recall urging her to get involved with the local council. She was clever enough and perceptive enough to make a contribution at that level, but like so many others of her generation, that was a task she preferred to leave to better-educated folk.

Unlike me, who couldn't wait to be fifteen and get out of school, Robert was a good student who passed his eleven-plus with ease and went on to Bedlington Grammar School. The teachers in Ashington believed he was sharp enough to have gone all the way with his education – if football hadn't got in the way.

2

FOOTBALL IN THE BLOOD

John 'Tanner' Milburn, my grandfather, got his nick-name from the fact that he was a small-time bookie in Ashington who would accept no bets less than a tanner. The era of the big bookmaking organizations hadn't arrived when I was growing up – hence the importance of the 'sixpenny operators' in the North of England.

They didn't have offices as such. Instead, they generally operated around the working men's clubs, and they were as sharp as razor-blades when it came to pulling strokes. They took bets on the horses and the dogs, and on the professional athletics meetings which served to fill the summer gap between the football seasons.

Virtually every village had its sprint handicap, and people would come from all over the North-East to run in them. To win, a runner had to be good enough to survive heats, quarter-finals and so on. Often the prize money for the winner could be as high as eighty to one hundred pounds, a king's ransom in those days – but the bigger money by far was earned in the betting. Bookies, dozens of them, would arrive on the day of the races to pit their knowledge and the tricks of their trade against the punters.

Tanner Milburn didn't own horses or greyhounds. But he trained sprinters, and with four sons earning a living as professional footballers, he started from a reasonably strong base when it came to sending out winners. Robert and I were allowed to join in the training, and it was there that we learned the rudiments of professional sport.

'Knees up, arms forward,' he'd bellow like a barrack-square sergeant as we bolted off the starting-blocks. What he didn't shout too loud were the various little ruses he had devised to extract money from his fellow bookies. If a lad won his heat, the starting price changed accordingly. So if Tanner had a fancied runner, he didn't want him to show his hand in the preliminary races. Now they knew their running in that part of the country, and anybody not trying would be spotted a mile away. Tanner's runners, to be fair, always appeared to be doing their best in every race – and I could never figure out how, after struggling into third place in the heats, they could improve so miraculously to win the final.

Then, unwittingly, I stumbled on the answer, while rooting around Grandfather's cupboard one day. I was already into fishing at the time, and one of my great problems was finding 'sinkers' to weight my line. Imagine my delight, then, when I discovered two big pieces of lead. Manna from heaven! I stuffed the two of them in my pockets, left without saying a word, and as soon as I got home, went to work with a relish. After melting them onto spoons, I ran a couple of pieces of bent wire through the lead – and for years afterwards, my 'sinkers' were the envy of all my contemporaries.

Then one morning I was having breakfast in

Tanner's house as he was making ready to go to a meeting, and I heard him yell at Grandmother, 'Where the bloody hell are they, who's taken my heavies?' I hadn't a clue when he was talking about, but I soon twigged. The leads I had taken were insoles, to be fitted into shoes when the lads were running heats. That way, they could run flat out in the preliminaries while still keeping something in reserve. Once the 'heavies' were removed, the form book would be stood on its head yet again.

I never did have the nerve to tell Tanner what I'd done, and he went to his grave without knowing what became of his heavies. But I reckon I was still his favourite grandson, and he proved it by choosing me to be part of his team whenever he had a coup lined up for a meeting. He would say, 'Jack, go and stand in the bookies' lines, and when I wave at you, ask such-and-such a bookie the time.' That was the signal for six or seven of his pals to descend on different bookies and place their bets at precisely the same time. That way, of course, they didn't have time to drop the odds on, say, Stan Milburn. And if you added it all up, six or seven winning ten-pound bets made it a very profitable day for our Tanner.

My Uncle Buck was a bookie's runner. He was my favourite uncle, who taught me how to poach, how to lay snares and, most important of all, how not to get caught. Now Buck's betting scams were ingenious and highly lucrative – until the day his luck ran out and he had to retire in some shame from the shady world of gambling.

His job was to collect bets from the various working men's clubs and then go and place them with a bigger bookie in the village. It was all very borderline stuff, of course, and every so often you'd see Buck disappear into the backyard of someone's house if a policeman chanced to appear on the street.

The rules were that when he collected all his slips, he would deposit them in a box in the bookie's office. They were accepted right up to the time the phone rang in the office to confirm the result of the race just finished at the local dog track.

Now picking winners at the dogs, as I've since found out, is not the easiest way of making money. But not only could my uncle nominate winners, he invariably got at least one big forecast at every meeting. And he had the bookie baffled.

Then, one unfortunate night for Buck, he was caught. A man using an upstairs toilet in one of the clubs heard this strange, gurgling noise coming from a cubicle. Looking over the door, he discovered my poor uncle suspended out of an open window, unable to get his head back in because the frame had trapped the back of his neck. More mysteriously still, there were rows of betting slips, already made out, neatly placed on the cistern.

Slowly the truth dawned. Buck would stand on the toilet seat, craning his neck out the window. If he listened carefully, he could hear the tannoy at the track call out the 1-2-3 as they flashed over the line. There were no photo finishes in those days, of course, and as soon as he heard the result, he'd leg it down to the bookie before the phone rang. Sadly, on this particular night, his feet slipped on the toilet seat, and he almost lost his life as well as his reputation.

A great character was Uncle Buck, a big strong man who, as his nickname implied, was always ready to have a go. As a youngster I remember him swimming across the river at night, laying the nets that would mean a nice little earner for him the following day.

That was the shadier side of the Milburn clan. But to thousands, perhaps millions, of football fans, they were known as the bluebloods of the game in the North-East, a family which fulfilled its destiny by sending out sons to become professional players.

Four of my mother's brothers, Jack, George, Jimmy and Stan, got their living from the game. And then there was the most famous Milburn of them all, our Jackie, the pride of Newcastle and, in time, England. A lot of people thought that Jackie was our uncle, but that wasn't quite the case. His father and my mother's father were brothers, which made him, I suppose, something like a second cousin of ours. But Jackie Milburn was 'family' as we termed it in the North-East, and we were proud, immensely proud, of what he achieved and the name he made for himself in the game.

Apart from a spell in Gosforth, Jackie Milburn always lived in Ashington. He was a nice man, who always had time for everyone. I remember walking with him in Newcastle as a kid, and being amazed by the number of people there who recognized him. Maybe it was this reflected glory, or maybe it was the England caps he'd show me when I pressed him that fired my imagination – but for the first time in my life I knew what fame was in his company.

In 1950, he'd stuck two in the net to give Newcastle United a famous win over Stan Matthews's Blackpool team in the FA Cup final at Wembley. That was the stuff of folklore at St James' Park, and of course he followed it by winning two more Cup medals in 1951 and 1955.

Jackie played thirteen times for England between 1949 and 1956, at a time when there were some fine centre forwards around – but I often wonder how many more caps he might have won had he played for a London club or, equally intriguing, how much a player of his class would make on today's transfer market.

He never did make a lot of money out of football, and apart from writing a weekly newspaper column, he earned precious little from it in his retirement. There was one occasion during my Leeds United days when I was asked to open a furniture store in Wallsend. When I told them I couldn't do it, they asked if I could suggest a replacement. I said, 'Have you tried Jackie Milburn? He's more popular with the punters in this area than both Charlton brothers put together.'

So they did. And the following day, I had a call telling me that they'd had to close off the entire street in Wallsend because of the crowds who turned up to see Jackie Milburn. That ought to have been the gateway to a big promotional career for Jackie. But he was a man who had always believed in letting his skills do the talking during his playing days, and I guess he saw no good reason why he should change in the twilight of his years.

Of my four uncles, Jack, George and Jimmy played for Leeds, and George later went on to play for Chesterfield and eventually became manager there. In that capacity he signed Stan, the youngest of the four and the closest to us in age. Stan was one hell of a good full back, who won an England 'B' cap and cost Leicester City something in the region of thirty thousand pounds, a huge sum of money for a full back in those days, when he moved to Filbert Street.

Although Jack or Jimmy Milburn occasionally

invited us to watch the training at Leeds, we never actually got to playing on the pitch. But it was a lot different on those occasions when we were put on a bus to Chesterfield, and George met us at the other end. There was none of the formality of Elland Road here. My uncle let us tog out in the club's strip – miles too big for the pair of us – and as well as being allowed to retrieve balls behind the goals, we even got to play in seven-a-sides on a couple of occasions. So if people tell you that Leeds was my first club, tell them they're wrong. The first club colours I ever wore were those of Chesterfield.

Remember how I mentioned earlier the problem of finding a football in Ashington? Well, my uncles George and Jimmy eventually took care of that, when they returned from the war and resumed their playing careers. In those days, the season ended in the first week in May and didn't restart until early September. Many of the pros in our area kept themselves fit by running in the sprint handicaps, but they would also do some ball work just to keep themselves in tune. And that meant that they were able to provide our kid and me with a ball, courtesy of Leeds United, to make us the envy of every other youngster in Ashington. After knocking a tennis ball about for all our young lives, we now had a ball, a real ball of our own – and suddenly our popularity with the other kids exploded.

Recreation time for every lad in the place started with a knock on the door at Number 114 Beatrice Street. And if we weren't in, my mother gave them the ball to take down to Hirst Park.

The game on Sunday mornings normally started around eleven, and it could go on for four or five hours. Depending on who had to go home for lunch or whatever, the two captains would then make their choice of replacements from the lads standing on the line waiting for a game. Robert, as I've said, was more than two years younger than me and considerably smaller. Yet he was always chosen to go on ahead of me, much to the delight of my pals. Strangely, I never took exception to that, even though it must have been a blow to my pride. The fact is that he was already regarded as an extraordinary talent. To this day, there are people in Ashington who will tell you that even as a nipper, Robert had been singled out as a boy who would one day play for England.

He was strong and he was skilful – and he could hit a ball harder with either foot than many lads twice his age. People often ask me, 'Which was your Bobby's natural foot in his playing days?' and I tell them, 'I simply don't know.' Normally, players have a preferred foot for striking the ball, but in his case the normal rules just didn't apply. He was capable of doing things with the ball that the rest of us could only watch and admire. And he had a swerve and a turn of speed to keep him out of trouble.

I went with my mother to watch him play for Bedlington Grammar School one day. The kids were so small that they ran a piece of string between the two uprights a couple of feet below the main crossbar to act as a new crossbar and give the titchy keeper a chance. Sometime during the game, Robert picked up the ball twenty-five yards out and struck it so hard that the kid standing in goal never even saw it as it whizzed past him.

The referee, probably as nonplussed as the rest of us, disallowed the goal on the basis that if the keeper hadn't moved, it must have gone over the makeshift bar. But I knew it hadn't, and after the match I went and showed that the ball couldn't have fitted between the crossbar and the improvised one.

If I needed any proof that my brother was out of the ordinary, that little cameo proved it. Robert went on to play for East Northumberland, Northumberland, and finally, the England schools team, while I never made it past the regional team. But never mind, I was enjoying a much more varied life. There was football and there was fishing. And then, when I reached my teens, there was shooting as well. My father had a gun, and every so often we would set out before daybreak for Cresswell, where the ducks came in off the sea onto an inland pond. We'd sit in the sand-dunes and wait for them as the sun came up. It meant a walk of five or six miles there and back, and getting up in the middle of the night – but when you had a pair of ducks to take home to your mother to vary the staple diet of chicken, bacon, rabbits and pigeons, it made it all worthwhile.

My father always had whippets too, and we'd go out chasing rabbits together. There was nothing he'd like better than to see a hare coursed across a field. The whippet would never catch the hare, but he loved the chase. In his old age, when he and my mother lived on a farm I bought for them in the Dales, he had a whippet called Bonny, and he used to walk it down to the pub every day, a distance of about a mile and a half, where it would sit peacefully under his chair. After my father died, Bonny would still arrive at the pub every day and sit under the chair. The landlord told me it used to bring tears to his eyes.

By the time I was in my early teens my mother thought I was old enough to go and watch football on a Saturday afternoon. Newcastle United were the big local team, and I've always been a Newcastle fan, still am to this day. Teams played only once a week in those days, so when Newcastle were away from home, we went and watched Stan Milburn doing his thing for Ashington. We'd never go and see Sunderland, who were the other big local team – in fact, the first time I ever went to Roker Park was when I played there with Leeds United.

On very special occasions, Jackie Milburn invited us to go and watch him play, and, of course, we made sure that all the other kids in Ashington were made aware of the event. He'd take us down the players' tunnel and stand us behind the trainers' box – and hell, did we feel big!

Other times, we'd go under our own steam. We'd have lunch in the British Home restaurant, and then time our arrival at the ground late enough to be passed down over the heads of the crowd to join the other lads at the perimeter wall.

There we stood, lost in admiration of the big names of the day. Stan Matthews, Stan Mortensen, Neil Franklin and Billy Wright – they all came and did their thing at St James' Park. But my special favourite was Sam Bartram, the goalkeeper of Charlton Athletic. Maybe it was because he wore a cap and was clad in a yellow sweater, I don't know, but somehow I was captivated by Sam Bartram. Ah, the innocence of youth. I mean, admiring a goalkeeper! Sam became a journalist with one of the Sunday papers. He used to visit me when I was with Middlesbrough, and became quite a good friend.

At that time, I was already becoming well known around Ashington – not, I hasten to add, for my football. I've always been a good earner, and between the ages of twelve and fifteen I was probably making between one pound and thirty shillings a week. In addition to the unpaid job of collecting swill, I had a milk round before school, delivered groceries for a local shop after – and then decided it was time for some private enterprise. So, apart from pinching daffodils and selling them round the houses, I'd go to the local colliery and collect the unused timber. Chopped up and neatly bundled, it made a nice little earner for lighting fires.

But my pride and joy in those days was my Sunday morning paper round. There were probably three dozen kids delivering papers in the area, and you took the round you were given at the start. Very soon, however, I discovered that it was a waste of time crisscrossing the place, delivering one paper in this street and then having to walk a couple of hundred yards to drop the next. So I sat down and drew a map. And by trading off with other kids, I arrived at a situation in which I started perhaps two miles away and then was able to walk in more or less a direct line back to my house. Already I had learned the value of planning and organizing a job.

That paper round was the earner I prized most. When I went away to join the ground staff at Leeds, I handed it over to Robert. Alas, when I came home for my first break, I discovered that not only had he wrecked the bike I gave him, but he'd given away the bloody round. He just wasn't interested, and I suppose that was another example of the difference between the pair of us.

We were still playing football together, for the Ashington YMCA Under-18 team. I was just approaching my fifteenth birthday and he was two years younger, so you can form your own conclusions about the quality of the side. We once drew 2–2 and nearly collapsed with excitement! More often than not, however, we lost by six or eight goals, and on one infamous occasion, we lost 18–0. Can you imagine that? A team including both Charlton brothers losing eighteen bloody nil!

Oddly enough, there was another youngster in the team, Willie Merryweather, who, like Robert, went on to play for the England schools team. Like so many others, however, he never made the crossing between gifted schoolboy and successful senior player, and eventually he came back to Ashington.

Me? I never got anywhere near the England schools team. Still, I must have impressed somebody when playing in that dreadful Ashington YMCA team, for soon afterwards, I got an offer to go on trial to Leeds United. My mother couldn't believe it at first, and thought they must have confused me with Robert. Of course, she was delighted for me as any mother would be, but she didn't think I was good enough to play professional football. I decided anyway that I was enjoying life too much in Ashington to leave home. So I told the man I wasn't interested, and on leaving school at fifteen, chose to follow my father into the mines.

3

THE PIT AND THE PENDULUM

I suppose I'd always assumed I'd go down the pit. I never really thought much about it, actually. I didn't think I was good enough to make it in football, and I don't think anyone else really did – despite the interest from Leeds United. I was just a big, gangly boy. I didn't want to go away to Leeds, or anywhere else for that matter. I liked home, I liked the countryside, and I was well set up with my 'rounds'. I was only fifteen then, remember.

So I went down the pit. In those days there was a tradition that if a son followed his father into mining, he would work down the same pit. My father worked at Linton, about four miles from our house, and to get there we took a special miners' train, known locally as the 'tankie'. When I arrived they gave me a miners' helmet and all the other gear, and put me to work 'screening'. This was a surface job for those not thought to be 'the full shilling': beginners like me, or old miners who'd been injured working underground. The coal came up the shaft, was loaded onto the conveyor belts – and there we stood for eight long hours, sorting out the stones and chucking them away. It was boring work, and soon I had grumbled enough to be moved to another job, weighing the wagons when they came in empty, then weighing them again when they were full, to work out the weight of the coal.

Now the sidings ran way out into the country, and soon, very soon, I found there were loads of rabbits around. Buck Milburn had taught me how to set a rabbit snare and the right sort of place to put it. I began to set snares regularly. Every morning I'd take the early 'tankie' to work, check my trap lines, and if I was lucky, I'd go home with three or four rabbits.

Miners would always take a rabbit off your hands. At a going price of a tanner, I usually left the pit at least two shillings richer than when I arrived. I think I would gladly have settled for that job for the rest of my life – but then I got a note telling me that I was required to start a sixteen-week training course, preparatory to becoming a fully fledged miner.

To be honest, I didn't like being underground. One day they took us along a seam only three feet high – we had to crawl on hands and knees to the coalface. I watched them bore a hole into the coal and place explosives there. When the moment came to blow out the coal, everybody had to get back thirty yards. Then came the shout: 'Hands over ears!' I've never, ever experienced anything like it. There we were, crouched on our hands and knees four hundred feet underground, and then suddenly this vast sound nearly takes our heads off. And then the dust! You couldn't see your hand for the dust – it's in the air, it's in your eyes, it's in your lungs. I don't mind saying that my first inclination was to bolt for the lift to get to the surface. Hell's bells, if this is what mining is all about, I just don't want to know!

One day they took us to see our fathers at work. After a five-mile journey underground from Ashington to Linton, I walked into a haulage way, and there was my father on a ladder, building a brick wall to support the roof. He didn't see me at first. Just then he dropped his hammer, and I heard him say 'Fuck!' for the very first time.

I went 'Father?' – and when he turned around and saw me, he went red beneath the black. 'Well, Jack,' he said apologetically, 'you know what it is when you're working and you do something stupid like that.' He was very, very embarrassed.

In fact, the only other time I ever heard him swear was when I returned home from Leeds for the first time. I was upstairs – he didn't even know I was in the house – when he came home from his pit shift and handed my mother his pay packet, as he did every week. And when she gave him his pocket money, he went, 'You mean old whore, is that all you're giving me?' Once again I said, 'Father?' – and this time he was just as embarrassed as he'd been before. 'Pay no heed, Jack,' he said, 'it's a little joke your mother and me have been sharing every pay day since we married.'

Later, they showed me a draughty, dimly lit place where two haulage ways met. Here the coal tubs coming from different directions were sent to the shaft head – they called it 'hanging on and knocking off'. And I said to the miner who was showing me the place, 'Am I going to be here eight hours a day?'

He said, 'Yeah.'

'Five and a half days a week?'

And he went, 'Yeah.'

And I said, 'Nah – I'm not going to do it.' I went and put my notice in and I left.

There was this stern-faced lady, the manager's secretary, sat in an outer office when I went to put in my notice. 'What do you want?' she rasped – and when I told her, she snapped, 'You canna' do that, you canna' see the manager.'

I mean, the pit manager was like God in a colliery town. He had a car, he lived in the biggest house, he wore the best clothes, he walked in a different world from the rest of us. Then the door suddenly opened and there he was, standing in that doorway, larger than life.

Many a grown man might have quaked at the sight, and if truth be known, my knees probably wobbled a bit in that moment. But I reckoned that if I was man enough to go underground in the first place, I was man enough to speak my mind.

'Can I have a word?' I asked. On being waved inside, I blurted out the words that had been burning inside me all morning. 'I want to resign – I'm not coming back any more.'

And I see immediately that he's not best pleased. 'You can't do that,' he says. 'We've just spent a fortune training you. If you walk away now, I'll see that you'll never get another job in a pit – anywhere.'

So I said, 'I don't want another job in the pit. I've seen it, I've done it, and I've had enough. I don't know what I'm going to do with the rest of my life, but it won't be that.'

I never wrote a letter of resignation. Come to think of it, I'm not sure if he even knew who I was, but walking back to my house that morning, I was content I'd made the right decision. I'm sure my father was disappointed when I told him what I meant to do, but my mother, bless her, was as supportive as ever. 'If that's what you want to do, Jack,' she told me, 'you do it.' And I did.

I had taken the precaution a couple of weeks earlier of applying to become a police cadet. Although I was only just a couple of months past my fifteenth birthday, I was already getting close to six feet in height. That, to my young mind, seemed as good a reason as any why I should try for the police.

What's more, they wrote back immediately, asking me to present myself for an interview in Morpeth the following Friday. So for the next forty-eight hours or so, I contemplated the prospect of swapping a miner's helmet for a policeman's one.

Then came a knock on our door one evening, and my life was stood on its head once more. The local scout for Leeds United was back, with the news that the club wanted me to go for a trial the following Saturday. I'd already told him once that I wasn't interested, but that was before I'd discovered what working underground was like. Now, the idea seemed a lot more attractive – even if it meant giving up my little earners.

When I'd handed in my gear at the colliery on the Saturday morning, I hadn't got a clue what I was going to do next. Now I had the chance of two jobs, or so it seemed until I discovered that I was due in Leeds early on Saturday morning to play against Newcastle N's, Newcastle's youth team.

Now Leeds at that time was a four- or five-hour rail journey from Ashington. And even if we had a car, which we hadn't, there was no way I could get to the game without staying in the city on the Friday night.

The choice was clear. Either I presented myself to the police board in Morpeth on the Friday afternoon, or else took a train to Leeds to play in the game. I chose the football match – and in that moment the prospect of PC Charlton on the beat was lost for ever.

My mother, as was her wont, had a few shillings put away for an emergency, and on the Thursday she took me into town and bought me a Burberry overcoat and a blue pin-striped suit – the very first time I owned a pair of long trousers. Whatever she thought about my football skills, she was determined that I should be as well dressed as the next player when I got to Elland Road.

So, with three pounds in my pocket and a million dreams in my head, I set off for Leeds. Of all the hundreds of games I played before or since, the one that Saturday morning had to be most important. If I didn't perform, I was on the next train back home, with my hopes of a professional career in ruins.

Strangely enough, I don't remember too much about the game itself, but I must have done all right, because as soon as it was over one of the coaches sought me out, and there and then invited me to join the ground staff at the club. I'd got my foot in the door, and I couldn't wait to tell my parents.

The instruction was to report for work at Elland Road on the Monday morning, and it was then that I met the manager, Major Frank Buckley, for the first time. I had heard of him only vaguely before that, perhaps from eavesdropping on conversations which my uncles Jack and Jimmy had with my mother when they came to visit. Everybody knew him as the Major, a tall stern man who commanded respect every time he appeared. You didn't take too many liberties with Major Buckley – but then again, I never felt inclined to do so.

It was, of course, my first spell away from home, but I wasn't fazed by the prospect, and my parents didn't worry too much either. After all, I had two uncles in Leeds at the time; and as I've said, we were a close-knit family who believed in looking after each other. Curiously though, they didn't ask either of my uncles to put me up. Instead, they sent me to a boarding-house on Beeston Hill, near the club ground, and there I lived happily for the next seven years with Mary Crowther, a lovely lady already in her seventies, and her spinster daughter, Laura. In time, Mary Crowther would become a second mother to me, a kindly old-fashioned woman who didn't stand for any hanky-panky.

She didn't believe in having a television set in the house either, and it was only after long hours of per-suasion that Laura and I succeeded in convincing her to get one. Mary loved her bottle of milk stout every evening, and the arrival of television in the house meant a sharp change in her practice. Her glass was replaced by a mug, and every time she took a sip, she re-placed the mug behind the chair. You see, she thought the faces on the television set were watching her.

Years later, when I was courting my future wife Pat, she'd often come to the house. Mary Crowther would watch us like hawks, just to make sure that nothing untoward took place under her roof. God rest her, nothing ever did, but there was one unforgettable time when Mary was convinced that if intimacy hadn't taken place, it was, at the very least, planned. For three long days, she never spoke a word to me, until at last I con-fronted her and uncovered the bizarre truth. 'I was making your bed this week, and look at what I found,' she blurted out, holding up a plastic comb case as if it was an exhibit at a murder trial. I was flabbergasted. Light slowly dawned. She thought she had discovered a condom! 'Yeah, Mary,' I said, 'the main pouch is for big 'uns and other one for small 'uns.' I think she was even more mortified when I showed it to Laura and asked her to confirm my innocence.

Still, my days with the Crowthers on Beeston Hill were happy ones. And one of the biggest bonuses of all was that after all those years, I got to sleep in a bed all on my own.

Out of the five pounds weekly wage I collected every Friday at Elland Road, I paid Mary two pounds and ten shillings for board and lodging. After I'd sent another one pound home to my mother, I didn't have a lot left over for my pocket money. In fact, I didn't need much. During my first two years in Leeds, I never once went into the centre of the city. I lived on Beeston Hill, I went to the pictures on Beeston Hill, I courted girls in the park on Beeston Hill – my whole life was lived within one mile of the Leeds ground.

My pal was Melvyn Charles, younger brother of the great John Charles, the biggest name at the club, but now, unfortunately for Leeds supporters, away doing his National Service. Melvyn was in digs just a couple of doors away, and we did virtually everything together. Sadly for me, Melvyn was to leave Leeds within another eighteen months to forge a fine career with Swansea Town, Arsenal, and, of course, Wales, and it would be another twenty years before we linked up again.

It was, as I've said, no big deal for a young lad from Ashington to go away to join a big club. Hundreds had done so before me, so it was not surprising that my going didn't cause much of a stir, even on our street. The more significant thing, by far, was any failure to take that opportunity. Cruelly, there was an implied shame for lads who were rejected and came home to spend the rest of their lives in the village. That was the fear which drove me during my first two years at Leeds. I didn't regard myself as anything special when it came to playing football, otherwise I'd have jumped at that first Leeds offer and never gone near the mines. But now I had been given a second chance, and I was determined that, come hell or high water, I'd take it. That's why I made a conscious decision to shun the bright lights of Leeds and immerse myself, body and soul, in my job. Perhaps that's why I developed very fast between the ages of fifteen and seventeen.

The lot of a ground staff boy at the big clubs in those days was far removed from the glamorous image of the modern game. We had to wait until the senior players had finished training before we got on the pitch in the afternoon, and the hours in between were filled with the most boring, thankless jobs.

Even at that point, there was a system of seniority in operation. The newer arrivals had to work outside, and that meant sweeping terraces, oiling turnstiles, cleaning toilets and then painting them with black-lead paint which clung to your clothes and your nostrils.

Promotion meant that you got to work inside and meet the senior players for the first time. You cleaned their boots, restudded them, put them neatly away and then pumped up the balls to make sure that everything was in order for the game on Saturdays.

Unlike the pros, we got just two weeks' holidays in the summer, and while they were away, our job was to remove the weeds from the pitch and replace them with grass seed. Let me tell you, that was monotony on a grand scale. I remember being sat out there one day with Keith Ripley, another ground staff boy, when

Major Buckley came over to us. We must have looked pretty forlorn, the two of us, and to gee us up he said he'd give us five shillings for every bucket we filled with weeds. Now that was an offer we couldn't refuse. By the time we were finished, we had filled six buckets, and cheeky bugger that I was, I marched straight up to the Major's office. And when he asked what I wanted, I told him I was there to claim my thirty bob for the weeds. He nearly blew a bloody gasket! 'Get out of here!' he bellowed. 'You're already getting paid to do that work – don't ever let me see you up here again with your buckets.' So much for on the spot agreements!

Yet beneath the gruff exterior, he was a kind man, as he demonstrated one morning when I met him on my way into the ground. My shoes must have been a sight, for when he looked down at them, he asked me if they were the only pair I had. I nodded. The next morning, he summoned me to his office and handed me a pair of his own. They were nearly brand new, a pair of Irish brogues, the strongest, most beautiful shoes I'd ever seen. And I had them for years.

We trained five days a week, and then on Saturday mornings, I played for the youth teams in the Northern Intermediate League. Not content with that, I would then go and ask if I could travel with the third team in the afternoon, just in case somebody didn't turn up. They frequently took me up on the offer, and sometimes I played twice on the same day. Now, the thirds played in the Yorkshire League – and that was the greatest learning experience I've ever had in football.

It was, in the main, a miners' competition, and you learned quickly, very quickly, that to survive you had to be able to take care of yourself. I was just sixteen, playing against hard, fully mature men, big strong buggers who clattered into you with no quarter given or asked. Later, I would play in every major competition in the world – but take it from me, none was harder or more physically demanding than the Yorkshire League. And it was the making of me as a footballer.

Obviously, the word of my Yorkshire League battles was getting back to the hierarchy at Elland Road, for in my second full season as a member of the ground staff, I was occasionally promoted to the reserve team and given the chance to play alongside people with a lot of senior experience. Raich Carter, one of the great names of football in the North-East of England, had replaced Major Buckley as manager by this time. He it was who would decide whether to offer me a professional contract at the end of the season.

The rules stipulated that clubs had to retain or release ground staff by their seventeenth birthday. And at noon on 8 May 1952, I presented myself at the office of the club secretary, Arthur Crowther, to await the fateful decision. The manager was away on tour with the senior team in Holland, and it was Arthur's job to deliver the verdict. At that point, I honestly had no idea what to expect. Nobody had ever said to me that I had a future in the game, least of all Major Buckley or Raich Carter.

So when I walked into Arthur's office, I could not guess what lay ahead. He got straight to the point. 'Jack,' he said, 'Raich has instructed me to offer you a contract. You'll have ten pounds signing-on fee, eighteen pounds a week in season and fourteen pounds off.' The first thought that entered my mind was, 'That's senior team money!'

I left that office feeling ten feet tall. When I walked

47

across the road to a newsagent's shop directly opposite the ground, the guy behind the counter asked, 'Have you signed then, Jack?' And when I told him I had, he said, 'Thank God for that! I've had half the scouts in the Football League in here this morning, wanting to know what you were doing.'

I asked how many. 'There must have been a dozen of the buggers, all wanting a word,' he told me. I was stunned. And in that moment, for the very first time in my seventeen years, I realized that I might have a real future in the game.

Within hours, I was on a train back to Ashington, to give the good news to my father and mother.

4

QUEEN AND COUNTRY

You needed to be fairly nifty to avoid the traffic of football scouts back at Number 114 Beatrice Street in the summer of 1952. And I hasten to add that it had nothing to do with me.

Our kid was still not turned fifteen, but it seemed his name was already on the hit-list of every big club in England. Big brother may have had to sweat it out until the moment Arthur Crowther told him he was being kept on – but not our Robert. As I've said, those who knew anything about football in Ashington had long since identified him as a lad who would go on to make it big in the game. The word gradually spread around the country of this remarkable talent in a remarkably fertile football area.

It would be another year before he finished school, but that didn't deter clubs from getting in early. At times, it became ridiculous. I mean, there might be representatives of two or three different clubs in the house at the same time. My mother would be at her wit's end trying to keep them apart. As a football woman, she knew what was what and who was who in the game – but so far as I know, she never tried to exert any influence on Robert about where he should go. The exception, curiously enough, was her aversion to

49

Newcastle United. When you think of it, that was strange. Newcastle was the club we lads had always supported, and my mother and father had given us their hard-earned shillings to go to St James' Park every second Saturday.

So why had my mother this barrier about allowing her son to play for Newcastle? She never spelled it out in as many words, but I think it may have had something to do with the club's reputation for not looking after kids properly. They went there in droves, but the rejection rate was high, and the word spread among concerned parents that Newcastle United was not a good place to send a promising young lad.

It would be another year before Robert yielded to Matt Busby's persuasive talk and joined Manchester United. As a kid, he'd never shown any affinity with the club, but perhaps it was the outstanding promise of the team that Matt was then building which persuaded him to go there. Matt Busby had introduced a policy of recruiting schoolboys and putting them through a proper apprenticeship with the club, and I think that swayed it for her. Given the enormous interest in our kid, my mother must have been offered money by several clubs to promote their interest. In fact, I know she was offered eight hundred pounds by one club, a vast sum in those days. But so far as I'm aware, she never got a penny when Robert went to Old Trafford. In later years, I often felt a bit guilty about that. She'd raised two lads who went to the top of their trade, she'd made a hell of a lot of sacrifices to get us there, and yet she and my father got no financial reward for their pains. Later I tried to make it up to them. When we won the World Cup in 1966, I bought them a house out of my bonus – but that's another story.

People often ask why the younger two Charltons never followed their brothers into a career in professional football. It doesn't usually work like that, of course, but having said that, I believe they too could have made the grade had they set their minds to it.

Gordon was taken on to the ground staff during my early years as a pro with Leeds United, but for all his talent, he just didn't have the dedication to go with it. Football was fine, but he didn't particularly like the menial work which went with the job. Time after time, the people at Elland Road would come to me with complaints that he wasn't doing this or that, that he wasn't showing up in the mornings to do the little odds and ends which were required of ground staff. They let him go after a year – and that was a terrible waste of talent. He might never have reached the standards of his older two brothers, but he certainly had the ability to make a living for himself in the game at a lower level. Later he went to work as a fitter in a colliery, before going to sea for a short spell. He is now sales director for a plant hire firm, and maintains an interest in football as a well-respected Sunday League coach in Leeds. Tommy too worked in a colliery, and like Gordon, he went into the navy for a time before getting a job in the mines. I suppose they got their love of the sea from my father, who had volunteered for the navy during the war, only to be rejected because he was classified as a worker in an essential service.

There are those in Ashington who will tell you that as a boy, Tommy had almost as much ability as our Bob. I cannot vouch for that, because while he was growing up, I was away playing at Leeds most of the time. According to the locals, Tommy had much of Robert's ability on the ball and my kind of pace. When you put the two together, he ought to have done something, but he fractured his knee as a boy and he never recovered sufficiently to play anything other than amateur football.

In many respects, Tommy was the brightest, intellectually, of the four of us. Not only that, he had hands that could do any job – a chip, perhaps, off the old block. There were times, I felt, when Tommy could have made it as a top trade union official, but he chose the quieter life, and who's to say that he didn't make the right decision?

My first season as a pro at Leeds was pretty uneventful. I did my physical work, and played in five-a-side games involving some of the senior players, but otherwise never came in contact with them. They were in one dressing-room, the young pros in another – and the demarcation lines were such that you never crossed over.

The old pros – or they looked pretty old to me – included Jimmy Dunn, Eric Kerfoot, Tommy Burden, Arthur Tyrer, Grenville Hair and, of course, the greatest of them all, John Charles. John had just come out of the army, and apart from his football talent, he had something else which made him different, a car. Now, it wasn't particularly big and it wasn't particularly flashy – but at a time when most players came to work either on a bus or a bike, that made him special. And we younger ones would cluster around it in the car-park, just to get a feel. I wonder what our extravagantly paid young pros of today would think of that?

By this stage, I was regarded as a regular on the second team, though it has to be said that on occasions I played with the thirds. Still, I was happy enough with my progress as we approached the last weekend of the season.

I've said that we never set foot in the senior dressing-room. Well, that's not quite true. You see, the manager never read out his teams to the players. He'd just post them on the back of the door in the senior dressing-room. All three teams played on a Saturday, so when you finished training on the Friday, you'd peep through the door and see where you were playing. And on Friday, 24 April 1953, I got the biggest surprise of my life. No sign of my name on the thirds or on the reserve team – but bloody hell, there it was, 'J. Charlton' in the first team, to play Doncaster Rovers the following day! And here's all these senior players looking at me, not saying a word.

Some of them had possibly never heard my name to that point. And when I looked again at the sheet on the door, I discovered that John Charles had been moved up to centre forward, and I was taking his place at centre half. Talk about going in at the deep end!

Incredibly, Raich Carter never came near me that day, never told me why he had put me in his team, nothing. And when I climbed aboard the first-team bus taking us to Doncaster the next day, I was left completely alone, without as much as a word from my new team-mates. I mean, nobody told me what I was expected to do, no tactical talk, nothing. I was left to my own devices until Eric Kerfoot, perhaps sensing my predicament, came across and said, 'Son, they've picked you because they think you're good enough. Now, go and prove them right.'

Fortified by those few words, I stripped and made ready for my big test. Doncaster didn't have a bad team in those days. I discovered that it was my responsibility to look after Eddie McMorran, a big, bustling Irishman who normally hit first and asked questions afterwards.

To be fair, however, he didn't abuse the raw kid playing against him, and the report in the paper the next day said that Jack Charlton hadn't let Leeds down in a 1–1 draw. And that was the first occasion that I had the doubtful pleasure of reading about myself in the papers. I had made it into the first team on the last day of the season – but nobody needed to remind me that I still had a lot of learning to do in the business.

Soon afterwards, I was informed that my country needed me – not to play football, but to do my two years' National Service. Thus, while the remainder of the Leeds players were kicking off the new season, I was on my way to Carlisle to start sixteen weeks' training. Afterwards, I had a week's leave back in Ashington before I joined my regiment, the Royal Horse Guards.

From time to time, you hear harrowing stories of people plucked from Civvy Street who suffered in the army. It didn't begin too well for me either, for when I arrived in Windsor for my first tour of duty, I was put in the 'clink' for seven or eight hours for supposedly going absent without leave – and take it from me, it wasn't a pretty experience. It turned out that I was supposed to have reported to Catterick to play football for Northern Command, but I never got the message.

That was a chastening introduction to the military life, but out of it came two of the happiest years I have ever spent. And that was down to the fact, I suppose, that for the first time, I had total freedom. It sounds strange, I know, but you have to remember that up to then I'd led a very sheltered life. At Leeds you had to be back in your digs by ten o'clock at night; trainers would come round to check up on what time you got in. Of course, there were army rules, a book full of them. But you can do exactly what you like in the army, so long as you don't get caught. And if that brief stint in the guardroom on my first day taught me anything, it was the necessity to keep my wits about me. If you broke the rules and got found out, you could get 'CB' – confined to barracks – and I hated that. You had to dress up, change four or five times a day, and report, just so an officer could walk up, take a look at you, and walk away again. If he didn't like the way you looked, he was liable to give you another couple of days.

Fortunately, the Horse Guards were not involved in tours of foreign duty at that time. Some of the lads who trained with me were posted to the Life Guards in Cyprus, and that wasn't fun at all. The only occasions I travelled overseas was to play football, which suited me fine. They appointed me captain of the Horse Guards team, the first private, I believe, to have been so honoured, and with two other professional players as well, we soon got a reputation as a handy side.

Membership of the football team bestowed all kinds of benefits. We could have late breakfast, for example, because it fitted into our training programme. In fact every conceivable excuse was dreamed up as to why we should have more time to train. In the end, we were like a professional team, and we duly repaid our debt by going to Germany and winning the Cavalry Cup in Hanover. In army terms, that was like winning the FA Cup. I remember they flew out plane-loads of soldiers to support us against the teams out there.

During those two years, of course, my career with Leeds was on hold. Depending on where you were stationed, it was possible for players doing National Service to fit in the odd game, but in my case there was an obvious problem in getting from Windsor to Leeds.

You needed a forty-eight-hour pass to get home to play, and normally you only got one a month. But inevitably, I devised a system whereby I was able to swap around and make it back every fortnight. In my second year in the army I even managed to squeeze in another first-team appearance for Leeds, against Lincoln City. But mainly I only played in the reserves. Sometimes I think I wasted two years in the army while I could have been becoming a better player. But really I had as much football as I could handle.

Lads in the army got four pounds a week retainer from their clubs. At Leeds, the rule was that you were paid six pounds when you came home on leave to play. It didn't matter whether you were in the first or second team, the fee was the same. The real 'scam' came in the expenses. People doing their National Service got chits to travel back to their families. But in the case of lads based at Windsor and living in London, these were pretty useless.

I soon discovered that I could buy them for a few bob, use them to get to Leeds to play games, and then claim four or five pounds travel expenses from the club. The weekly wage in the army was something like twenty-five shillings, but thanks to my football, I was making between twenty-five and thirty pounds a month. And every now and then, I'd receive a parcel from my mother, with maybe a cake or something and a ten-bob note inside. In time, I got a reputation as a lad with a few quid to spare, and I became a money-lender. That, too, yielded a small profit, and by the time my service was finished, I was doing nicely, with around four hundred pounds in the bank.

Windsor, with its easy access to London and all that went with life in a big city, was an eye-opener for me.

There were loads of girls around. Windsor seemed to be full of them, because they used to come up to see the castle or walk along the river. I started going to dances for the first time, and I met plenty of girls there too. I had a girlfriend in Slough and a girlfriend in Maidenhead – but it was never very serious. If you didn't have a car it meant catching a bus back. And it was a long walk back from Slough or Maidenhead if you missed the last bus home.

Windsor was also full of gays – we used to call them queers. It was quite a well-known thing that young soldiers would go off with businessmen and suchlike, and we used to exploit this to a degree that was criminal at times. We used to go to a certain pub where they would buy you drinks all night. They would become very friendly at closing-time, but we'd just say, 'Well, thanks very much, see you now,' and walk off.

And then there was the Royal connection. We soldiers were always taught that if by chance we found ourselves in the presence of Her Majesty, we were to address her as 'Ma'am'. Apart from seeing her drive in and out of Windsor Castle, I never got anywhere near her – but I did have a close encounter with Prince Philip on one occasion. Part of our duties – I think, in fact, it may have been a little 'earner' – was to walk the polo grounds in Windsor Great Park the day after a game, flattening out the ground and replacing any loose divots. On this occasion, a friend and I decided to nip across a path into the woods for a smoke. We then found that neither of us had any matches, so I went back out on the path and hailed this man who was just walking past: 'Excuse me, have you got a light?' – and who turns round, but Prince Philip? I tell you something, my mate and me scarpered out of that place fast!

I learned all my bad habits in the army, and smoking was one of them. I'm still a smoker to this day, though I've never been what you'd call a heavy smoker – we used to buy them in tens in those days, and ten fags would last me two or three days. Through most of my career as a player, I'd stop smoking when I reported for training before the start of a new season, and I wouldn't start again until the season was well under way. I've given up smoking at various times since, but I always drift back onto them.

I remember my last train journey from Windsor, travelling back to Leeds with another lad from the club, Ronnie Powell. At one point in the conversation he said, 'If I don't get a regular place in the second team this season, I'm leaving.' And I told him, 'If I don't get a regular *first*-team place this season, I'm off.'

That kind of talk would have been anathema to me before I set eyes on the bright lights of London. But it's amazing how two years in the army can change the way you see things. For the first time in my life, I had been living on my own, making all my own decisions, and generally living an adult way of life. I liked the Jack the Lad bit – and I was in no mood to change when I reported back to Elland Road.

5

FINDING MY FEET

I came back to leeds two years older and much more self-assured. You could say that I went away to the army a boy of eighteen, and came back a man of twenty. After what I'd experienced away from the club, I wasn't in any mood to let myself be pushed around. Maybe I was a bit too full of myself. I remember one run-in I had with John Charles, of all people, when he came back for a corner against us and started telling me where to go, sort of saying, 'You go over there and I'll go here.' I soon told him where to go, in the way that he couldn't have misunderstood.

After the game he put me up against the wall and pointed a finger at me. 'Don't ever speak to me like that again!' he said. I took his advice to heart.

Although I'd missed the pre-season training, I was quite fit by the time I got back to Leeds. In my last two months in the army I'd worked hard to get myself back into shape. I came back into the side for a home game against Rotherham on 24 September 1955, and from then on I was a regular in the Number 5 shirt. Raich Carter had decided to move John Charles up to the centre forward position again, and I took his place as centre half.

It was a wonderful season for Leeds United. We'd

been not far off the pace in the Second Division for several years without managing to win promotion, in spite of all the goals that John Charles kept scoring. The trouble was, as fast as he scored them, the Leeds defence had been letting them in at the other end. Now we established a home record of thirty-four games without defeat, finishing second to Sheffield Wednesday and winning promotion to the First Division for the first time since 1947.

John Charles was a team unto himself. People often say to me, 'Who was the best player you ever saw in your life?', and I answer, probably Eusebio, Di Stefano, Cruyff, Pelé or our Bob – but the most effective player I ever saw, the one that made the most difference to the performance of the whole team, was, without question, John Charles. He could defend, he could play in midfield, he could attack. He was quick, he was a very, very strong runner, and he was the greatest header of the ball I ever saw. His power in the air was phenomenal. Normally when a player heads the ball his eyes close automatically, but John's didn't, they stayed open. If you tried to challenge John in the air, he'd always jump a fraction of a second earlier, and he seemed to be able to hang in the air. He'd lean on you, he'd put his chest on your shoulder and lean on you, while heading the ball into the net.

The balls you used to head in those days were nothing like the ones today. The balls today don't absorb water, they stay the same shape throughout the whole game. In those days, a keeper often had difficulty punting the ball out of his own half of the field because it was so big and heavy. On a really wet day, the ball got heavier by the minute. If you headed it wrong, you sort of stood there groggy for five or six minutes before you recovered.

John was always known as the Gentle Giant. He'd never go through somebody or kick them from behind, as centre backs often did in our day. But John used to run with his arms stretched out, and he was so big and strong, you just couldn't get close to him without being whacked. I remember one guy getting too close to him and being knocked clean over by these massive, powerful arms.

They may have called him the Gentle Giant – but when it came to the tricks of the trade, John was right up there with the best of them!

I learned loads of things from John. I remember him saying to me, 'When the centre forward's got the ball and he's coming at you, just turn sideways on slightly, just slightly, make a little dart towards him as if you're going to tackle him, and he'll push it the other way. Then check, turn and go the way he's running. You'll have a yard or two's start on him anyway, so you'll get to the ball first. You'll get him.' That was one of the great lessons I learned in my early twenties.

He taught me another trick, which was not to head the ball where you're looking. 'When you go up to head the ball,' he said, 'just change your mind where you want it to go at the last moment. All you've got to do is turn the head, and the ball will follow. It's as simple as that. The keeper will be watching which way you're looking and he will say to himself, "Oh, it's coming that way." You'll send him the wrong way and then just change your mind.' John taught me how to do it, but I was never as good as he was.

I picked up something else from John, which has become a bit of joke with me – and that is the habit of cadging cigarettes from other people. On a lot of occasions I don't carry any, on the basis that if I don't have any with me I won't smoke them, but then I weaken when I see somebody I know smoking and I say to them, 'Go on, give us a fag.' It's a good way of introducing yourself and joining in the conversation. Cloughie's always teased me about it since.

Apart from John, there were some tremendous senior players around in the League in those days, people like Stan Matthews, Tom Finney, Len Shackleton and Jackie Milburn.

At the end of the 1956–57 season we finished eighth in the First Division, but that summer John left us to go to Juventus, for what was then a record fee of £65,000. I was going through a roughish spell at the time, with a bit of the army still sticking with me – staying out late, boozing, girls. Perhaps that was why I was dropped from the first team for much of the second half of the season. But then I met the woman who has been at my side, supporting and encouraging me, ever since.

Pat Kemp had never been to a game. She knew absolutely nothing about football or those involved in it when I walked up and asked her to dance with me in the Majestic Ballroom in Leeds.

Talk about fate! I'd gone to the cinema directly below the Ballroom with a couple of the Leeds players, and almost as an afterthought I went upstairs and stuck my head in the door just to see what was going on.

As I've said, Pat hadn't a clue about football, so when I introduced myself as Jack Charlton, the Leeds United player, she wasn't very impressed. She just raised her eyebrows as if to say, 'Go on, tell me another one.' If I'd said Joe Bloggs of Leeds it still wouldn't have made any difference.

Then there was a dance, one of those novelty

dances, in which a guy leaves the stage, closes his eyes and picks out somebody for a spot prize. He puts his arm on my shoulder and then announces, 'We've got a bit of a celebrity here – Jack Charlton.' And suddenly, Pat realizes that I hadn't been leading her on.

Pat had been inveigled into going out that night with her sister, and strangely enough, out of that decision came two happy marriages, because her sister also met her future husband that night.

We were married at St Peter's Church in Bramley, Leeds, on 6 January 1958. Robert was my best man, and among the guests were his Manchester United mates, Tommy Taylor, Billy Whelan and David Pegg. God rest them, they would be lying dead on a Munich airfield within a month.

I didn't have a car at the time, so I borrowed a pal's to get me to the wedding. I only discovered it had a flat tyre when I set off for the church, so we had to change it then and there, and eventually arrived in a lather of sweat and confusion. Nor was the honeymoon any great shakes either – for after two nights in Scarborough, I had to be back to watch a game. I wasn't playing – it was an FA Cup tie between York City and Birmingham City – but, honeymoon notwithstanding, I felt I needed to be there to keep an eye on form.

That was Pat's introduction to the hardship of life with a professional football player, but bless her, she has adapted superbly over the years. I was away from home when our first son John was born in January 1959, and away again when our only daughter Debbie arrived some two years later. Coward that I am, I deliberately absented myself from the birth of our second son Peter, just a week after the World Cup finals in 1966 – chickening out on the premise that it would be better if I took the two children to stay with my mother. I am a bit superstitious about things like that.

I settled down once I met Pat, and regained my place in the Leeds team. In October 1957 I was actually picked to play for the Football League against the League of Ireland. I remember we won with a bucketful of goals, and I scored one of them. That was my first introduction to an Irish team, and to be honest I wasn't much impressed, but later when Don Revie took over at the club we started to go over to Ireland and play some pre-season matches, and I remember that we had some very competitive games.

Leeds United could not have been described as a glamorous club at the time – unlike Manchester United, who were the most talked-about team in England. Everyone knew about the 'Busby Babes', about Matt Busby's policy of encouraging young players, and the wonderful talent that he was nurturing at Old Trafford. I remember them beating us 5–0 at Old Trafford, and Duncan Edwards was so strong, he was absolutely unbelievable.

Our Bob was just starting his National Service when I came back from the Horse Guards. He was posted to Shrewsbury, and somehow he managed to wangle much more time off than I ever did, because the following year he made his début for Manchester United. That season he played fourteen games as part of that championship-winning team which came close to winning the double. They probably would have done, too, had their keeper, Ray Wood, not been carried off after only six minutes of the 1957 FA Cup final against Aston Villa.

Our kid was still only nineteen when he played against Real Madrid in the 1957 European Cup semi-final, and the following year he was a part of the Manchester United team which beat Red Star Belgrade in a two-leg European Cup quarter-final. It was on their way back from this win, on 6 February 1958, that Matt Busby's young team had to change planes at Munich airport.

I was drying myself in the dressing-room after a training session when the news came through to Elland Road. I can remember to this day exactly where I was standing, stark naked at the time. Arthur Crowther, the club secretary, walked in and announced, 'The Manchester United plane has crashed and they don't know if there are any survivors.' Then he left the dressing-room. One of the lads looked at me and said, 'Your kid's on that plane,' and I said, 'Yeah.'

I got dressed as quickly as I could and went up to Arthur Crowther's office, where five or six of them were sitting talking about it. I asked if anyone had any information about the crash, and they tried phoning around, but nobody knew what had happened. So I decided to go back to Ashington. There was no phone at my parents' house, of course – but my mother later told me she knew I'd come. I phoned Pat, and we arranged to meet at the station. It was bitterly cold, with thick snow lying on the ground. Some guy was talking about the crash on the train, but I couldn't speak to him. The bloody train journey lasted ages.

From Newcastle station we took a taxi to the Haymarket, where we could catch a bus to Ashington. The taxi dropped us off, and as we walked to the bus stop I saw a guy selling newspapers. I could read the stop press in the papers folded over his arm: *Bobby Charlton among the survivors*. I shouted, 'Bloody hell, he's OK!', though of course we didn't know if he had been badly injured – the paper just said that he had been taken to hospital. When we got home, my mother had already heard the good news. The local police constable had come running up the street smiling and waving a piece of paper, a message from the Foreign Office that our Bob was safe. A few minutes afterwards a neighbour arrived to say that the plane was 'a burnin' inferno', and that there were no survivors. 'If that woman had arrived a few minutes' earlier,' my mother said, 'you could have buried me at home.'

Later we heard that our kid had asked one of the survivors, the goalkeeper Harry Gregg, to get a message to us, before collapsing and being taken to hospital.

There was relief, of course, that he was going to be OK, but there was also sadness as news came through of those who had died. I knew them all: Tommy Taylor and David Pegg had been at our wedding only a month earlier, and Duncan Edwards and Billy Whelan had often driven over the Pennines with our kid for a drink on Sunday mornings. Matt Busby himself was seriously ill, being treated in the same hospital as our Robert.

My mother wanted to fly straight to Munich, but she was just recovering from a breast cancer operation and the doctors advised that it wouldn't be safe for her to travel. Matt Busby's assistant, Jimmy Murphy, had taken over while Matt was in hospital, and he suggested that she should come and help out in the offices at Old Trafford, where there was plenty of work for her to do. I think it helped to take her mind off things while she waited for our kid to come home. The buses had been cancelled because of the snow, but she

66

managed to beg a lift over the Pennines early the next morning from a newspaper delivery driver.

I can't remember how long our Bob was in hospital, but it seemed weeks and weeks. I went down to London to pick him up from Liverpool Street Station and drive him back to Ashington. He was very quiet in the car. Then he said, 'I know you want to know what happened and I will tell you, but I don't want you to ask me again.' He told me about the plane trying to take off and then checking and going back to clear the ice off the wings before trying again. 'Finally they started for the third time, and as we gathered speed I looked out of the window and realized that we weren't going to clear the fence at the end of the runway. That was all – I don't remember a bang or a crash or anything like that. The next thing I remember is seeing Harry Gregg pulling people out of a big hole in the side of the plane. I was still belted into my seat. I realized I was outside on the runway, but I didn't really know if I had been thrown out or if someone had pulled me out.' Then he told me how he had fainted and been taken to hospital, and coming round to hear the terrible news of the others who had died. 'Now I want to forget all about it,' he finished.

Our Robert has said he felt drained after the accident. So many of his friends and team-mates had been killed, he couldn't really understand why he was still alive. He looked as though he was going to cry all the time. He kept asking himself, 'Why me?' The press were hounding him, which made it worse. For a time he declared that he wouldn't have anything to do with football any more. Then our family doctor sorted him out, and he went back to Old Trafford.

I would often go and see him in Manchester or he

would come across to see me at Leeds. On one occasion, less than three months after the accident, I'd been staying a couple of days with him in his digs. We'd been to the pictures in the afternoon, and when we came out I bought an evening paper. I was looking at the back page while we were walking down the main street in Stretford – and there it was in the stop press: *Bobby Charlton has been picked to play for England against Scotland at Hampden Park*. I let out a whoop, and he just turned to me and smiled. I was absolutely overjoyed for him, I really was.

Leeds had two more seasons in the First Division, but we were always struggling, not helped by the musical chairs in the manager's job. Raich Carter left in 1958, and then two managers came and went in the next three seasons.

While all this was going on I'd started to become involved in coaching. I'd met an ex-Leeds player called George Ainsley who coached in schools, and one day he invited me to go along with him. George sat all the Batley Grammar School kids down in the gym and asked one of them, 'How many times do you want me to head this ball?'

The boy just went, 'Um, five?' George told me later that the kids usually said five or six, never more than ten. 'OK,' George said, 'I'll do a hundred.' And he did. The kids couldn't believe it, it made them laugh, and it taught me a lesson, which is that when you're coaching young people, you've got to make it fun, otherwise they'll not want to do it. You must entertain, you must be a showman. Words mean nothing in football, George told me. You must show them how to do a thing and why, and then they'll all want to do it like you. George taught me too that you've got to vary your coaching, you can't do things repetitiously or you'll lose their interest – and once you've lost their interest, you're wasting your time.

He'd certainly got my interest, and with his encouragement I took my prelim badge as a Football Association coach, and a month or so later I went away for a week on the FA summer coaching course at Lilleshall. I couldn't get my full coaching badge that year, so I went back the next year, and I liked it so much that I soon became a regular there. Bill Shankly and Bob Paisley and people like that used to come and talk to us. You discussed football, you looked at the way different people played, you looked at different patterns. It opened me up to thinking about football in a completely different way, it gave me all sorts of ideas. There was a great change sweeping through English football at the time. For those that had the eyes to see what was going on, it was very exciting. At Lilleshall I mixed with many of the young coaches who went on to become managers, people like Bobby Robson, Lawrie McMenemy, Dave Sexton and Malcolm Allison. I got to know all the players who were interested in coaching at the time – and I must have known someone at practically every club in England. If you look back, you'll see that almost every player who went on to succeed as a manager had been to Lilleshall – those that didn't, like our Bob or Bobby Moore, never really made it as managers. The same was true of most of the players who were with me at Elland Road in the great Leeds teams.

Walter Winterbottom was in charge when I first went there, and after him Alan Wade. I remember Alan introducing a guy from college one day. This counsellor spent all afternoon giving us advice about how to handle players, and I have to say it was pretty boring. Then he said, 'We're going to play a game.' We divided into two teams and trooped off to the dressing-room to change. Before we went out to play this counsellor came round to see each of us individually; he just sat down with us quietly and said, 'I'm going to give you a word to remember, and at half-time I'm going to come and ask you what it is.' Then we went out to play football, and at half-time he came round to see each of us in the dressing-room again. Not one of us could remember the word he had given us. 'OK,' he said, 'I'll give you the word again. But this time, try to remember it.' So he repeated the word, and then we went out to play the second half. At the end of the game, he came back – and again no-one could remember their word!

We couldn't really understand the point the guy was trying to make until he got us all together again. Then he explained. 'The game of football wipes everything from your mind; you're so engrossed that you think of nothing else. So don't tell your players, "I want you to do this," or "I want you to do that," and expect them to remember what you say, 'cos they won't. Players react to situations automatically. Unless you programme them differently, they'll do things the way they've always done them. You have to be prepared to work with them for weeks and months to get an idea to stick. In a dead-ball situation players have more time to remember what you've told them, but even then you've got to practise with them for weeks to be sure that everyone reacts the way you want them to.'

The point has stayed with me throughout my life – that you must programme players in what you want them to do until it becomes second nature to them.

And the best thing is to keep it very simple. The less choice you give a player, the more likely he is to make the right decision. If you keep it very simple, each player will know what he has to do, and will know what the other players are going to do and the positions they will take up. Football is really a very simple game – you just have to programme the players beforehand.

Soon I was an FA-approved coach, working in schools and boys' clubs in the Leeds and Castleford areas. In those days the FA paid you thirty shillings an hour to work in schools, and I was working as many afternoons as I could, for the money as much as anything. At the end of the month I might get a cheque for sixty or seventy quid, which was good money to me, when I had a young family and was buying a house, and I was only earning twenty quid a week from the club.

Strangely enough, all this coaching didn't make me any happier at Leeds. Raich Carter wasn't a coach, and he didn't employ coaches. Everyone respected him as a great player of the past, but he didn't understand that you might need help to work on your game. Maybe Raich was such a good player that he didn't understand how things that came easily to him might be difficult for other people. The only training we used to do at Elland Road in those days was to run down the long side of the pitch, jog the short side, sprint the long side, and so on. We used to have five-a-side and eight-a-side matches on the cinder surface of the car-park. But no-one ever coached you, there was nobody you could talk to about your game, we never went out and practised free kicks or corner kicks or anything like that. We never really had any team talks, and we never had a run-down on the opposition. Leeds United wasn't

71

what I would call a professional club in those days. You trained in the morning, you went home – nobody bothered what you did the rest of the day.

An ex-army guy called Bill Lambton took over from Raich. Bill was a nice enough man, but he wasn't a player, he wasn't a coach, he wasn't anything. If you ever saw Bill walking about he always had a piece of paper in his hand – nobody ever found out what was written on that paper, but it made him look as though he was doing something. Bill was a fitness fanatic. I remember one windy day, when we complained about the balls being too hard during a training session. Bill told us that anyone worth his salt ought to be able to kick balls in his bare feet and never feel it, so one of the lads said, 'Well, go on then.' Now Bill wasn't a pro, he'd probably never kicked a ball in anger in his life, and yet here he was running up to kick the ball in his bare feet, and of course you could see him wincing afterwards. This is the manager who's just been appointed, and he's making a fool of himself in front of his players. He finished up hobbling off the pitch, with all of us laughing at him. Bill never recovered from that day. A few weeks later we had a meeting, and after some of the lads had their say, the chairman asked if we wanted the manager to leave – and every one of the players said yes. Bill said pathetically, 'If you let me stay, we'll have a new start,' but nobody said a dicky-bird. He was sacked that same day.

I felt sorry for Bill. I didn't take him seriously as a football man, but I got on all right with him. I used to see him later from time to time when he was running a pub on the Leeds–Grimsby road, and he seemed much happier.

Then we got a manager called Jack Taylor, and his

brother Frank joined the club as coach. In those days managers didn't wear track suits, but Frank did. He was the first guy who ever took me out on a pitch and taught me how to kick a ball properly – following it through, keeping it low, chipping balls, that sort of thing. One thing he did was to lay down two bricks and place the ball between them, then ask you to run up and hit it full on. You soon learned to keep your eye on the ball! I could talk to the Taylors about the game, and suddenly I felt I had kindred spirits within the club. But the other players didn't respond well to the new approach. Their general attitude was that they came into the club to do their bit of training, played their matches, and then buggered off. They just weren't interested in developing their skills or any theory or anything like that.

Meanwhile I was still very involved in coaching, reading the literature on football theory and suchlike to get my qualifying badges. I used to go away in the summer to Lilleshall for the managers' and trainers' week, and a group of us used to meet in the Griffin Hotel to discuss football. When George Ainsley moved away from the area I took over his schools, and I became so involved that I sometimes used to squeeze in a session in the morning before I went to the club for the ten o'clock training. The schools were often a bit disappointed to have me instead of George, because he used to go into the classrooms or the common-rooms before a coaching session to tell jokes and make them laugh.

Leeds were still in trouble, and at the end of the 1959–60 season we were relegated to the Second Division. That was bad enough, but we were in free fall. By the 1960–61 season we were struggling to stay up in the Second Division. Jack Taylor resigned, though he still had time to run on his contract. We had never really replaced John Charles. John did in fact come back to us in 1962, but he wasn't the force he had been and he only stayed eleven games.

One thing Bill Lambton had done for us in his three months with the club was to sign a couple of good players. One was a Scots lad called Billy Bremner, only just seventeen – the other, almost twice his age, was Don Revie. Don was a bit older than the rest of us. We all knew of Don because we'd all heard of the Revie Plan, which was quite famous at the time. It was what you call a deep-line centre forward, actually. At Manchester City, even though he wore the Number 9 shirt, Don operated from midfield delivering the ball to people. Good striker of the ball, good passer, was Don – though he couldn't tackle to save his life. Then he went to Sunderland and then he came to us.

I suppose I was feeling rather sorry for myself at the time. It irritated me when Don said that I was spoiling it for the others, 'with that chip on your shoulder'. Maybe I had a bit of a chip, maybe I just needed some discipline, I don't know. I remember what Don told me during one practice match. I used to go charging up the field for corner kicks and I ran about all over the park during the play. The crowd liked it when I ran with the ball, although half the time – no, 90 per cent of the time – I'd overrun the bloody thing. Totally unprofessional. Anyway, I'd gone charging up the field with the ball and Don said to me afterwards, 'If I was manager, I wouldn't play you – you're always messing about.'

'Well, you're not the manager,' I said, 'so what the hell?' And then, lo and behold, Don became manager!

I was, well . . . I couldn't have been one of Don's favourites in those early days.

The first year with Revie was an interesting one. The day after he took over, he moved me up to centre forward. I tried my best, but the Number 9 shirt didn't feel right to me. I didn't know what to do, and nobody showed me. I remember Joe Shaw of Sheffield United laughing at me, I was making such a mess of it. After I protested Don switched me back to centre half.

Don created a more professional backroom staff, bringing in Les Cocker as trainer, Syd Owen as coach, and Maurice Lindley as assistant manager. I should have welcomed that, because, as I've said, I had been disappointed at the lack of professionalism within the club up till then. There was no coaching, no work that went into the game, no development of players, no pattern or structure. But I still had a bit of an attitude problem. I used to call Les Cocker 'Cocker', which annoyed him. He stopped me in the car-park one day and said, 'My name is bloody Les!'

'Oh?' I replied. 'I always thought your name was Cocker.'

I was just being facetious and nasty.

I got so upset with Syd Owen shouting at us during practice matches that I offered to take my coat off to him. I told Don that if Syd didn't get off my back, 'I'll not be responsible for my actions.' I suppose I was going through a difficult period of my life. Leeds United were a very average Second Division side, I was just a young pro with a very famous brother who was making headlines at the time. I didn't consider myself to be a particularly good player, I was just a typical young footballer like hundreds of others in the League. I felt I was in limbo, with a club that wasn't going anywhere. I had my own thoughts and ideas about the game – and perhaps that made me a bit more argumentative and less eager to listen to people who were telling me things I didn't want to hear. I was unsettled, I wasn't very happy at the club, and I didn't do anything to hide my discontent. Don later said that at the time I was one of the most awkward customers he ever had the misfortune to meet.

I remember a half-time incident during a game against Rotherham. We had a keeper called Tommy Younger, a Scottish international, at the time. There'd been a corner against us in the first half, and their centre forward had sent in a floating header from the edge of the eighteen-yard box. Tommy should have collected it easily, but as the ball hit the ground he dived over it and it bounced into the net. When Don came into the dressing-room at half-time he was not best pleased. He pointed at me and said that I should have picked up the centre forward on the edge of the eighteen-yard box. 'Wait a minute,' I said, 'the bloody ball was headed from about twenty-five yards away. I'm not bloody responsible. If a guy gets in and heads a ball within ten yards, that's my responsibility. If I'd have gone out there and somebody else had headed the ball where I should have been positioned, then you would have bollocked me!'

I had a teacup in my hand and I threw it against the wall. It missed Don by about a foot and smashed to pieces. Everyone else went quiet while I went ranting on. Then Don just walked out of the dressing-room. After the game had finished, we all sat down and Don said, 'If I want to discuss things we do wrong in any game, we'll discuss it on a Monday morning when we've all had time to settle down and had a weekend to

76

think about it.' And that's what we did from then on.

People don't realize how hyped up players can be when they come off the football field. You're full of adrenalin, you get high, and you can do silly things. So right after the football match is not the time to talk about things that you may have done wrong.

I had more words with Don after somebody had scored a goal against us while I was up the other end for a corner. I had got a reputation for being a good header of the ball, and I used to go to the goal for dead-ball situations near the box. Even if the ball went some-where else, just my presence distracted the other side's defences. The crowd began to call me 'the giraffe' because my neck would stretch up above the others in front of the goal. Well, you can't be in two places at once, so if the centre back goes up, somebody has to fill in for him. I argued about this with Don, and in the end I said, 'Bugger it, if you want me to be a centre back I'll be a centre back, and I won't go charging up front any more.' For a while I refused to go up forward, even though I enjoyed it. I was just making a point, that I couldn't do that and this as well.

The next season Don moved me up to centre for-ward again, and brought in Freddie Goodwin in my place. Freddie was a very nice lad, a big, steady centre half, but he always had the idea we should play what he called man-to-man marking, that everybody, all the defenders, should pick a man and stay with him. I totally disagreed with this – you could see it wasn't working. We had a bloody awful spell and went very quickly down the League. At the end of the season we finished nineteenth, and only just avoided relegation to the Third Division by winning the last game against Newcastle 3–0.

Revie called me into his office one day and announced, 'I'm prepared to let you go.' I said, 'Wait a minute, are you letting me go as a centre forward or a centre half, 'cos I've been playing for you for fifteen games or whatever as centre forward, which is not my position? But I've been doing it because you asked me – when really I should be coming back to my own position if I'm in the side.'

'Well,' he said, 'I'm quite happy with the way Fred Goodwin is doing it.'

I said, 'OK, please yourself,' and walked out of his office.

I started playing for the reserves. The funny thing was that though Don had said that he was prepared to let me go, he never did put me on the transfer list.

Bill Shankly telephoned me to say that he was negotiating with Leeds to buy me for Liverpool. 'I have offered them £28,500 and they want £30,000,' he said. 'I'm not going to be held to ransom – so the deal's off, for the time being. I'm sorry, son, but that's the way it is.'

I'd been told Manchester United were interested in signing me, too. They were on a tour of America at the time, but it seemed they were going to come in for me at the end of the summer. So I refused to sign a new contract with Leeds. It caused an unpleasant feeling at the club. Syd Owen took me by the arm and asked me what the problem was, but I told him to 'shove off'. Then I got a message to go over to see Matt Busby. We sat talking in his office, and he explained that while they were in America they had played a young lad at centre back, someone who had just come into the side, and Matt wanted to wait until the new season started so that they could have a good

78

look at this lad before giving me a decision.

I couldn't believe what he was telling me. 'I have caused ructions at Elland Road, I have refused to sign a contract, nobody there is speaking to me,' I said. 'I have caused bloody havoc in the club, I have been offered a deal and turned it down – and now you are telling me I have got to wait until the beginning of the new season, until you have had a look at someone else? No,' I said, 'I am not going to do that, I am going back to Elland Road, and I am going to apologize for what I have done. I am going to sign a new contract with the club and I am not bloody well coming here!'

I was most upset when I walked out of Busby's office. I went straight back to Leeds to see Don. 'Have you got a contract you want me to sign?' I asked him. He said yes, he had. 'I have caused you enough problems at this club,' I told him, 'and I won't cause you any more.' And I signed.

6

'ALL FOR ONE AND ONE FOR ALL'

Late in the 1961–62 season, that season we nearly went down to the Third Division, Don called me into his office and said he was bringing me back into the side as centre back. He talked for a bit and then he said something which astonished me: 'Listen, if you screw the nut, you could play for England.'

'What?' I said. 'You must be kidding, one minute you're prepared to let me go and the next you tell me that I'm good enough to play for England?'

I laughed at him then, you know. I never dreamed then that I would one day play for England – but within a few years I had.

'Screw the nut' meant more than just trying harder. It meant changing your attitude, becoming more professional in your approach. It meant becoming part of the set-up.

Don was starting to put the club on a more professional footing. The travel arrangements improved, and we stayed in better hotels. We felt looked after. Don's attitude was that the players are the important people. Leeds United was just a lump of ground – the team were what mattered.

Don scrapped the rule book. Before Don took over we had this rule book, which acted like a pass letting you into other grounds for nothing, but it also had all these rules. Don scrapped all that. 'The only rule we've got from now on is common sense,' he used to say. It wasn't that he was lax with us – he used to phone me and demand an explanation if I was seen in a pub in the days leading up to a game, but he seemed to be able to impose some discipline without laying down formal rules. I don't ever remember him fining anybody, as so many managers do.

The coaching was different. Suddenly we were starting to do all the things I'd learned about at Lilleshall. I found that I could work with Syd and Les – though we still had our shouting matches, when Syd would shake his head and walk away. Don never coached himself, but he was always there, he always knew what was going on. He started giving us team talks before we went on the field, and he would go round before the game to have a word with each player individually.

There was a game against Swansea, in September 1962, that marked a turning-point in my life. Don had left a lot of senior players out of the side, a very brave thing to do at the time, and he brought in a lot of new young players he'd just signed – Gary Sprake in goal, Norman Hunter, Paul Reaney, and a fellow called Rod Johnson. I said to Don, 'Well, I'm not going to play the way you've been playing with Fred, I don't want to play man-to-man marking, I want to play a zonal system where you pick up people in your area. I'll sort out the back four for you the way I want them to play' – and Don said OK.

That, for me, was the moment when I stopped being one of the awkward squad and came on board the Leeds United ship. It was a sign that I would be one of the key players in the new team Don was building. I was sort of the organizer at the back, I was the pusher, I was the one who told the young lads where to go, when to cover, and how to pick up positions. I'll never forget something that happened a few years later: Norman Hunter suddenly rebelled against me telling him what to do. 'I've been with you long enough and I've learned me bloody lesson now,' he said. 'I wish you'd let me do things my way instead of you bloody telling me all the time.'

And I said, 'Norman, now you're reacting that way, you're fine. Get on with it.'

He reminded me of me.

I even became captain for a bit, but I didn't like it because I like to be the last out of the tunnel. Captains in football do very little anyway, and I was happy just to be organizing the back four.

Don was a very superstitious man. Everyone knows about his lucky suit that he always wore at matches. He'd heard that there was some sort of gypsy's curse on Elland Road, so one of the first things he did when he took over at the club was to bring in a medium to lift the curse. Some of the lads laughed at him – but from then on things at the club started to improve.

I must have been a bit of a Revie addict, because I got to the stage where I needed to follow a ritual before every game. I would always put on my left boot first, followed by my right boot, my jock-strap and my shorts. Then I would take a programme and go and sit on the toilet for three or four minutes. I'd always leave the programme on the left-hand side of the toilet before I went back to the dressing-room. I wouldn't put my shirt on till I was ready to go out on the field. And, as I've said, I liked to be the last out. In the end it was ridiculous, it was taking me more than an hour to get ready.

Before the game at Swansea there was another crucial change at Leeds, another moment that marked the change from being a mediocre Second Division team to one of the most feared in England – and that was the arrival of Bobby Collins in March 1962. We were still struggling to avoid relegation, and in the last few games of that season Bobby played a vital part in ensuring that we stayed in the Second Division. From then on the only way forward was up.

Bobby Collins was a thirty-one-year-old former Scottish international when Don signed him from Everton. He was only a little guy, about five feet six inches tall, but he was a very, very strong, skilful little player. But what marked him out, and what made the difference to the Leeds sides he played in, was his commitment to winning. He was so combative, he was like a little flyweight boxer. He would kill his mother for a result! He introduced a sort of 'win at any cost' attitude into the team. Probably because we had a very young side at the time, the other players were very much influenced by his approach to the game.

I got on all right with Bobby, but I didn't like to play against him. Even when we were playing five-a-side practice matches, you never knew what he was liable to do because he always wanted to win so much. But that was the attitude we needed at the time.

In Bobby's first complete season with us – the season we played that game at Swansea and brought several new young players into the side – we finished fifth in the Second Division. At the beginning of the following season, 1963–64, Don signed another key player, Johnny Giles, and we finished top. Many so-called experts thought that we would struggle in the First Division, but we didn't, we were right up there with the leaders, finishing second to the eventual winners, Manchester United, at the end of the 1964–65 season. Bobby was named Footballer of the Year, and regained his place in the Scotland squad after an absence of six years.

Bobby introduced a much more professional attitude to winning. In the past we'd often score a goal but then let the other side back into it. Now we'd score a goal and that would be it – we'd lock it up, that was the end of the game. Our defence was rock-solid and we tackled hard. Nobody liked playing against us. It wasn't very popular, of course. Teams like Arsenal and Spurs might play to the gallery by chasing bigger scores, but not Leeds United. We beat all the London clubs that year, and I don't think the London press ever really forgave us for that.

Bobby might not have been captain, but in those early years he was the real leader of the team. He introduced a new spirit, which Don encouraged – 'all for one and one for all'. We all looked after each other, so that if you kicked me, I wouldn't kick you back, but somebody else would. Eventually it all went too far. A game against Everton at Goodison Park – Bobby's first return to his old club since he transferred to us more than two years earlier – had to be abandoned for ten minutes after scuffles broke out on the field between the players. There were lots of tackles going in and fouls such as I'd never seen before – going in over the top, boots hanging in late – sneaky things. I didn't like it. It was nice to be successful, of course, and the crowd at Elland Road loved it. But the way we were achieving that success made me feel uncomfortable. We were getting a reputation for intimidating teams rather than outplaying them – which was wrong, because we had some good players. I'm a Geordie, and I was brought up with good, honest, hard football. You kick me as hard as you like when you're trying to get the ball, I'll kick you as hard as I like when I'm trying to get the ball – that's OK. But don't nip my legs while the ref's looking the other way.

Norman Hunter was like that, too – despite his ferocious reputation as a man who 'bites yer legs'. Norman tackled hard, very hard, but he always went for the ball. If he sometimes missed the ball, it was an honest mistake. Norman was a bit like Tommy Smith of Liverpool. When you tackled Tommy, it was like running into a brick wall – it shook every bone in your body. But I never saw Tommy commit a nasty foul, and I never saw Norman commit a nasty foul. When they tackled, they tackled with everything they'd got, but you could never accuse them of being dirty players.

Revie wasn't a hard man himself, but he was very protective of his players, and maybe that led him to turn a blind eye to some of the things that were happening on the field. He certainly instilled the will to win in us, the idea that only winners are respected.

We made a lot of enemies in that 1964–65 season. I remember lying on the treatment table in the Leeds dressing-room with one of the young lads, Jimmy Lumsden. He was talking about a reserves match the night before, and he told me that he had gone in over the top of the ball to a guy who then had to be taken off. 'I gave him a beauty,' Jimmy said. Don murmured something approvingly.

'Jimmy,' I told him, 'Jimmy, you live by the sword, you die by the sword. That guy might some day play against you again, he will remember you and he might just go over the top to you when you're not expecting it. You might finish up breaking your leg.'

I remember playing against Brian Clough that season. It was his first game back for Sunderland after he'd been out of the game for a long period after a very nasty injury. I was loath to tackle him, to be honest. But when he stuck two goals in, I changed my mind! I learnt a lesson, which is that there's no give and take in this game. No matter what the injury, if you're playing on the field, you've got to accept what's handed out.

Brian was what we called a goal poacher, always hanging around the penalty box – very similar in style to John Aldridge. He didn't hit spectacular volleys, but he'd get a lot of goals through headers close in or little nudges with his toe. Brian was considered to be a very selfish player. If he had a chance to score, he'd take it – even if there was a guy standing next to him who was certain to score.

I admit that I was still a bit of a hothead at the time. I would certainly say my piece in the dressing-room, and sometimes do some silly things on the park. I had a famous falling-out with Jimmy Greenhoff. There'd been an incident when I'd dived in to head the ball and collided with the keeper. The ball bounced out, and all Jimmy had to do was to knock it into the net. But he pulled his head away because someone else was coming in. I went crackers. 'I nearly got killed,' I said, 'and the ball was there for you, and you pulled out of a header that could have won us the game.' I called him 'chicken' in front of the other lads, and I don't think he ever forgave me for that.

The 1964–65 season was marked by an intense rivalry between ourselves and Manchester United. Both teams seemed to have a chance of the double until very late in the season. We went to the top of the First Division and enjoyed a run of twenty-five games without defeat before Manchester United beat us at Elland Road – a defeat that eventually cost us the League championship.

But we were League leaders right up to the last game, when we played Birmingham City away. Manchester United were playing at home that same night. We knew we had to win, but in fact we went a goal behind after only four minutes, and soon after half-time we conceded another two goals. We fought our way back in the last fifteen minutes, and four minutes before the end I scored the equalizer. But we couldn't get the win we needed. I don't know whether it was nerves or not. Having to go to a place and win your last match is a different thing entirely from going to a place needing to draw. Being such a high-profile game probably helped them more than it did us – they had a chance for glory in an otherwise lacklustre season. If we'd played Birmingham earlier in the season we'd probably have beaten them. But that game at Birmingham started the notion that Leeds United choked under pressure.

We ended up losing the League on goal difference. Even though we'd won a massive sixty-one points, enough to win the Championship in most seasons, we hadn't clinched it.

We had a chance for revenge against Manchester United when we were drawn against them in the semi-finals of the FA Cup. The first semi-final, at Hillsborough, was a bad-tempered game which ended in a 0–0 draw. I had a number of clashes in the penalty area with Dennis Law, nearly pulling the shirt off his back on more than one occasion. You had to hang on to Dennis, because he was so sharp and so good in the air. I used to hate playing against him, though I've always regarded him as a good pal of mine.

Dennis was a great competitor. I'll never forget going for a cross coming in at Elland Road, and as I went to volley the ball, suddenly Dennis was diving over me and heading it into the net. I kicked Dennis right in the mouth, I really walloped him – not deliberately, of course, it was an accident. Anyway, I remember Dennis lying on his back, and there's blood and everything coming out of his mouth and nose, and the trainer is sponging him down. I was standing over him as he started to come to. He looked up at me and smiled, and he asked, 'Did I score, big fella?'

Matt Busby had rebuilt Manchester United into one of the greatest teams in the world. It was about this time that they went to the Stadium of Light and beat Benfica 5–1 – and not many sides have done that! As well as Dennis Law they had our kid, of course, and he was a very dangerous player. He scored some tremendous goals against us in those early days – the power of his shots was amazing. Most of the time I played against him, he was always running towards me, and he was liable either to 'nutmeg' you – to push the ball through your legs – or to go past you. If he had room he would run at you and try to go past you, which is probably why he never needed anybody else to play the ball off. You had to try to get close to him if you could. Whenever I played against our kid my mother always used to say to me, 'Take care of the little one.' Some hope!

Their other star player, of course, was George Best. George was a very, very gifted player. There were better headers of the ball, there were better passers of the ball – but there was never anyone better on the ball than George. He could dribble better than anyone I've ever known. He was so sharp that when you tried to get the ball off him, he'd turn and he'd be off. He seemed to have a sense of where you were all the time, he had frightening pace, and he had an eye for squeezing through a little gap that nobody else knew was there. He was very slim in those days. Strangely enough, we had a player called Paul Reaney who was very quick, probably even quicker than George. When we played Manchester United, Paul used to stick to George throughout the game – virtually the only time Don ever designated a player to mark anyone. But if George ever got away from Paul, he was a threat to everybody.

Every day there was a story in the papers about George Best – but most of the things we were reading were not about what he'd done on the field, but about sleeping with three Miss Worlds or whatever. I cancelled the *Daily Mirror*, because I was sick to death of reading all their stories about George.

George is still, to this day, a legend – but in my opinion he wasn't a great player. To be a great player, you've got to be a Bobby Charlton, a Billy Bremner or a Dave Mackay – players who stayed around in top level football for ten to fifteen years. George didn't hang about that long before running off to America. It was a great loss to the game.

I remember meeting him much later in Lisbon when he came back to Manchester United. It was Eusebio's testimonial match, and we had been invited to go and play for an international side at the Stadium of Light. Tommy Docherty had taken over at Old Trafford, and he was desperately trying to sort George out. I walked out onto the hotel balcony, and there was Tommy Doc with George. I went and sat down with them, and I remember thinking that some of the things George was saying were out of order – things like, 'There's no way I'm going to do this,' and 'There's no way I'm going to do that.' I was so disgusted, I got up and walked away. He was just a fat little fella who had been wasting his time in America.

We won the semi-final replay 1–0, after a goal by Billy Bremner only two minutes from the end.

We went to stay the few days before the Cup final at a hotel near London, the Selsdon Park in Crystal Palace. I remember playing a little five-a-side game on the Friday. Norman Hunter volleyed the ball, and it hit Bobby on the face, making his nose bleed a little. It was clearly an accident, not deliberate or anything. Then the game restarted, and when Norman got the ball Bobby just flew at him. It was obvious Bobby meant to do him harm. I yelled, 'Norman!' – and he looked up and turned just as Bobby hit him in the middle with both feet. Bobby finished up on top of Norman, punching him. I yanked him off, and I had to hold him at arms' length because he started trying to whack me. 'Come on, Bobby, calm down,' I said, 'we've got a Cup final tomorrow.' But that was Bobby, you couldn't stop him when he got worked up.

I wasn't particularly nervous before the Cup final. I'd played at Wembley before, though not with Leeds – it was the first time we'd been there as a team.

In the first twenty minutes or so of the final itself we found it very difficult to hang on to Liverpool. We were still very inexperienced, and they looked a much better side. Gary Sprake kept us in the game by making some superb saves. But we had a good side too, and both teams were good competitors – neither would let the other side really play.

At full time the score was still 0–0, but only three minutes into extra time Roger Hunt put Liverpool into the lead. About ten minutes later I went up for a cross and headed the ball back across the box from the far post for Billy to score with a great volley. From then on we were back in the game, and it was tightly contested. Then Ian St John headed the winner for Liverpool.

Don's attitude was, 'Well, we'll win it next year.' I wasn't disappointed. We'd had a great season, and I felt we'd achieved a great deal, even though we hadn't actually won anything in the end. We were still building, and there would be plenty of chances in the years to come.

The following season, 1965–66, we were again second in the League, this time to Liverpool. It was our first season in Europe, since we'd qualified for the old Inter-City Fairs Cup (now the UEFA Cup). Bobby Collins broke his thigh bone in the opening match against Turin. I remember it very vividly – Bobby was lying there, the referee wanted to move him off the park, and the Turin players were trying to bundle him off. I wouldn't let them move him; I knew that if Bobby Collins wouldn't get up, he must have something broken. I stood over him, whacking one Italian and punching another to keep them back, until eventually the referee realized that Bobby must be seriously hurt and called for a stretcher. We won the game 1–0, and afterwards a few of us went by the hospital to see Bobby. It was only hours after the game, and he was lying in bed with what looked like a tent over his leg, a weight-and-traction thing at the end to hold his leg straight. He smiled when he saw us, and then he said,

'Take a look at this.' He threw back the tent thing, and there was a bolt through his leg – not a shiny silver bolt, but something that looked like it came out of the scrapyard. Bobby thought it was funny. That was the sort of guy Bobby was – tough. But he was never the same player for Leeds again. Soon afterwards Johnny Giles took over his role as the midfield general.

In the third round of the Fairs Cup we were drawn against Valencia. The first leg at Elland Road ended in a bit of a barney between myself and their defender Vidagany. I'd come up for a corner kick, like I always did at the time, and as the ball was cleared, he just kicked me across the ankles. I stumbled and fell, and then I got up and went after him. He ran towards the goal and hid behind the net, with three or four Spanish players blocking my path. I was trying to get past them when the goalkeeper punched me in the mouth, so I went after him instead. The keeper backed away, kicking to keep me off – and then a policeman brought me down.

The referee took us all off the park, and then he came into the dressing-room and told me that I would not be coming back when play resumed. Vidagany didn't come back either.

The press lads had a real go at us afterwards. There was an FA inquiry. Don defended me, saying that I'd been provoked by being constantly kicked. The referee, a Dutchman called Leo Horn, flew into London and gave evidence. To his great credit, he took some of the blame. 'I actually saw the player kick Mr Charlton and I didn't do anything about it,' he said. 'I maybe should have done something about the incident, but I turned away as the game was still going on. Then I looked back and I saw that Mr Charlton was chasing that man with madness in his eyes.' The FA fined me twenty pounds.

The press built up the second leg in Valencia as a possible bloodbath, but in fact it was a perfectly normal game and we went through to the next round. Eventually we reached the semi-final against Real Zaragoza. It was 2–2 after the first two legs, and we were lucky enough to draw the home advantage for the replay. We were expecting to take the game to them at Elland Road, but in fact it was exactly the other way round, and we were 3–0 down after only half an hour. After that we didn't really have a hope. But we were learning how to play in Europe and we'd had a number of hard, competitive battles. We found that in Italy especially, you've got loads of time on the ball, nobody seems to put you under any pressure – but when they come at you it's fast, and you suddenly think, 'What the hell's going on here?' – and then they've scored.

The day I got the news that I was playing for England was the day we beat Manchester United at Nottingham Forest's City Ground in the 1965 FA Cup semi-final replay. It was a sweet moment for us, but for the Manchester United team it spelt the end of their hopes of a double.

Right after the game Don told me that I had been selected to play for the national squad. I was so delighted that I didn't think, I just had to tell our kid. I went straight round to the Man United dressing-room and said, 'Hey, I've been selected to play for England!'

I'm smiling all over me face, and there's all the Manchester United team sitting round looking miserable. There was a bit of a pause, and then Bobby went, 'Ah, yeah, well, congratulations, great.'

'Now fuck off out of here,' said someone else.

And I suddenly realize what I'm doing, so I said, 'Excuse me,' and left. That's the tact I'm famous for.

7

RAMSEY'S ENGLAND

I once asked Alf what made him pick me to play for England. After all, I was getting on for thirty when I made my début in 1965. I'd played for the Football League against the League of Ireland as long before as 1957, but it hadn't led to anything. Our Robert, who was younger than me, had been established in the England side for more than five years when Alf picked me for the first time. It never even occurred to me, to be honest, that I might make the grade as an international player until Don Revie suggested it.

Anyway, we were in this hotel bar one night, just the two of us, when I asked Alf the question. 'Well, Jack,' he said, 'I have a pattern of play in my mind – and I pick the best players to fit the pattern. I don't necessarily always pick the best players, *Jack.*' That was his way of boosting your confidence!

Later he explained a bit further. 'I've watched you play, Jack,' he said, 'and you're quite good. You're a good tackler and you're good in the air, and I need those things. And I know you won't trust Bobby Moore.'

I said I didn't know what he meant, Bobby Moore was a tremendous player.

'Yes, Jack,' he replied with a superior smile, 'but you

and he are different. If Gordon Banks gives you the ball on the edge of the box, you'll give the ball back to him and say, "Keep the bloody thing" – but if Gordon gives the ball to Bobby, he will play through the midfield, all the way to a forward position if he has to. I've watched you play and I know that as soon as Bobby goes, you'll always fill in behind him. That way, if Bobby makes a mistake, you're there to cover it.'

He was absolutely right, of course. It was how I used to play with Norman Hunter at Leeds.

That was probably the longest conversation I ever had with Alf. People often ask me, 'What was Alf Ramsey like?' and I say, 'I don't know, I was only with him six years.' Alf was a very difficult man to get close to. He spoke a bit like a schoolmaster, with the clipped tones of a man who had once taken elocution lessons. He was not the sort of manager you could sit down with over a couple of beers at the bar to discuss things, like you could with Don Revie.

Alf was a stickler for time. With Don, if you were playing a hand of cards or watching a movie the night before a game, he would let you finish before going to bed. Not so with Alf. He would come in and announce, 'Bed! Time to go' – and you had to go. One night he packed us off to bed while we were watching *Butch Cassidy and the Sundance Kid*, so that we never saw the end. I'm still trying to find out if they got away!

He was very much The Boss – you didn't argue with Alf. But he never shouted at us, either. If he was disappointed with the way you'd played, he just wouldn't speak to you – and if he came over and smiled, you knew you'd done all right.

He didn't involve himself much in the training. Alf was always adamant that we kept possession and didn't

Me as a young professional for Leeds United, aged 17.

(Provincial Press Agency)

Charlton family gathering, just before the outbreak of war. I am standing with my legs apart at the centre of the picture. Bobby stands at the extreme left, his fingers in his mouth.

Football in the backyard of Beatrice Street, Ashington. Mother Cissie kicks the ball towards Bobby; my younger brothers Gordon and Tommy watch admiringly. (Newcastle Chronicle)

Still only fifteen, I spent sixteen weeks training to become a miner before deciding it was not for me. (David Barry)

National Service in the Royal Horse Guards, around 1954. I stand to the right of the picture.

Tea in the Leeds dressing-room, 28 April 1956. We are celebrating the victory over Hull City that took us back into the First Division after nine seasons in the Second. By this time I was a regular in the Leeds first team. Manager Raich Carter stands on the left; John Charles is the gentle giant towards the right. (Colorsport)

Socializing over a pint with John Charles. Uncle Tommy Bailey leans over the table, and my father Bob sits on the right.

With my bride Pat Kemp.
(Y.E. News Photo)

Wedding day at St Peter's Church, Bramley, Leeds, 6 January 1958. On my right is best man Bobby, then my father, with my mother sitting in front. On the edge of the picture are my two younger brothers. Also present at the wedding were Bobby's Manchester United team-mates Tommy Taylor and David Pegg, who were to lose their lives in the Munich air disaster only a month later. (Y.E. News Photo)

Munich airport, 6 February 1958.
(P.A. News)

In action for Leeds United, early 1960s. (Yorkshire Post)

Training at Elland Road. Look at the state of the balls.
(Photopress (Leeds) Ltd)

Leeds United line-up, around 1960. In the front row is senior player Don Revie, later to take over as player-manager. Don was often critical of my attitude in this period. (A. Wilkes & Son)

Shaking hands with new manager Don Revie, March 1961. Away from the cameras our relations were often strained, and I nearly quit Leeds United in the next couple of years.

(Y.E. News Photo)

Line-up at Lilleshall, probably early 1960s. I am visible at the centre of the picture. Other young coaches visible in the picture include Malcolm Allison, in the back row behind me, and Bobby Robson, far left, second row from the back. (Arden Studios)

Leaving the Professional Footballers' Association meeting in Manchester, November 1960, with brother Bobby and Maurice Setters, later to be my partner in management.
(Syndication International)

give the ball away – that was virtually all his team talk. He didn't give much away, either. No matter what you asked him, he'd never answer you immediately. He'd look at you with a little smile, and then just say yes or no. You knew then that it was a waste of time trying to carry on the conversation. Maybe because I was a coach, I would try to draw him out, but I wasn't very successful.

Alf would never accept suggestions or ideas from any of us players. If you wanted, maybe, a different approach to a free kick, it was common practice to outline it to somebody else within Alf's hearing; then later perhaps Alf would introduce it as his own idea.

I remember having a big argument at Lilleshall with Jimmy Armfield, who would still play occasionally at right back when George Cohen was unavailable. It was all about how the centre back could cover for a full back if he chased between opposing players. Jimmy was that sort of player, he liked to dart around – but I was saying to him that if a full back stays with one man, I know exactly where I should be, but if he chases between players, I'm lost. Alf came across when he saw us arguing and listened to what we both had to say. But instead of going on to work through it as Don would have done, Alf just said, 'Well, whatever you do, sort the bloody thing out between you, and get it done as quick as you can,' and then he walked away.

One of the most disconcerting things about Alf was that you never knew if he was serious or not. That night I talked to him in the hotel bar, for example, I was just standing there having a quiet drink when Alf came in and said, 'We're still on the pints then, are we, Jack?' I didn't know how to react, I've never been a big drinker and I was just having a quiet pint before going to bed. Maybe he didn't mean anything by it – or maybe he did.

I never thought he liked me, to be honest. But I learned a lot from him. Just as he told me that night in the hotel, Alf always picked his teams to fit the way he would play them. I've been a method man ever since, I've always tried to design my teams to cause the opposition the maximum problems in handling what we were doing.

He'd developed the 4-4-2 system when he was manager of Fourth Division Ipswich, and he'd taken them straight up through the divisions to win the League Championship. It was an unbelievable achievement, and it really shook a lot of people up. Most of the teams at the time played the old 'WM' formation, with one centre back and the full backs covering him. Then, all of a sudden, Ipswich's wingers weren't wingers any more, they were midfielders, and they had another centre forward up front, so the other team's centre half was now marking two players. When teams first came up against Alf's system they didn't know what to do – and they panicked.

I made my début for England against Scotland at Wembley on 10 April 1965, just a few weeks short of my thirtieth birthday. The England-Scotland games were always high profile, and to make your début in one of them was a bit special. Funnily enough, Nobby Stiles made his début in the same game. I'd played with Nobby only a month earlier, for the Football League against the Scottish League at Hampden Park – a game in which I scored, even though I was ill with flu. I remember walking into the dressing-room and seeing Nobby sitting there wearing nothing but his glasses and a jock-strap. He looked up at me, and we

Secretary:
DENIS FOLLOWS, M.B.E., B.A.

Telegraphic Address:
FOOTBALL ASSOCIATION, LONDON, W.2

22 LANCASTER GATE, LONDON, W.2

Ref: SLW/DMN

31st March, 1965

J. Charlton, Esq.,
c/o. Mr. C.J. Williamson,
Leeds United Football Club,
Elland Road,
<u>LEEDS, 11.</u>

Dear Mr. Charlton,

<u>INTERNATIONAL MATCH</u>
<u>ENGLAND v. SCOTLAND</u>
<u>SATURDAY - 10/4/65</u>
<u>WEMBLEY</u>

I have pleasure in advising that you have been selected
to play   for England in the above match at Wembley on Saturday,
10th April, 1965, kick-off 3 p.m. Your Club has already been
informed of your selection.

An itinerary card is being prepared and will be sent to
you in due course, but, for your information, it will be necessary
for you to report at The Hendon Hall Hotel, London, N.W.4. by 9 p.m.
on Wednesday, 7th April, 1965. There will be Training and Match
Practice Thursday morning on a London Ground, and a visit to Wembley
Stadium Thursday afternoon. The programme for Friday will be
announced from Headquarters.

The fees for the match will be £60 per Player and £30
for the Reserves. The fee will be paid through your Club for the
purpose of deducting P.A.Y.E. Expenses should be claimed on the
appropriate form and will be paid to you by cheque.

After the match at Wembley, both Teams will be the guests
of The Football Association at Dinner at The Cafe Royal. Will you
please let Mr. Ramsey know immediately on your arrival on Wednesday,
7th April, 1965, if you will require accommodation at The Windsor
Hotel, Lancaster Gate, London, W.2. for the Saturday night, 10th
April, 1965.

You are entitled to two Complimentary Tickets for the
game, and, in addition, may purchase the following :-

2 @ 30s.
4 @ 25s.
4 @ 15s.
2 @ 7s.6d

If you require these tickets please forward a remittance of £11.15s.0d.
by return of post.

Yours sincerely,

D. Follows

Secretary

said hello. Then I watched him start to put his contact lenses in – not the little bits of plastic that you put in front of your pupils nowadays, but great big ones the shape of an eyeball, which needed a stick with a suction pad on the end to pull them out again. Nobby had to use a lot of lubricant to get his lenses in, and until they were settled, he was virtually blind. Even then he couldn't see more than about fifteen yards. He used to say to our Robert, 'You've gotta stay within a fifteen-yard range of me, 'cos that's as far as I can see.'

Nobby's prime task in the England midfield was to win the ball. He was always harassing the other side, always getting under people's feet. Some of the tackles he made were horrendous, but they were always honestly made – he never went for anyone deliberately. Then he would either pass the ball to our Bob, or go on one of his surging runs forward. Nobby was such a competitor, and he was a lot quicker than people expected.

Our Robert was the fulcrum of England's midfield. His role was to pick the ball up from the backs, to control it, and to pass it to a player going forwards, or to run forward himself. He was so well equipped as a player, he could do almost anything; he could go past players, he passed the ball well, he turned well, and of course he had a phenomenally powerful shot with either foot.

I spent some time with our Robert before my first international, mainly because the press lads were very keen on the idea of two brothers playing for England together. They liked it even more in the match itself, when I passed the ball to Bobby and he scored. Ray Wilson twisted his knee and had to be carried off just before half-time; then Johnny Byrne was injured as well, so we were effectively down to nine men. There were no substitutes in those days. When Ray went off, our Robert went and played at left back, something I'd never seen him do before. He did it well, too. In a way, it suited me that we had to struggle, because I had to get my head down and battle and I didn't have very much time to think about what I was doing. We held out to draw 2–2.

Despite all the pressure, though, I found the pace of the game slow compared with a League match. The Jocks had some very good players, like Ian St John, Dennis Law and of course Bobby Collins, and you had to work like hell to get the ball off them. But when I wasn't involved in a tackle or picking up a position, I found it quite easy. It wasn't a case of having more time on the ball, it was a case of there always being somebody around you to give the ball to. We played what I called knockabout football, keeping possession and passing the ball about. We wouldn't just hump the ball up the field, hoping that one of the forwards would pick it up.

The next match, also at Wembley, was against Hungary. We beat them 1–0, with a goal from Jimmy Greaves. But they were not as good a side as the one that had beaten us 6–3 in 1953, when Alf Ramsey had been part of the losing England team. Looking back, I reckon that defeat was good for English football – although it was a terrible shock, the first time a Continental country had beaten us on our own soil. People suddenly started to look at our game and compare it with the way they played on the Continent. It was apparent that the game in England was falling behind, especially when England again lost to the Hungarians, this time 7–1, in Budapest six months later. The European sides were getting stronger, and people realized that we needed to change if we were to go on competing at the top level. It's probably those defeats by Puskas and his side which kick-started all the coaching business in England. By the time we beat Hungary in 1965, the English game had adapted to cater for the way the Continentals were playing.

In George Cohen and Ray Wilson we had two really quick attacking full backs. George in particular used to tear up and down the field. We used to laugh at George, because he was a bloody awful crosser of the ball. I mean, he would run three-quarters the length of the field with the ball – and then cross it in behind the goal! We used to shout, 'George, just keep it in play!'

George would tear down to a guy at the corner-flag position, he'd tear back up the field if the ball was knocked back to somebody else, and then he'd tear down the wing again. I remember having much the same sort of argument with George as I'd had with Jimmy Armfield at Lilleshall. I told him, 'George, don't chase between people, just pick up one of them. Let the wing half pick the other one up and I'll cover the pair of you.'

Ray Wilson was built like a whippet, and he was very, very quick. He didn't come forward as often as George, but he would occasionally go up on the overlap and play the ball through to someone like Martin Peters stealing into the box. He always picked out the guy and played it in front of him, and he was a better crosser of the ball than George.

So we had two very quick full backs. I wasn't slow myself. I wasn't as quick as some over three or four yards, but over a distance I could catch virtually anyone. Pace was never one of my problems.

102

Bobby Moore never had any pace; in sprint training he was always the last. But he was such a good reader of the game that he would often be already in position before the other guy had decided he was going to play the ball there. And he was a very good passer of the ball, at a time when centre backs were not supposed to be good passers of the ball. You've got to remember that Bob played most of his career with West Ham in midfield, but with the introduction of the 4-4-2 system, he later dropped into the back four. Some people argue that it was this system which allowed a good player to develop into a great one.

I've always argued that the relationship between the centre back and the goalkeeper is crucial. So it was very important to me that Gordon Banks agreed with any position I took up. Banksy was a good organizer, and his sense of positioning was tremendous. If somebody shot from outside the eighteen-yard box, 90 per cent of the time it would just fly into his hands. He very rarely had to dive – it was one hell of a shot if he did have to dive. But if he did, he was like lightning. At Leeds, we kept dossiers on players, and Don had noticed that when Banksy had to jump for the ball under pressure, he would never catch it, he would either punch it or throw the ball back in the direction it had come. So when I used to go up to challenge Gordon for a cross coming in, we always had Billy Bremner waiting for the ball that he tried to punch clear, and we scored a lot of goals against him that way. But it didn't matter when I was playing with him for England because other teams didn't exploit him the way we did at Leeds. Don Revie's attention to detail was such that he picked up these points.

After beating the Hungarians we went on a short

European tour, playing the Yugoslavs in Belgrade, the West Germans in Nuremberg and the Swedes in Gothenburg. This was Alf's opportunity to have a close look at players and assess them, to get his mind settled on who he wanted to play in the World Cup. He brought in Ron Flowers for a game, and just before the World Cup he played Flowers instead of me, but it didn't upset me in any way, shape or form, because by that time I knew I was Number One. Alf sorted out the back four quite quickly, and I think he knew his midfield, with the exception of who he would play wide on the right. But he'd swap forwards around all the time. Forwards came into the side, played, and didn't play again. We always assumed that Jimmy Greaves was going to be one of them, but we never knew who else was going to play alongside him.

Alan Ball came into the team for the Yugoslav game, which we drew 1–1. He was a sparky little fella, very competitive, shouting a lot during the play in his little high-pitched voice. I remember a game against Everton at Elland Road when I went for a ball and Bally yelled at his team-mate Johnny Morrissey, 'Get the big bastard!' A few minutes later, I deliberately went straight through the ball and kicked Bally right up in the air. He looked up at me from the pitch and asked, 'What did you do that for?' And I told him, 'Teach you to mind your own business.'

But I liked Alan, though later when we both became managers we had a lot of arguments about tactics. I've always thought that you should play to the strengths of your team, and it seemed to me he sometimes didn't remember that the players he was coaching didn't have the skills he had. He never agreed with the way my Irish team played the ball into the space behind people, and he used to say, 'I'll never have a team that will play the way your team plays.' And I used to reply, 'But, Bally, the results are there.' We've crossed swords on several occasions, but we've always remained good pals. I knew his father quite well, a very volatile little man like Bally, and I often say to him, 'You get more like your bloody old man every day.'

As a player, Bally was always yapping at people's heels and always on the move. He was a great one-touch player, playing the ball first time and then getting it back – something that our Robert never did, perhaps because he found it so easy to go past players himself. Nobby and Bally ran and ran and ran – they became the engines of the England midfield. Bally was a great pincher of the ball. Nobby would go and win the ball off the other fella with a crunching tackle, but Bally would just nick it off you.

We beat the Germans and the Swedes, and then we had a break before coming back and drawing with Wales at Cardiff Arms Park. Then we lost 3–2 to the Austrians at Wembley, and that was a big surprise. It was one of only two games I played for England which we lost – the other one being against Scotland in 1967. Gordon Banks didn't play against Austria, Alf brought Ron Springett in instead. I think it was Ron's lack of height that did for us. Ron wasn't a very big goalkeeper, and when one of the Austrians shot from about thirty yards out, he got caught off his line. The ball sailed over his head and dipped under the bar. It was one of those games where the three things they did right fitted. Sometimes you get those games, and there's not a lot you can do about it.

After that we beat Northern Ireland at Wembley, and then went to play Spain at the famous Bernabeu

Stadium in Madrid. I'd never experienced a stadium like it – it was stacked on three tiers and the crowd seemed to be looking down on you. It was a strange feeling to be that close to the crowd. The game ended in quite a comfortable win, 2–0, but it attracted a lot of comment beforehand because we went into the game without any out-and-out wingers, just players who got forward down the flanks when necessary. The press called us 'Alf's wingless wonders'. We played a sort of 4-4-2 combination, something that was virtually unheard of at the time. Alf had in fact been playing teams like this for a while, but they hadn't really cottoned on to it in Europe. The Spanish didn't know how to handle it. Full backs in those days were used to marking players who went wide, and we didn't have anyone who went wide. Their full backs just stood there, not knowing what to do.

A month later, on 5 January 1966, we played Poland at Goodison Park. Alf had chosen me to come up and take any free kicks in forward positions. The lads looked at him a bit sideways over that, because we had players like our Robert who were acknowledged as excellent strikers of the ball. But Alf insisted it should be me. So when we got a free kick about ten yards outside their box, I came up to take it. I smacked the ball pretty well, and if it hadn't hit the goalkeeper it would have gone straight into the net. That was one of the things about Alf. Sometimes he would see things in you which you didn't know you had.

In the second half Poland were leading 1–0, and though we were all over them we couldn't score. Alf pushed Bobby Moore forward, and in fact he scored the equalizer. That was a classic case of Bob going forward and me filling in behind him, just as Alf had described. Though for dead-ball situations, for free kicks and corner kicks, the roles were reversed. I would go up and Bob would stay back.

After that we played West Germany again, and again we beat them 1–0. It was Geoff Hurst's first game. Geoff didn't have a particularly impressive début, but he began to establish himself as a part of the side in the next game, against Scotland at Hampden Park, where he scored in a 4–3 win. It was a terrific game, and a terrific atmosphere. You were talking about crowds of well over 100,000 in those days.

Alf was still shuffling his forwards. He had dropped Jimmy for the game against the Jocks and instead played Roger Hunt, who scored twice. It was beginning to look as though it would be between Geoff and Roger for the final place alongside Jimmy.

We had one more game at Wembley, a comfortable 2–0 win against Yugoslavia, before the World Cup finals. That was Martin Peters's début. He was more of a left-sided midfield player than an out-and-out striker, though he was very good at stealing goals. Many of them came from his ghosting into the box at the last moment. Otherwise there was nothing spectacular about Martin. He just did the job the way it should be done.

After the Yugoslav game Alf gave us three weeks' holiday before gathering together the party of England players for the World Cup at Lilleshall in early June. I took the family to stay with a friend in Weymouth, a former Leeds player called Bobby Forrest. I kept in shape by running on the beach every day.

Lilleshall was hard to take – training and preparation all day, and nothing to do in the evenings, because we were confined to the hotel grounds. I used to walk down the drive leading to the main road with Nobby and Bally and a few others. It was a couple of miles or so to the gate, and we just used to stand there and watch the traffic go past. I remember sticking my arms through the wires and shouting, 'Let us out, let us out!'

A few of the lads used to nip over to the golf club-house for a pint. You could get there by going across the playing fields, over a fence, over a wall and then across the golf course. I wasn't brave enough to go myself. Inevitably, Alf found out and called a meeting, where he said that if anybody else did it again, they'd be out of the door immediately. Nobody went back after that.

The England party spent three weeks together before embarking on a four-match tour of Scandinavia and eastern Europe. I scored my first goal in a 3–0 win over Finland, a shot which deflected off one of their defenders. Then I didn't play in the next match, a 6–1 victory over Norway. Greavesy scored four times – he was absolutely unbelievable that day.

Our next match was against Denmark in Copen-hagen, and I scored again in this game, a header at the far post after a corner kick.

The last game we played before the World Cup was against Poland, a match in which Roger Hunt poached the only goal. About ten minutes before the end, we gave away a free kick not far from the box. It was always Nobby's job to organize the wall. Nobby would stand as near the ball as he was allowed, to stop them taking the free kick quickly, telling everyone where to go, then checking with Gordon that the wall was in the right position. Alf had nominated our Robert to be in the wall, and Nobby had objected at the time, because although our kid loved to whack balls at people, he wasn't too keen on people whacking balls at him. Our Robert tended sort of to squirm a bit, and of course this opened up gaps in the wall. I wasn't one of the ones Alf had said should be in the wall myself. Anyway, I remember Nobby leaning over to pull our kid tight into the wall for the third or fourth time, shouting at him to get in close, when the fella took the free kick. It whistled past where Nobby should have been, and hit the outside of the goalpost. I remember shouting at Nobby, 'You silly little prat, why don't you watch what's going on?'

Nobby stared hard across the eighteen-yard box, and then he started to walk towards me. I remember this as if it was yesterday, he had his socks round his ankles, a little bit of hair dangling over his face, no teeth except his two big incisors – and he snarled at me. I remember thinking to myself, hell, you've made a mistake here, Jack. My nerve broke when he was about five yards away, and I turned tail and ran off the field. Before I always used to wonder why people were afraid of Nobby Stiles, but I never wondered about it after that!

We came home on a high, having won all three games of the World Cup warm-up tour. Our first match of the World Cup itself was against Uruguay. They had some very good, gifted players, and it surprised me that they didn't come for a result. They played for a draw and the game finished 0–0. Jimmy missed a couple of really good chances, they had just one shot over the bar, but that was that. It was a very disappointing start for England. We got a lot of stick from the press for not winning the opening game, but Alf had said that the one thing we must not do is lose, so we resisted the temptation to push men forward and over-commit ourselves.

Five days later we played Mexico. We knew we could not afford to drop another point and we battered away at them, but somehow we just couldn't get a goal. Then all of a sudden, about ten minutes before half-time, our Robert scored one of the best goals ever seen at Wembley. He picked up the ball in our half of the field, turned, and started to run with it. The Mexicans backed off him a little bit, then he dipped his shoulder and went past one of them. I was right behind him, and I wanted him to shoot, but he didn't, he went past another guy – and then he struck the ball with his right foot, about ten yards outside the eighteen-yard box. It just flew, it was a goal from the moment he struck it. Tremendous goal.

After that the game changed a bit. Now they had to come forward and play, instead of just defending. The game opened up, and when Jimmy's shot was palmed away by their keeper, Roger Hunt was there to tap it in. The game finished 2–0, which meant that we were virtually certain of qualifying. Then we had a fairly easy win against France, with Roger scoring both goals. I remember jumping for a ball by their far post as it was crossed in. I headed the ball down, it hit the post, ran across the goal and bounced off the other post, before Roger knocked it over the line.

Greavesy had still not scored in the tournament. I remember seeing him on the treatment table after the French game – he had a cut across his shin, right across the bone. I can picture it today, the cut was about three or four inches long, and his shin was swollen blue and yellow. I couldn't see any way that he was going to play with that injury. Now whether Alf would have left him out if he hadn't had the injury I don't know, but I couldn't see how Jimmy was going to play with that leg.

I felt for Jim. How could Jack Charlton come into the team only a year before and end up with a World Cup winners' medal – and Jimmy Greaves, a fantastically gifted player who played for England seventy or eighty times or whatever it was, not get one? People have said since that Jimmy's disappointment at being left out made him drift to the drink, but I've no idea whether this was in fact the case. It was a great surprise to me when I found out, years later, that Jimmy was an alcoholic. I never had any inkling of it until I read it in the paper. I'd often been out for a drink with Jimmy, and he only ever had a pint, or a couple of pints at most. We used to call him 'Simple Jim' – not because he was dim, Jimmy's a very bright lad – but because he liked the simple things of life: his family, his pipe, his pint of beer. No extraordinary food or anything like that, just the simple, uncomplicated things of life. Sensible man. That's why I couldn't believe it when I first read that Jimmy was an alcoholic.

The quarter-final against Argentina was a strange game. The Argentinians didn't seem to want to play – and yet they had some tremendously good players and they had looked like a really good side in their qualifying group. They contained us very well to start with, knocking the ball about without letting us gain possession. They were ruthless defenders. I remember going up for a corner kick and getting battered and then kicked when I fell to the ground. But generally they weren't dirty players in the accepted sense, it was just that they were past masters at stopping other people playing. Their centre half, Rattin, was a huge giant of a man. He seemed to feel that he could run the game by intimidating the referee, and he spent a lot of time walking alongside the ref, pointing at things and giving him the benefit of his advice. Eventually the referee got tired of telling him to go away and ordered Rattin off the field. There was an uproar, with all the Argentinians protesting. We just stood there watching – we didn't want to get involved. Rattin refused to go, and even when the police came on he continued arguing. The interruption lasted seven minutes before he finally left the field. Even after he went off Rattin kept on walking up and down the touchline, waving his arm at the referee and shouting in Argentinian or whatever language it is they speak there. I thought it was stupid and unnecessary, but at the same time we were delighted to see him go, because he was a bloody good player.

Then the game restarted, and the Argentinians' game became completely negative. Later they virtually admitted that from then on they were holding out in the hope of winning the game on the toss of a coin after extra time. For a while they held us off, but then came the only goal of the game. Ray Wilson passed a short ball to Martin Peters, who ran forward and sent in a cross, which Geoff Hurst headed past the keeper.

I was glad when the game was over. Alf was furious, calling the Argentinians 'animals'. He didn't want us to swap shirts with them. I swapped with one of their lads who'd played up front and hadn't been involved in any of the crap. Not all the Argentinians were that bad. But there were four or five players that day who would let nobody past them. The ball could go past them, but you couldn't.

I remember a hammering on the door of the dressing-room after the match. One of the training staff rushed in and blurted out, 'The Argentinians are here, they want a fight!' I said, 'Well, let 'em in. They want a fight, OK, now we're off the park.' I was all for opening the door, but the police arrived and cleared them away.

While we were playing Argentina the scoreboard displayed what was happening in the other quarter-final between Portugal and North Korea. At one stage Korea were 3–0 ahead. I remember looking up at it during the game and thinking, I can't believe this. Then the scoreline kept changing, until it finished 5–3 to Portugal. Eusebio ended up with four goals. It meant that in their four games before meeting us in the semi-final Portugal had scored a total of fourteen goals. And we had yet to concede one.

Eusebio was a truly great player, strong, beautifully balanced, and very quick, as good as Pelé in my view and an exciting player to watch – unless you were playing against him. He struck the ball extremely hard off a very short back-lift, which threw you off balance because it was so unexpected. He was the sort of player you had to get close to and hang on to – you couldn't let him dictate to you, you had to dictate to him.

Portugal had a thrilling, attacking side, but we had a superb defence – and in Banksy, the outstanding goalkeeper of the tournament.

I was probably more anxious about the semi-final against Portugal than I was about any of the other games. Portugal had this big centre forward, Torres, about six foot six tall. He wasn't the most mobile guy in the world and he wasn't that good on the ground, but I knew it was going to be a battle trying to win balls in the air against him.

Nobby handled Eusebio brilliantly that day. He didn't let him settle on the ball, he was at his heels the whole time. There was an incident late in the game, almost at full time, when the big guy beat me in the air and knocked the ball down across the goal. Eusebio was coming in on the right-hand side – and Nobby Stiles just flew. I have never seen Nobby move so fast, and as Eusebio went to hit the ball Nobby tackled him. It was a certain goal if Nobby hadn't got there.

Our kid scored two tremendous goals in that game. The first came after the Portuguese keeper had blocked a shot from Roger Hunt. It ricocheted out to our Robert, who calmly side-footed it back into the net. After that Portugal had most of the play, but we defended well and kept them out of the box for most of the game. In the second half Geoff Hurst made a break, and then held the ball up while our Robert came charging forward in support. As he arrived, Geoff crossed the ball to him – and our kid slammed it so hard, it screamed in.

We were winning 2–0, but the big lad was still causing me quite a few problems in the air. Late in the game he chipped the ball over Banksy's head and I was forced to handle the ball, giving away a penalty. Under the modern rules I would have been sent off. Eusebio scored from the penalty kick, his eighth goal of the tournament, and that's how it finished, 2–1. At the end I was in tears as I hugged our kid. We were through to the final.

8

30 JULY 1966

I was quite confident that we could beat the Germans in the final. We had beaten them a couple of times in the previous year or so, and I saw no reason why we should not do it again. To be honest, I was glad that West Germany had beaten Russia in the semis, because I felt that the Russians would have been more of a threat to us.

So it was a terrible blow when we went a goal down. I remember it to this day. It was a fairly simple cross into the box, and instead of playing the ball on, the way he should have done, Ray Wilson headed it back up the middle, something you should never do. He mistimed it, it fell to Haller who had plenty of time to shoot – though funnily enough, he didn't hit it that well. I remember standing there, and as the ball came past me, I could have stuck a foot out and stopped it. But it looked as if it was going straight to Banksy. Now as I've said, normally I had a very good understanding with Gordon, but as it happened, it sort of sneaked in between me and him. Maybe he thought I was going to stop it, I don't know. Afterwards I always felt I should have stopped it. But when you're a centre back, you let lots of balls go which you could stop because you know your goalkeeper's got it covered. Only this time he hadn't.

Then we got one back, when Bobby Moore took a quick free kick after he had been fouled. It was something Alf had spent a lot of time working on, encouraging us to take those free kicks quickly. Anyway, Bob put the ball down, looked up, and sent a beautifully flighted pass to Geoff Hurst, who just nodded it in. It was quick thinking, it was brilliant. If Bob had never done anything else in those ninety minutes, that was enough, because we needed a goal to get back in the game.

The second goal came after Geoff's shot ricocheted off somebody and came over the top of the centre back just as I was coming in behind. I was thinking to myself, this is coming to me – and then all of a sudden Martin Peters runs in front of me and knocks the ball into the net.

The last ten minutes of the game were an anxious time, with us leading 2–1. And then there were only seconds left. The referee was upsetting me because he kept pulling his watch out of his pocket and then putting it back again. It breaks your concentration when the ref does that. Then he'd get his whistle out and put it in his mouth. I remember thinking: when is he going to blow that bloody thing?

I remember going for a ball that bounced right up in the air. I never took my eye off the ball, and as I jumped to head it I fell on top of somebody. I hadn't even known he was there! But the referee gave a free kick, about ten yards outside the box, in the last seconds of the game.

It might be different if you watch it on telly, I don't know, but what I remember is the guy drove the ball at the wall and it hit George Cohen on the knee. Held ran in for the rebound, and his shot flew across the goal, about five feet in the air, before hitting Schnellinger under the arm, which killed the pace on the ball. I remember looking across, seeing Bobby Moore putting his hands up in the air to appeal for handball. It was a race between Ray Wilson and Weber for the ball, and Weber got there about a hundredth of a second earlier, then just toed it in by the far post. I remember thinking, handball! and looking round for the referee, linesman, anybody. But it was 2–2. Our kid was just standing on the goal-line looking at the ball lying at the back of the net, with the tears running down his face. All he could say was fucking hell, fucking hell. There was so little time left that the referee blew full time only a few seconds after we had kicked off.

Alf came out to us but he didn't say very much – just, 'Well, you've won it once, now go out and do it again.' We sat on the ground for a couple of minutes and rubbed our tired legs. Then Alf got us up and we got on with the game.

People have been analysing that third goal and arguing about it ever since. The referee wasn't sure about it and asked the linesman, and the same question has been asked again and again over the years. Just because it bounced back out doesn't mean it wasn't a goal. You see, when a ball hits the bar and bounces down, the spin on the ball often brings it back again. That happens all the time in football. But no-one ever got a clear picture of the ball over the line, so I suppose the argument will go on for ever.

When Nobby whacked the ball the length of the field to start the move which led to the third goal he had no idea what he was doing. As I've said, Nobby was too blind to see more than fifteen yards. I told him after the game, 'Hey, Nobby, that was some pass you made into the corner for little Bally – I didn't think you could see that far.' And Nobby replied, 'To tell you the truth, big fella, I never saw him, I was just playing for time.' Anyway, Bally chased it towards the corner, and when he caught up with the ball he crossed it first time to Geoff, who knocked it down with his back to the goal, swivelled to his right, took a couple of steps and then struck it hard with his right foot. The ball hit the bar and bounced down towards the line. Roger Hunt was only two or three yards off the goal-line, and I don't know to this day whether he could have knocked the ball in the net if he'd had any doubt about the goal. But he sort of went, 'Ah, it's over the line,' and turned away. I saw Roger's arm go up in the air to celebrate. Later I asked him, 'Was it over the line, Rog?' and he smiled at me with a big grin on his face and answered, 'Miles over the line.'

The second half of extra time seemed to last for ever. Then came Bobby Moore's bit of magic. It was typical Bob. He was under pressure in the box when he took the ball on his chest and pulled it down. I couldn't believe it when he passed the ball to Bally, who ran a bit and then passed it back again. I mean, you just don't do that when you're defending in your own box – especially not in the last minute of a World Cup final! Any ball that came to me in that situation got humped as far as I could up the line or into the crowd, anything to get it away. When you're under pressure, get rid of the ball as far away from your goal as possible, waste as much time as you can, but don't try to play your way out of trouble. Which is what Bob did, and then he stopped and turned and looked upfield, before delivering the perfect pass for Geoff Hurst to run on to score the fourth goal. I didn't actually see the goal, because I was looking at Bob and thinking, I will never be able to play this bloody game, because Bob has just done something that is unheard of.

The final whistle went just after Geoff's goal, the game was over, and Geoff stood there with his hands in the air. I ran the whole length of the field just to get hold of him, but as I came near him he ran off and I was too knackered to follow. I flopped to my knees, totally exhausted, and my head fell forwards onto my hands. I don't remember saying a prayer – I probably just said something like, 'Thank the Lord that is over.'

When I rose to my feet our kid was standing beside me. We just put our arms around each other. He wasn't smiling at all, yet I knew in my heart he was overjoyed. 'What else is there to win now?' he asked me – and I laughed. 'We shall have to win it again.'

We were on the field a long time; all the England players shook hands and hugged each other. Alf had a big smile on his face, a genuine big smile on his face. Alf grinned a lot, but sometimes when he grinned you didn't feel it was a real grin, like when he was telling you that you couldn't do something. But this time Alf had a real grin on his face – and he looked very, very happy.

The Germans were still there as well, and we shook hands. I didn't swap shirts, it wasn't the sort of shirt you would want to swap and in fact I still have it somewhere.

I looked up to see where my mother and father were. Pat was at home, because she was pregnant and expecting a baby any day. Then we started to go up the steps to collect the trophy and our medals. I slipped a couple of times and stumbled on the way down; the steps up to the Royal Box are brick, not wood, and

119

quite difficult to walk on in studs. The Queen was waiting at the top, I remember she had white gloves on, and I wiped my hands before she handed me the medal.

Back on the field there seemed to be hundreds of photographers. We started a lap of honour. Bobby Moore came over to me and handed me the trophy. I held it for a bit and had my picture taken waving to the crowd. I remember Nobby skipping, looking happier than I have ever seen him in his life.

Eventually we left the field. As we filed down the tunnel, a guy suddenly appeared and told me I had to go and give a urine sample. I said, 'Not again!' because it had happened to me after four of the six games, but I followed him into a little room where the doctors gave me a bowl with a rim to wee in, shaped like a bowler hat. After a game it is sometimes very, very difficult to go and I was in there for ages, they had to give me drinks before I was ready. When it was all over the doctors presented me with a plastic hat, it had the England colours all around the edge and was signed by all the doctors. Written on it in big letters was, 'For one who gave his best for England – the Jimmy Riddle Trophy'.

The bus took us back to the team hotel, then we changed and climbed back on the bus to go to the Royal Garden Hotel in London, where there was going to be a reception in the evening. I remember we had to take our gear with us because we were staying in the Royal Garden that night. The driver couldn't go very fast because there were people lining the pavements waving at us. When we reached the hotel there were thousands of people waiting, and my mother and father were there in the entrance. Then a guy ushered us upstairs and the whole team went out onto the balcony to wave at all the supporters standing in the street below. My mother and father were with us and waved at the people down below as if they too had just won a World Cup final.

Afterwards there was a formal reception, with a meal and speeches. The whole thing finished about eleven o'clock that night. All the other lads were going out with their wives to some nightclub, but I was on my own. Coming down the stairs I met an old friend of mine, Jimmy Mossop, standing in the foyer. We stood talking for a while, and then he said he was going to go back to Manchester. 'Now?' I asked. 'Yes,' he replied, and I said, 'No, you're not, we're going out, me and you. I have a few hundred quid in my pocket and we'll go and have a night out.'

We could not get out of the hotel at first, but I finally found a waiter who let us out by a side door. We ducked round the back of the crowd and opened the door of a taxi waiting to drive past. It was only then that I realized that there was a guy in the taxi already! I asked, 'Do you mind if we share your taxi until we get out of here?' and he said, 'Certainly not, get in.' So we jumped into the taxi as the traffic started to move. It turned out that the guy was a professional musician, a violinist who had just finished a concert. He hadn't heard about the football. The taxi took us a couple of miles down the road and then dropped us off somewhere where we could get another taxi to a nightclub I knew. It was a place that all the England team used when we were in town because you didn't need to buy champagne, you could get a jug of beer on the table. Anyway, we arrived and had a few drinks and then a guy called Lenny, a complete stranger, came over and asked us to join him and his friends at their table. We got right stoned with them and then we went back to Lenny's house, somewhere near Leytonstone, where we had some more drinks and a bit of a party. Eventually Jimmy and me slept on the settee.

The next morning, we were having breakfast in the garden when this woman pops her head over the wall and says, 'Hello, Jackie.' I couldn't believe it! It was one of our neighbours from Ashington, and she was visiting relatives who just happened to live next door! 'How are you getting on, Jackie?' she asked, a little suspiciously. I think she was wondering what I was doing in a garden in Leytonstone.

We didn't get back to the hotel until about midday, and as I walked in my mother was standing in the foyer. She was a bit short with me. 'Where have you been?' she demanded. 'I have been up to your room this morning and the bed has not been slept in.'

I had to laugh really, because we'd just won a World Cup and my mother's telling me off for going absent without leave!

9

THE FAMILY

On the Sunday after the world cup final a friend who
had a car drove us home. On the way back up the A1 I
said I felt like something plain to eat, after all that
luxury hotel food I'd been having with the England
squad. We stopped at a transport café, where I had
some egg and chips, with a nice bread roll – and do you
know what? It was the best meal I'd had for weeks. It
was funny to sit there in a transport café with four or
five hundred quid in my pocket, part of my bonus for
winning the World Cup.

I put that money to good use not long afterwards. A
company was building some new houses on Wembley
field at Hirst Park, and they asked me to open the show
house. I liked it so much that I asked if I could buy one.
Then I walked round to Beatrice Street, where my
mother was hanging out the washing. 'I've bought you
a house, Mother,' I told her.

'You haven't!'

'I have,' I said. 'Come on, leave the washing and put
your coat on. We'll go round and see which one you
want.'

My mother and father had lived in two-up, two-
down coal houses all their lives. They'd never had a
bathroom, they'd always had to make do with an

123

outside toilet, coal fires, washing and cooking in the pantry. Now they had a new three-bedroom house with a proper bathroom and a fitted kitchen. They called it Jules Rimet, after the World Cup trophy.

The new season was about to start, but as I'd been playing through most of the summer Don Revie gave me a couple of weeks extra off. I took the kids to Filey, where we had a caravan. Then it was back to the grind of League football.

Some new players were establishing themselves in the Leeds United side. Peter Lorimer had found a permanent place in the first team the previous season, and in 1966–67 Paul Madeley and Eddie Gray began to play for us regularly. Terry Cooper was in and out of the side, looking for the Number 3 shirt which he would claim the following year.

It was another frustrating season. We finished fourth in the League, and lost the semi-final of the FA Cup to Chelsea. I didn't play in that game, because I'd been injured in an international against Scotland in April. The games against the Jocks were always very competitive. Dennis Law had put them ahead after half an hour, and that's how the score remained for much of the game. Then, with only ten minutes to go, there were four more goals. I'd been hobbling for most of the match, since an early tackle on the touchline with little Willie Johnson which had done something to my toe. After that I couldn't put any weight on my foot. Ray Wilson was injured as well and Jimmy Greaves was suffering from a swollen ankle, so we were up against it. I went off for a bit, and when I came back Alf moved me up to centre forward. Ten minutes before the end they went two ahead, but then I pulled one back, the second goal I'd scored in successive internationals, because I'd headed one in our 5–1 win over Wales back in November. Almost immediately the Jocks scored a third, but we didn't give up and Geoff Hurst headed the final goal just before the whistle to make it 3–2.

It was a disappointing game and a disappointing result for us, ending a nineteen-match unbeaten run. The Jocks were saying they'd won the World Cup after beating the champions – their supporters went mad, running onto the field and removing the crossbar. I went to the hospital to have my foot X-rayed, and I was surprised when they told me there were no bones broken. When I went back to the hotel I still could not put any weight on it.

So they took me back to the hospital again for more X-rays. I was outside the room waiting for the results when the doctor put his head round the door and said, 'Will you come back in again please, Mr Charlton?' He showed me the X-rays and told me, 'In all the history of medicine, nobody has broken the bones that you have broken.'

I asked him what he meant. He said that I had broken the – what do you call it? – sesamoid bones, two small bones only about half an inch long, not attached to anything, under your big toe. 'The impact of the tackle must have pushed the stud through and broken them. They will probably never knit together again, but they will repair themselves and the pain will ease.'

So I had to go and sit through the FA Cup semi-final against Chelsea at Villa Park in plaster. I made my way to my seat in the stand with a walking-stick. When the referee disallowed a perfectly good goal by Peter Lorimer I was furious, and when the final whistle went I was bloody raging. I smashed the stick on the chair in front of me – and it broke in two! I had to hobble out of Villa Park without anything to lean on.

I got the Footballer of the Year in 1967. Our Robert had won it the year before, and this time I believe it was a very close contest between me and Geoff Hurst. I felt a bit guilty about that, because the one thing I couldn't do was play. I was very good at stopping other people playing, but I wasn't a player in the sense that our kid was, Dennis Law was, or Geoff Hurst was.

I knew in advance that I'd won it, and I was told I had to make a speech at the dinner. I had been to plenty of these dinners before, of course, and normally the person receiving the award didn't say much, just a few thank-yous really, before sitting down. Anyway, I'd written out something like that before I drove down to London with a friend, an ex-rugby player called Dave Croft. On the way down, we came to a place where the road was up on one side, and there was single-lane traffic controlled by traffic lights for about two hundred yards. We were at the head of the queue, and when the lights changed to green we started driving through, but suddenly a guy on a moped appeared coming in the other direction. Dave had to slam on the brakes, and the other guy fell off his moped. Dave was very angry. He rolled down the window and shouted, 'What the hell are you coming through for? Didn't you see those lights were red?'

'Yes,' said the other guy, picking up his bike, 'I did see the lights were red, but I chose to disregard them.'

I just collapsed laughing.

I sat next to the chairman at the dinner. When the time came for me to speak I didn't read the notes, I just started telling them about the guy on the moped. They all seemed to enjoy that, so then I told some other stories. Apparently I spoke for fifteen minutes or so, and it went down extremely well. No other footballer had ever made a proper speech, apart from the usual thank-yous. I got a standing ovation at the end.

This talk completely changed my life, not in a football sense, but because I suddenly started getting invitations to speak at functions. To begin with I was rather naïve; I would go out to speak at little football clubs and I would just claim a small amount to cover my expenses. Then I was doing a dinner at Burnley with Fred Trueman, and he asked me how much I was getting. 'Just my expenses really,' I said, 'about fifty quid.'

'You have to get more than that,' Fred said, 'You are a star now. I tell you what I do. When they phone me up to do a dinner, I say, "How many people will be there?" When they say two hundred, I say, "OK, add an extra pound on the tickets and pay me two hundred quid."'

I did what he advised, and it became more and more part of my income and still is to this day – except that my fees have gone up a little bit now. It never would have happened if I hadn't been made Footballer of the Year.

I also had a couple of gents' outfitters in the Leeds area, which I ran with Pat. They never made much money, but they sort of paid for themselves. It all sprang from a time in the early 1960s, when we had a young family and we were quite short of money. I used to go and work in the summer for a guy named Fred Barlow who had a mill near Bradford. This gave me access to cloth in a limited sort of way. I used to buy off-cuts and seconds, any kind of leftovers – but it was good stuff. Those were the days when you couldn't buy a suit off the peg, and I started making a few quid on the side by selling on cloth lengths, mainly to other players. If you ask any of the players from my era, they'd probably say, 'Yeah, I bought some of Jack's cloth.' I used to have a roll in the car when I went to Lilleshall, and all the lads would come and have a look at it. Terry Venables used to buy cloth from me when he had his tailor shop.

There came a time when I was making a sight more money on the cloth than I was making at the football. It was a lean period at Leeds United, when we were stagnating in the Second Division, going nowhere. I was tempted to pack in the football and go into the business full-time.

Later on we started a souvenir shop at Elland Road. It was just a little hut where we sold badges and scarves and stuff, but it became a very good business, especially when we started selling programmes and went into mail order. I remember when Pat came back home with about two hundred pounds of takings in a carrier bag. A while later the girl from the sweet shop came to the door with the carrier bag, saying, 'Is this yours?' It seems that our Peter, who must have been about five years old at the time, had gone off with the carrier bag and was giving his friends fivers to buy sweets!

In the end Leeds closed us down, because they saw how well we were doing and they wanted to run it themselves. I felt annoyed about that, because they'd had a shop before but they hadn't made a go of it. Don stuck up for me. He said to them, 'Look, it's Jack's business. He built it up, and you're not going to take it away from him.' In the end they gave me notice to quit, but at least I managed to get them to buy all my stock. Later Pat ran the souvenir shop at

Middlesbrough, not for us but for the club.

We'd qualified again for the 1967 Inter-Cities Fairs Cup, and this time we got right through to the final. The match was held over until the late summer, by which time I'd recovered from my injury. Our opponents were Dinamo Zagreb, and we had a tough away leg, losing 2–0. We still thought we were in with a chance in the home leg at Elland Road, but though we threw everything at them, somehow we just couldn't score a goal. I had an effort disallowed, and a shot cleared off the goal-line. The final score was 0–0, leaving us runners-up yet again.

By this time we'd invented the situation of standing on the goal-line in the near-post area and having in-swinging corners, which became a great ploy – and still is a ploy used in the Football League today. It's something that became my trade mark, but it came about purely by accident, while I was training with the England squad at the Bank of England's ground in London. We were just filling in time, practising crosses before the proper coaching began. Jimmy Greaves and our Bob were taking turns in goal. Now our kid always fancied himself as a goalkeeper, and just to be annoying I went and stood in front of him as the balls were being crossed, which blocked him from running out and taking the ball comfortably. 'What are you doing?' he said irritably. 'Get out of the way!' I just stood underneath the crosses and nudged them on so they dropped in behind him. And I thought – I wonder if that'd work? When I came back to Elland Road I went to see Don and explained what had happened. And he said what he always said, 'Well, we'll take a look.'

So we went out on the field, and I got Peter Lorimer and Eddie Gray bending the balls in towards the near

129

post. We hadn't told Gary Sprake what to expect. He couldn't see the ball being crossed in because I was standing in front of him, and to make it even more difficult I was backing in to him as the ball came in. And Sprakey couldn't handle it. He finished up on top of me, starting a fight – in the middle of the training session! When we stood up laughing and explained what we were doing, he nearly flipped his lid. But Don said, 'There's a bit of merit in this.' And we started doing it in competitive games. It became a very, very important part of our game, and we scored loads of goals that way. Although I didn't score a great many goals myself, I did get the odd one, but more important was when I'd flick it on and Peter or Billy or somebody else would wallop it in – what they call 'assists' in America. I'd jump for every ball, and sometimes I left it, sometimes I flicked it on for someone else to score, and sometimes I'd score myself.

Within two years we were famous for our in-swinging corners, and the talk in the League was all about how to handle me at the near post. Just the sight of me loping up for corners caused panic in the other side's defences. In those days, it caused a tremendous amount of hassle, and some defences reacted with open hostility. I was accused of 'cheating' by television pundits – though they never explained how what I was doing was against the rules. Managers were known to spend their entire pre-match team talks on the problem of how to cope with me and what to do to make sure I didn't get near the ball. Clubs got so uptight about it, they'd put a player marking me on the inside, a player marking me on the outside, and another in front of me, so that I was surrounded by three players. What they didn't realize was that they were actually making it harder for the goalkeeper by putting more and more people in front of him, so that he had to go over four people to get to the ball instead of just me. I used to get hold of the goalpost, because then nobody could push me out of position, and I found I could use it like a lever to get a bit higher. Even the referees had to adjust to my new technique; they came and stood behind the net to see what I was doing.

Eventually this became standard practice in the game. It gave me great satisfaction, knowing that I had introduced something fresh to the game which other people picked up and used.

The problem for the defenders was solved so far as I was concerned in a game against Everton. I'd already scored once in the game, a flick-on header. Then we got another corner, and I heard their keeper, Gordon West, say to the backs, 'Get out of the way and leave him to me.' He went and stood at the far post – and I thought, oh Jesus, he's a big strong lad, is Gordon West.

When the ball was crossed in at the near post, Gordon ran across the goal and as he leaped to punch the ball away, his knees hit me a painful blow in the back. He finished up on top of me – and I'm lying on the ground winded, thinking, that's the end of that ploy!

It wasn't of course, though I maybe didn't try it against Everton too often after that.

There was another incident with another goalkeeper called Gordon, my England team-mate, Gordon Banks. We were playing Stoke City in a League game, and, as usual, Banksy was keeping goal for them. On this particular day I had come up to the goal-line for a corner kick, as I always did. Gordon was getting very agitated, hopping about, telling his players the positions they should take up. He was pointing here and there, and as he gestured in front of my face, I couldn't resist taking a nip out of his finger. 'Let go!' he shouted, bouncing about even more, trying to get his finger out of my teeth – but I just grunted, 'Nah.' The referee, who was only a few feet away behind the goal, could see it was only a bit of fun and was laughing his bollocks off. Being the nice man I am, I let go of his finger once the corner was ready to be taken – and the ball was cleared.

People often said that Leeds United were a dour team, because once we got a lead we tended to lock things up at the back. What they didn't recognize was that we had plenty of good players in the side who could play attractive football when the occasion demanded. Such an occasion presented itself early in the 1967–68 season, when we played Chelsea just after their manager, Tommy Docherty, had walked out on them. Chelsea weren't exactly our favourite team in the League in view of what had gone before, so it was nice to beat them 7–0. We finished the First Division race in fourth position for the second year running, and we were beaten in the semi-finals of the FA Cup by Everton when Johnny Morrissey scored from a penalty – but at last we tasted some success when we won the League Cup final against Arsenal. Terry Cooper scored the winning goal after dreaming that he would do so for three nights in succession. The Arsenal lads weren't best pleased with me because I'd been up to challenge for the ball on a corner crossed in by Eddie Gray – and they're complaining that I pushed the goalkeeper, which in fact was never the case. All I was doing was making it difficult for the keeper to see and get the ball, like I always did.

After that we had to face a whole lot of 'cheating' allegations from the press and self-styled 'experts' on television. I didn't mind what they said so long as we kept on winning. The more successful we were, the more the press, especially the London press, hated us.

The 1968 League Cup was our first trophy, and after so many years of coming close and failing, it was nice to win something. It wasn't long before we had another trophy to add to it, because that year we again reached the Fairs Cup final, this time against the Hungarian side Ferencvaros. We won the first leg at Elland Road 1–0, and we managed to hang on to this slim lead in the away leg and so win the Cup – after being runners-up the year before and reaching the semi-finals the year before that.

The 1968–69 season was the year we finally shook off the label of second-best. We lost only two League games all season – to Manchester City and Burnley, funnily enough – and clinched the title when we drew 0–0 with Liverpool at Anfield on 28 April 1969. You've got to remember that Liverpool were *the* big team of the time, and they were pressing us hard in the championship even though we had built up a record number of points. The atmosphere in the crowd was incredible, and we were still out on the field enjoying the cheers twenty minutes after the end of the game. I have to admit it surprised me that Liverpool fans reacted the way they did that night; I hadn't expected them to be so generous. They called me 'Dirty Big Giraffe' – but it was affectionate, and Anfield became my favourite away ground after that. Shanks came into the dressing-room to congratulate us afterwards. 'You're worthy champions,' he said generously. 'If it wasn't going to be us, you're the next best.'

Don won Manager of the Year that season, and he went on to win it again the next year. He'd made Leeds United into one of the most professionally run clubs in Europe. If I had to sum up Don's qualities as a manager in one phrase, it would be attention to detail. He compiled elaborate dossiers on our opponents, and for an hour or so on the morning before a match he'd analyse every one of their players – their weaknesses, their strengths, whether they were quick or slow. Sometimes it got a bit hard to bear. If someone started nodding off, he'd shout, 'Pay attention! I've spent fortunes sending people all over Europe to watch teams and bring back reports, so you bloody listen!'

Don had the idea that we were a family club, that all the players would look after each other on and off the field. He was delighted when all the lads went out for a drink together, though he would never come with us himself.

Don liked his players to be married, he wanted you to settle down. He was pleased to have the wives at dinners, and he always made sure they were well looked after if they travelled with us. But he didn't want women around before a game. He encouraged us to go and stay in hotels on Friday nights, to get a good night's sleep before the games on Saturday – particularly if you had babies at home. And he tried to talk us out of having sex on Fridays. He said that it weakened you.

That summer Don signed Allan Clarke, who soon formed a deadly partnership up front with Mick Jones, a centre forward who had come into the side a couple of years earlier. The classic Leeds United line-up which everyone remembers to this day was complete: Sprake, Reaney, Charlton, Hunter, Cooper, Lorimer, Bremner,

Giles, Gray, Clarke and Jones. We won the Charity Shield at the beginning of the 1969–70 season, and we extended our unbeaten run to a record thirty-four games, playing a more positive style of football that at last began to win us some credit with the press. As the season progressed it seemed that we had a chance of a unique treble of League championship, FA Cup and European Cup, especially after we started our first ever season in the European Cup with emphatic 10–0 and 6–0 wins.

The team which finally won the League that season, Everton, were the ones who ended our great run, beating us 3–2 at the end of August. The strain of playing too many games was beginning to tell, and once it became clear that we were not going to win the League, Don was anxious to spare the players for the assault on the FA Cup and the European Cup – especially after Paul Reaney broke a leg in a League game against West Ham. On Easter Monday, Revie fielded a reserve team for a game against Derby, which we lost 4–1. The FA didn't like that, and fined the club five thousand pounds.

We were having a great run in the FA Cup, but it was gruelling, especially the semi-final against Manchester United, which needed two replays before we got a result. That was the time when we played eight games in fifteen days. I remember coming out of the third semi-final at Bolton late in March and seeing Pat waiting at the gate. 'Where are you going?' she asked, and I said, 'Well, me and Billy are going to book into the Queens Hotel and we're going to get stoned, 'cos I feel stretched like an elastic band. I'll be home sometime tomorrow. Do you mind?' And she said, 'OK.'

Six days later we had to play the first leg of our first European Cup semi-final against Celtic at Elland Road. We'd played them once before, in a friendly at Hampden Park just after the World Cup which I think we won 1–0. But we'd already played fifty-two games that season, and we were desperately tired. You've got to remember that in a club like Leeds United, virtually everybody went away to play at least seven or eight internationals every year, on top of League matches and all the Cup competitions.

The game began badly, when Celtic went ahead after less than two minutes of the first half. It was a very disappointing goal. A simple little ball was played through – and for some reason Paul Madeley missed it, George Connelly got a toe to it, and it went in off the far post. I remember that we pounded away at Celtic for the rest of the game, but it just wouldn't go in for us. To make matters worse, Everton won that same night to clinch the League title.

Before we played the second leg in Glasgow we had to go to Wembley for the FA Cup final against our old enemies Chelsea. The playing surface was diabolical after the Horse of the Year show had been held there – the horses had broken the surface and heavy rain since had made the ground sodden. It was the first time I'd ever seen mud at Wembley. Normally, the grass was so lush and tight that you played in short studs – because if you played in long ones and they went through the surface, you could do yourself an injury. You'd try to turn, and your feet would stay planted in the tight soil. But that day against Chelsea it was like a pudding.

We should have won, because we dominated the game from start to finish. I headed the first goal from a corner kick, but then Chelsea equalized after Gary dived over the ball. Then, only seven minutes from the end, Clarkey's shot hit the post and Mick Jones scored on the rebound. We thought we had it won, but then they got a free kick, the ball got played in, and Ian Hutchinson suddenly appeared at the near post to make it 2–2. Everyone was looking accusingly at Gary, but it wasn't his fault, he was expecting a cross, not something flicked in at the near post. You can't be everywhere at once. Somebody should have picked up that position at the near post, but they didn't.

Extra time failed to produce any more goals, so we were in for a replay. Four days later we had to go to Glasgow to play the European Cup second leg against Celtic. The 136,505 spectators made for a tremendously hostile atmosphere, especially after we took an early lead through a cracking Billy Bremner goal. I was stood right behind Billy at the edge of the box when the ball was laid back for him, and he hit a thundering shot which flew into the corner. Then they came back at us with a vengeance, and it felt as if we were under siege. The equalizer came two minutes after half-time. Gary was carried off after a collision with big John Hughes, and then Bobby Murdoch scored the winner for Celtic to make them 2–1 victors. Poor David Harvey, our substitute keeper, didn't have a touch of the ball before he had to pick it out of the back of the net.

I remember being disappointed in the performance of one or two of our Scottish players that night. Billy gave it everything, but I thought that Peter Lorimer and Eddie Gray hadn't performed anything near what they were capable of. Maybe they froze a little. The press had built it up into 'The Battle of Britain' – and playing in front of such a hostile home crowd might have intimidated them, I don't know.

The replay of the FA Cup semi-final took place at Old Trafford at the end of April. At Wembley Eddie Gray had run 'Chopper' Harris to bits, but in the first few minutes of the game Chopper gave Eddie a beauty. Eddie stayed on the field, but he was virtually a spectator after that.

Clarkey went on a brilliant run before setting up Mick Jones to score the opening goal. But twelve minutes before time, Chelsea equalized through a Peter Osgood header. I blame myself for that goal. I'd been waiting on their goal-line for a corner kick when one of the Chelsea players – someone who'd better remain nameless – whacked me in the thigh with his knee. After the corner was cleared I started to chase him, way over to the right. Then the ball was knocked in long to our box and I started to run back, but I was still hobbling after the whack in the thigh and I couldn't get there in time to stop Peter Osgood heading his second goal.

So we were again in for extra time. Ian Hutchinson did one of his long throw-ins, and I remember jumping and heading the bloody thing. Then John Dempsey climbed on top of Terry Cooper to flick the ball on, and somehow it finished at the far post for Dave Webb to nod the ball in. It was the first time they'd been ahead in 224 minutes' play, but that was how it stayed. It seemed written in the stars that we were not going to win the FA Cup that year.

The disappointment was incredible. I went straight to the dressing-room and kicked open the door. I've never been more upset over losing a game, maybe because it was partly my fault. Nobody else came into the dressing-room, and I just sat there and sat there for ages, before all of a sudden the lads started to drift in with their losers' medals. It was only then I realized I hadn't collected my own medal. To this day I'm not sure if I ever got it – though I suppose I must have done.

Leeds United had started that season with hopes of a unique treble, only to end up with nothing. In a way, we were victims of our own success. We had played far too many games that season. All we seemed to do was to go from one high-profile game to another, for months on end. We had no time to settle, to relax, to get one important match out of our system before going on to the next. Had we been able to go on and play right through May or into early June as they do now, we probably would have won everything. I used to say to Don, they want to get the season finished so they can go and watch bloody cricket.

I feel players are expected to play too many games, even today. People in the higher echelons of football think, they should be able to play two matches a week, no problem.

And I've always said, 'No, it's not two matches a week – it's three matches in seven days.'

All the knocks you get, all the niggles, all the little taps on the ankle, the knees in the thigh, all the hammering in the back when you're jumping and heading balls, all the little elbows and contact blows, and all the little strains – they all build up and build up to a stage where you know you're not performing at your best. Because you're always carrying something – and managers are having to wait until a Friday or a Saturday morning to decide if you're fit enough to play. And most of the lads, who want to play, will say, 'Yeah, I'm OK,' when really, they aren't fully fit and should have three or four days' more rest to get over it.

139

People say Leeds United should have won a lot more – and maybe we would have won a lot more, if we hadn't been involved in every competition right until the end of each season. I mean, we got used to losing things, but we always came back the next year. Don used to say, 'Well, we didn't win it this year, but we'll do it next year.' We went for years and years and years, competing in virtually every competition till nearly the end. We eventually won everything – except the Cup Winners' Cup and the European Cup. Yes, there was a lot of disappointment – but there was a lot of pride, too – pride and passion and discipline which kept the Leeds family together when we might have fallen apart.

10

'I'VE GOT A LITTLE LIST'

I never had a black book. that was just a term I chose to use when I was asked to do a half-hour, one-on-one interview on Tyne Tees Television. I felt the interview went well, and they seemed quite pleased with it at the time. It was just about football, about the realities of the game. I mentioned that if a player did something nasty or unnecessary to me, I wouldn't forget it. His name would go down in my black book. If the chance of retaliation came, I'd tackle him as hard as I could. I'd kick him five yards over the touchline if I had the opportunity. But I'd do it within the laws of the game, when the ball was there to be played.

Note that phrase 'within the laws of the game'. I didn't say I'd deliberately kick the guy in the air in any circumstance. What I did say was that if the opportunity presented itself, I'd pay him back, in a hard but perfectly legitimate tackle. You can be as hard as you like in the game of football. There is no rule to say you cannot tackle as hard as you want – but within the laws of the game, when the ball is there to be played.

The purpose of the remark was not to shout my mouth off about what a hard man I was. I was merely explaining some of the professional practices prevalent in the game at the time. Fine, perfectly reasonable. But then this local reporter in the Newcastle area is invited to a preview of the programme, takes my remarks out of context, and puts a lot of quotes on the wire to all the news agencies in London – things like 'Jack Charlton says he would kick a player five yards over the touchline', 'Jack Charlton says he has got a black book with names in it of players he will get before he finishes his career' – quotes like that. Suddenly the tabloids are running stories with headlines like 'Kick Jack Charlton Out Of Football' or 'Ban This Man For Life'. All those journalists who hated Leeds United had a wonderful opportunity to bad-mouth us. I got so much press, it was ridiculous. For about two weeks I got pilloried in every newspaper in the world. The worst of it was that the FA took the reports at their face value – and soon I found myself on the carpet in London.

None of these journalists had even seen the programme. They didn't take the trouble to check if I had been quoted correctly. Acting as judge and jury, they rushed to condemn me. I refused to speak to any of them. I'd say, 'If you see the programme, I'll talk to you. Ask the questions about the programme, but see the programme first.' None of them could be bothered – or perhaps they didn't want to know the truth.

At the time, there were in the Football League a lot of players whom the critics liked to call hard men. I suppose I was one of them. But I was never what you consider a dirty player – in my position I couldn't afford to be, because you can't afford to give away free kicks near the box.

Everybody thinks that defenders are the dirty ones in a side. That's not true – defenders are committed to getting the ball, that's what they're there to do. Defenders have to be *more* careful, because if a defender commits a silly foul in the box, he can give away a penalty. In fact, giving away a free kick anywhere around the box is not likely to please the manager.

In my experience, it wasn't the big lads who were the culprits. People like Tommy Smith were as hard as nails – but they were never nasty. They usually tackled hard, but providing the ball was there to be won and their timing was right, that was OK. The ones you had to watch out for were the little fellows, the ones who normally played on the wings or in midfield. They were invariably late in the tackle, always leaving something there for you to hit. A guy has left his foot there, and when you follow through, you hit six studs with your shin. Let me tell you something, it doesn't half hurt.

Referees and linesmen follow the play, and very often miss the incident which happens a split-second after the ball has been struck.

There was a spell in the Football League when full backs were getting sent off regularly for attacking wingers. And nobody in authority ever questioned the reason. But those of us playing the game knew what was happening. And it had to do with incidents like the one I've just mentioned.

And there were other nasty ploys in the game. As a centre back, my job was to pick up a position for a cross, challenge for the ball and win it. But the opposing centre forward didn't necessarily have to win the ball, and the number of times people have clattered into me late with their heads or their elbows doesn't bear recounting. You finish up with your face slashed, elbows in your eye, fingers stuck up your nose, and so on. I tell you, you get a few headaches. In a lot of cases, the guy hitting you knows exactly what he's doing. It isn't accidental.

When I first went to Leeds, I played with a lad called Albert Nightingale. He was an inside forward who used to play alongside John Charles. Albert was notorious in the six-yard area. As the ball was being played into the box, he would tap his opponent on the ankle, the fellow would howl and grab his foot – and our Albert would be free to knock the ball into the net. Nine times out of ten, the referee didn't spot it because he was following the ball, but the other players knew exactly what had happened, and I saw them chasing him around the pitch or complaining to the ref.

Clarkey was a bit like that. Off field he was a great lad – but he could be a little bit sneaky, with a bit of a mean streak in him. He would leave the boot in just a bit longer than he should have done. It caused us loads of aggravation – suddenly all the other side's defenders would come running after him and we'd have to go and bail him out. Tommy Smith used to say to Clarkey, 'I'll break your back.'

John Giles used to do some awful things to players, too. We would have rows about it in the dressing-room. I once said to him, 'What do you do it for, John?' And he said, 'Well, I once got my leg broken, and I'm gonna make sure nobody ever does it again' – meaning that he was going to 'do' everybody before they did him. I said, 'Sure, every bugger in the League is going to get punished because you once got your leg broke.' But it wasn't just them, it was us he was putting at risk. John caused us a lot of hassle at Elland Road over the years. It was all so unnecessary, because he was such a skilful player.

Playing as a kid of seventeen in the Yorkshire League had taught me that if you didn't learn how to take care of yourself on a football pitch, you'd soon get run over. The reality of the game at the time was that you were responsible for looking after yourself, first and foremost, and then you looked to the referee for protection. And watching referees' performances these days, I sometimes get the impression that they think they are officiating at an amateur game. They frequently miss the mean fouls, the professional fouls. It begs the question of why more professional players are not encouraged to become involved in refereeing. I'll tell you why – because the powers that be just don't want to know ex-pros. The way the system is currently structured, a guy with an uncle on the Northumberland FA or some other FA has more chance of becoming a Football League referee than a player with a dozen England caps. It's sometimes who you know, not what you know that counts.

Sports like cricket or rugby league use former players as officials. I think it's high time that young professional players with no obvious future on that side of the game were encouraged to take up refereeing. That way, a lot of the unseemly things we see in the game today would not go unpunished, while at the same time referees would be more understanding of the realities of the game, having experienced it themselves as players.

These were the sort of points I emphasized in the Tyne Tees interview. And I confirmed that there were, of course, vendettas. When a player's gone and nearly broken your leg, you don't forget it. When somebody does something that is nasty, you don't forget it. And when the chance of retribution comes, you take it.

Any one of a hundred players could have told the FA that, but still I'm summoned to London to explain myself. Don Revie and the club solicitor accompanied me. We took a tape of the television programme with us. As a point of principle, we refused to go to Lancaster Gate. It had to be a neutral venue for the meeting, away from the eyes of the media.

And the first thing which struck me when I walked into the room was the pile of newspaper cuttings in front of the FA Secretary, Dennis Follows. It must have been six inches high! 'I'm not having that,' I said. 'I'm not going to be judged by the reports of newspaper people acting on second-hand information.' Don and the solicitor agreed with me. We told the FA officials that if they wished to adjudicate fairly, they'd have to watch the film. At that time, television evidence was inadmissible in FA hearings. But in this instance, we weren't prepared to budge. They sent us out of the room for almost an hour while they talked the matter over among themselves. Eventually, we were called back in to be told, yes, they would watch the film.

That set a precedent which would soon become standard. Of course, having watched it, they could only come to the conclusion that my remarks had been taken out of context, that I had been unfairly reported in the press.

But still they insisted I apologize. 'What for?' I asked. I hadn't done anything wrong. They'd just gone through the television evidence and exonerated me. And now they wanted an apology! We must've sat there for another hour discussing whether I should apologize. 'The people who should apologize', I said, 'are the guys who wrote that pile of crap in front of you.' Anyway, we had a little meeting outside, and Don said, 'We've got to apologize in some way.' He said it was in my best interests to make some kind of gesture. I'd have stayed there for ever rather than give in to them, but eventually I agreed.

Only Don could have got me to do that. As a manager, he was never better to me than at that time, when I was under a lot of pressure and I needed sound advice. He stood with me through the whole episode – and I shall always remember him for that.

What I had to do was to find a way of apologizing without admitting that I'd done anything wrong. And I remember to this day the final statement that was sent to the newspapers, the same newspapers which had made headlines of the story for weeks: 'I apologize for the fact that through me, the press was given an opportunity to knock football.' That was the apology we sent to the press – and you can imagine where they printed it.

The FA tried me, and I was found not guilty. I was never fined, never suspended – though I'd suffered two weeks of being pilloried and having my name blackened all over the world. This was virtually the start of the sort of bloody journalism we have now. If I pick up the phone and find there's a journalist that I don't know from one of those papers on the line, I just put the phone down.

Strangely enough, while all this was going on I had a conversation about it with Lord Harewood, who was President of the FA at the time, as well as being President of Leeds United. George knew I liked shooting, and I go and shoot at Harewood House every year. I remember sitting with them, and Patricia, George's wife, saying to me, 'We thought you'd been under enough pressure, Jack, so we haven't asked you before now what this is all about.'

'I don't really know what it's all about,' I said, and I explained about the television programme.

'Ah, I understand at last,' she said, when I had

147

finished. 'You know, you've been unlucky.'

'Why?'

'Well, there's been no other big news story to take the weight off you,' Patricia said. When she and George first met he had been married to someone else, and it was a time when something like that about the Queen's cousin was big news. 'We had lots of bad press,' she said, 'just like you – but it didn't last long. Funnily enough, what took us off the front page and out of the public eye was that somebody shot President Kennedy.'

Unfortunately, there was no big news to take the pressure off me. On a personal level, the 'black book' incident earned me a reputation as someone who speaks his mind, someone who says things when he feels it's necessary to say them. Now, whether I've been naïve in this over the years or not I don't know, but personally I don't think I have. I think I've come through my career with a reputation as an honest, straightforward guy who doesn't pussyfoot around. And I think that's the image most people have of me.

And the names in the book? I didn't mention any names in the programme, and I don't really want to start mentioning names now. As I've said, I didn't really have a black book – but I did have perhaps five or six players in mind who had committed nasty tackles on me and whose names I wouldn't forget in a hurry. You always remember the names of people who have done you wrong, you never forget them. I'd get them back if I could. But I would do it within the laws of the game.

A lot of people thought that Peter Osgood topped the list in my black book, but that wasn't the case. Ossie and me did have some good battles – but I don't remember doing anything untoward in my duels with him and I can't recall him ever doing anything untoward to me. The same was true of Dennis Law, who's always been a good pal of mine. I've got two or three of Dennis's shirts at home that I ripped off his back.

Still, I couldn't say the same for Peter's Chelsea clubmate, who 'did' me in the sneakiest way possible in the 1970 FA Cup final replay when I wasn't even watching him. I haven't caught up with him yet, so I won't give you his name. As I've said, there was no reason for it except that I was doing my usual thing of standing on their goal-line. He got away with it at the time, and I can assure you, that rankled for a while.

George Kirby, a very competitive centre forward at Southampton, was another you had to watch out for, frequently a split-second late with the header and always liable to hurt you. I didn't like that kind of player, and I remember walking off at the end of a game at the Dell with a bad headache. Looking back, they were still treating him on the pitch.

It's more than twenty-five years since the black book was news, and it wouldn't serve any useful purpose now to start trotting out names. I'll give just one more example, purely because the player involved, John Morrissey of Everton, knows the score. We were playing at Goodison Park one day and John, a short, stocky little lad, was on the wing. I came across to make the tackle, he went through me, and I ended up having my foot put in plaster after the game. I still wouldn't have given the tackle much thought had I not encountered him again on the way out of the ground.

Picture the scene – my foot is in plaster, and I'm hobbling towards the coach with the aid of a stick. He's stood at the door asking, 'How's the leg then, big fella?' And I look across at him and see this cynical smile on his face – and I nearly flipped. I mean, if I could have done him then, I would have. 'I'll tell you something,' I said, 'if it takes me ten fucking years, I'll get you back for this.' And I did. But then he got me back, and I got him back, and so it went on till we finished playing.

I suppose you could say that I was a bit short-tempered. If somebody did something to me which I thought was unnecessary, I would react very quickly. That Fairs Cup game against Valencia was a case in point. I was being abused by some of the Spanish players and I wasn't having that.

There was another incident, I think it was in Rome or in Naples, when one of their guys just turned round and gobbed in my face. I couldn't help myself, I punched him right in the mouth, and he went down. The referee turned and saw the guy lying on the floor – you know the way they do, rolling and holding his face – and he ran back and looked at me as if to ask: what happened? I didn't say anything, I just pointed to my face. He could see the gob still there, and he said, 'OK, free kick,' and he just left the guy lying there.

You have these moments of madness when you let fly or go chasing somebody all over the park after they've done something nasty to you – until somebody grabs you and slaps you on the face and says, 'Hey, settle down.' People forget that in football you're 100 per cent concentrated on the game, you're looking at the game, you're reacting to the game, your position changes as the ball moves around – and then somebody does something really nasty, and it snaps your concentration. That's what happened to me in the 1970 Cup final replay.

It's just hypocrisy to pretend that a professional foot-baller can just forget when somebody does something like that to him. In no way, shape or form can any pro just 'forget' when somebody's nearly broken his leg, or split his eye, or smashed his forehead. You know in a split-second if it's deliberate. And as I've said, if you have a chance to get even later on, you take it. Everyone in the game knew that – except, apparently, the FA.

11

LEEDS AT THE PEAK

I missed a lot of games for England in the late 1960s because of the pressure on Leeds. The further we progressed in all the competitions, the greater the pressure. I don't think Don ever said to me, 'I don't want you to play for England next week' – but I dropped out of a lot of international matches because of niggling injuries. In other circumstances they might not have been enough to stop me playing, but if we had a big match coming up, it was very much in the interests of the manager – and it still is to this day – to say, 'You'd better pull out of this one.' So one way and another I missed a lot of England games.

But I played in most of them, of course, including our great 5–0 win over France on 12 March 1969. Another nice memory was our 1–0 win over Portugal in December that same year. Our kid took the corner, and I was in the box to jump and head the winner.

Brian Labone was the one who played in my place when I was out of the side. He always thought, and I thought too, that he was filling in for me. We reckoned that when it came to the defence of the World Cup in the summer of 1970 I would be the one to play, maybe because I had played in the team that had won the World Cup in 1966. I still considered myself the first choice. It's true that at thirty-five I was getting on a bit, yet I'd just finished what was probably my best ever season at Elland Road. After all the punishment we'd taken in 1969–70, I was confident I'd be able to handle the heat and the pressure in Mexico.

Alf took us on a warm-up tour of South America, playing Colombia and Ecuador in late May, just before the finals began in early June. I didn't play in either of the two warm-up games, and I began to suspect that Alf wasn't planning to play me in the finals. Alf probably thought I was coming to the end of my time with him, I don't know.

That was the trip where our Bob and Bobby Moore were accused of stealing jewellery from a shop in Bogotá. Our Bob had been released after the initial inquiries, but he was still very nervous as we waited for the plane to take off. The other lads were playing tricks on him, and I told them to lay off. We had to leave Bobby Moore behind for a few days. But he didn't seem too upset when he rejoined us in Mexico – he seemed to regard the whole business as a laugh.

Alf got a bit uptight while we were in Mexico. He was very adamant, and he was perfectly right of course, that we shouldn't stay in the sun too long, so we were only allowed half an hour's sunbathing by the hotel pool every day. Trainer Harold Shepherdson would blow the whistle to indicate that we could start sunbathing, after fifteen minutes he'd blow the whistle again to tell us to turn over, and after another fifteen minutes he'd blow again to tell us it was time to go inside.

The hotel we were staying in was one of those ones divided into little houses, and somebody kept pushing anonymous letters under Alf's door, full of outrageous

153

stories about what the players were getting up to. I still don't know to this day who it was. But Alf did his nut. He called us in and said, 'If I find any of you behaving like that, you'll be on the first plane home.' It was hard not to smile.

I was not surprised when Alf announced the side for the first game and I found that Brian had been picked instead of me. Brian came to my room and said, 'I am sorry, I thought you would be playing.' I told him, 'Don't worry, Brian, it's not you that picks the team, it's Alf. If he thinks you're the man for the job, that's fine.' And I wished him all the best.

Alf never said anything about leaving me out, he never explained anything to anyone.

Some of Alf's other selections puzzled me, too. Alf had said before we left for Mexico that anyone who couldn't handle the heat wouldn't play – and yet Franny Lee played in virtually all the games. And Franny was the one player in the England squad at the time who couldn't handle the heat. The one guy who was really at the top of the tree as a player at the time, that we all felt would have a big part to play in the World Cup finals, was Peter Osgood – but I don't think Peter was in the starting line-up for any of the games. In all our practice matches Peter seemed to me by far the best player; his laid-back style was ideally suited to the heat. But Alf never used him – except as a substitute.

Our first game was against Romania. They fouled us constantly, but our lads didn't retaliate. Our kid was brought down in the box in the first five minutes, but the referee waved play on. He looked a constant threat throughout the game, and several of his powerful shots only narrowly missed. But it was Geoff Hurst who eventually scored the only goal, skipping round the defence before smacking the ball into the net from a very tight angle.

Then we played a pulsating, thrilling game against Brazil. I'll never forget that day, because I felt that England were so unlucky to lose. We dominated in the early stages, but then they came back strongly early in the second half, and a brilliant move by Tostão and Pelé set up Jairzinho to score. But we came back at them, and missed two or three of the best chances. Franny Lee had one on the line – and I said to him afterwards, 'If you'd dived and headed that ball as it bounced you would have scored' – but he put his foot up to kick it instead, and somebody hooked it back off the line. Then Jeff Astle somehow missed an open goal, side-footing the ball past the post from only twelve yards out. Bally had several chances, including one only ten minutes from the end – all he had to do was to chip it over the keeper's head, but he hit it too hard, and it cannoned back off the crossbar. The final score was 1–0 to Brazil.

Brian Labone was playing all right – he wasn't the quickest player in the world, but he was strong in the air.

Alf took our kid off during that game, as he did later against West Germany. On the way home he explained his thinking. Our Robert had been playing so well, and he was such an instrumental part of the way that England were playing, that Alf thought he should save him for the semi-finals. Which was perfectly under-standable, because Bobby had played in all the previous games.

Alf played me in the next game against Czechoslovakia. For some reason the crowd was very hostile, and we gave a disappointing performance after the great game against Brazil. Allan Clarke scored the only goal of the game from a penalty, after one of their defenders had brought down Colin Bell in the box and then handled the ball for good measure. They nearly equalized when Banksy couldn't hold on to a shot from their striker Adamec, and I remember having to make a desperate tackle to stop him early on. I found the game very hard, not having played in any of the build-up games, and I must have looked a bit jaded.

Our 1–0 win meant that we qualified for the quarter-final against West Germany. The stage was set for a rerun of the 1966 final – but this time round, I wasn't even on the bench.

Just before the game Banksy reported sick. He'd been taken ill the previous day, and there'd been newspaper reports that his food might have been tampered with. Now it was obvious that he wouldn't be able to play, and Peter Bonetti was drafted in at the last moment. It was hard for Peter, having to replace the guy who was acknowledged to be the best keeper in the world. Gordon had made a thrilling save to deny Pelé a goal in the game against Brazil. It had to be bad news for England that he was out of the game.

After a nervous start we began to control the midfield, pushing the Germans back when we broke from defence. Alan Mullery put us ahead with a great goal in the first half, and just a few minutes into the second Bobby Moore started a move which ended with Martin Peters ghosting in to score once again. We were 2–0 ahead with twenty minutes remaining when Alf took our kid off. It's normal practice to bring on an extra midfield player when you're leading at that stage of the game – but what happened was that suddenly

Beckenbauer could stop worrying about our Bob, and instead of playing at the back in his normal sweeper role, he pushed upfield.

I remember watching Geoff Hurst chasing the ball. He headed it past the goalkeeper, and as it bounced slowly towards the goal he could have dived and he probably would have knocked the ball into the net. But it looked as though it was going to hit the post and rebound back to him. Geoff hesitated, just for a second, to see the ball scrape past the post. Had he scored we would have been 3–0 ahead, and into the semi-finals.

Then Terry Cooper made one of his runs. I was yelling from the stand, 'Stay where you are! Don't give the ball away!' But Terry overran the ball and it rolled through to the goalkeeper, who picked it up and threw it to his left. The next thing we knew was that Beckenbauer was running forward with the ball, while Terry was still trying to get back. Caught on his own, Alan Mullery didn't know whether to stick or twist, because he had Beckenbauer coming towards him and another German moving up on his right. Beckenbauer dummied to play the ball to his left, and when Alan took the bait, Beckenbauer came inside and hit a shot from about twenty yards away. It seemed like the most innocuous shot, but Peter Bonetti had come off his line and was stranded in a dangerous position. The ball bobbled underneath him and carried on into the net. It was 2–1.

I couldn't stand it any more. I walked out of the stadium and sat down in a café. I was looking at my watch waiting for the crowds to come out when I knew the game was supposed to finish – but they didn't come out. Shit! The game must have gone into extra time. I walked back to the ground, just in time to see Brian Labone mishit a clearance straight to a German player. His cross came over deep, before being nodded back, for Gerd Muller to volley the ball into the net from near point-blank range. That put them ahead 3–2, and that's how it remained. We'd lost the World Cup.

I've never seen a team come off the field so down. I went into the dressing-room afterwards, and Alf was just walking round saying, 'We can all go home now, we will be leaving tomorrow.' I don't think he was annoyed – I think he was just disappointed, like the rest of us. I remember Tommy Wright, the Everton full back, buying a crate of beer on the bus to the airport. By the time we boarded the plane he was stoned out of his mind, and that's how he stayed all the flight home.

I had been very disappointed when Alf announced the team for the West Germany match, and I knew then it was time to call it a day. When I saw Alf sitting alone on the plane I decided to speak to him about it, but I had to pluck up courage by downing a few drinks first. I went over and told him, and he hardly looked at me. 'Yes, I totally agree,' he said. I was all got up and walked away. Strangely enough, our kid had also played his last game for England. Alf had taken him off to save him for the semi-finals, but in fact he never played for England again.

It was another disappointing season for Leeds United. For a long time we were seven points ahead in the League, but then Arsenal made an unbelievable late charge, winning virtually every one of their last six or seven games 1–0. When we beat them at Elland Road in our last but one game of the season, I thought we had it won. My first shot ricocheted off the post, and I just sort of dived in and forced the ball over the line. But Arsenal had the last laugh, scoring a last-minute goal against Spurs in their final game of the season to clinch the championship, in the year they won the double. We finished runners-up with sixty-four points, the most ever scored by a team finishing second.

We'd had a bit of bad luck in a home game against West Brom late in the season, when Jeff Astle scored a crucial goal. Norman Hunter had played a ball forward which rebounded to one of their players who looked yards offside. Everyone just stood and looked. The linesman flagged him offside, but the referee overruled him, and the guy played it forward to Jeff, who scored. If he hadn't we'd have drawn the game and most likely won the League.

We crashed out of the FA Cup early that year in an embarrassing 3–2 defeat by Fourth Division Colchester United. The conditions were dreadful that day: the wind was blowing a gale, there was virtually no grass on the ground, and the pitch was very bumpy – what we call a great leveller. Good teams are always at risk on days like that. Don was very upset, we were all most upset. It was one of those games that you hate afterwards, because they are for ever showing it on television.

But we were doing well in the Fairs Cup, reaching the final that year. Our opponents were Juventus, and the first leg was played in Turin. In fact the first match had to be abandoned halfway through, because the pitch became so waterlogged. Instead of going home and rearranging the fixture for a later date, we stayed on to play three days later, which caused a problem, because quite a few of the players had brought their wives over – and as I've said, Don didn't like the players mixing with their wives before a game. Whenever we went away, he always insisted that the wives travelled on a different flight and stayed in a different hotel. They were looked after properly, they were taken on a bus to the ground, but they were kept away.

We had a meeting after the abandoned game, and several of the players insisted that their wives should come and stay with them in the hotel. But Don was adamant, and he threatened to resign if he didn't get his way. I didn't mind, myself, because I'd been married long enough to know that Pat wouldn't worry whether we were together or not for a couple of nights. But some of the players, I can't remember which but some of the younger players, were very unhappy about it. As far as I can remember, it was the only time Don ever threatened to resign.

I agreed with him, actually. There's a place for men and there's a place for women – but certainly not a place for women on the night before you play a big game. There's always a problem when you bring a lot of women together – one of them's bound to say something about somebody else's husband that shouldn't be said. Although the lads might know everything about each other, it's sort of kept in-house. Once the wives know, it's outside the family.

Three days later the weather had cleared up enough for us to play. Juventus were the favourites, but our experience in international competitions had taught us how to handle the Spanish and the Italian teams. It's called international knowledge. Although Roberto Bettega put them ahead, we came back at them and just before half-time Paul Madeley hit a cracking shot from thirty-five yards away to put us level. Two more goals in the second half left the final score 2–2. We felt pretty confident going into the second leg at Elland Road. Allan Clarke spun round to shoot and beat their keeper Tancredi after only twelve minutes, but they equalized seven minutes later. Then it was a case of battling through, and both sides had their chances but there were no more goals, leaving the final score 1–1. Leeds had won the Fairs Cup on the away goals rule.

The Juventus coach was disappointed that his team should have failed to win the trophy despite not losing a game. But people don't appreciate how much away goals count in competitions. If you go away and draw 0–0, then it's a good result. But if you go away and draw 1–1, it's a great result. If you can get a couple of goals away from home, that really gives you an advantage, because even if you get beaten 3–2, you only have to win 1–0 back at home and you're through. We actually lost a game 2–1 to Dynamo Dresden in the second round of the Fairs Cup that year, but we went through on the away goals rule.

Don made us very much aware of the importance of not giving goals away at home. You've got to be patient, you can't go charging off trying to score at the other end. You've got to keep your shape and fill the midfield. The main thing is not to over-commit yourselves, because they'll draw you in and then they'll beat you on the break. If you're patient, the chances will come. The number of times I read in the papers that our 1–0 lead might not be enough! Nobody ever beat us by two clear goals – that was a sort of thing with us. It might not have been popular with the press, but it worked. I don't think there was a better team in Europe than we were between about 1968 and 1972. Nobody fancied playing Leeds – it was very difficult to get a result against us.

Unfortunately we had a lot of crowd trouble that season. After West Brom beat us with that controversial goal in April, the fans invaded the pitch and the referee was jostled by angry fans. The FA responded by closing Elland Road for the first four games of the 1971–72 season. But things were going better on the field. We had a great run in the League, with some famous victories: 5–1 over both Newcastle and Manchester United, 6–1 over Nottingham Forest, and, most famous of all, 7–0 over Southampton on 4 March. We absolutely murdered them that day. The movement, the pattern – everything seemed to go right. Some of the moves included twenty-four or twenty-five passes. Seven of us scored, including me.

The game was shown on *Match of the Day*, and people started to look at us in a different way. They started calling us 'Super Leeds' and comparing us to Real Madrid. I reckon that was the game when people took a look at us and finally said, 'Yeah, this is a good team.'

I was making good money in football by this time. I'm not a great spender, I don't drive ostentatious cars, and I've always been careful with my money. The only thing I've ever spent money on, really, is property. I'd always fancied a house in the Yorkshire Dales, and now I had enough money to buy one. My father had retired by this time, so my parents moved in there – the fresh air was good for his lungs.

We often used to take the kids to stay with them in the Dales, or we'd go to Filey, where we'd kept a caravan since we were newly-weds. Eventually we bought a fisherman's cottage on the sea there. Another place we used to go at the time was Torremelinos. Fred Pontin had a hotel there, and he'd let footballers stay at special rates. There were always loads of players there, with their wives and kids. It was generally the gathering-point for footballers on holiday. We'd sit in the bar and talk football. The kids used to play football on the beach, and some of the Spanish waiters might join in. There was an occasion when I was watching a game and talking to Chris Nichol, the big centre half for Southampton, when one of these waiters ran right in and flattened his kid. Chris just stood there looking at him, and he said, 'He can't do that – that's my boy.' He went on and started playing, and he kicked this Spanish waiter all over the place.

Our rivalry with Arsenal was renewed when we met in the final of the FA Cup. It was a good game, but we were in control for most of the time. Allan Clarke scored the only goal with a header, and we had several other near misses – though they had some chances at the other end too. Charlie George hit the crossbar with a tremendous shot from way out, Paul Reaney had to kick an Alan Ball shot off the line, and David Harvey saved from Frank McLintock. Charlie didn't cause me as many problems as I thought he would – in fact, apart from that shot, I was very disappointed in his per-formance. Centre forwards cause you problems when they're making runs and drawing you out of position, but Charlie just played straight up the middle.

In making the cross to Clarkey which led to the goal, Mick Jones fell and dislocated his shoulder, and he had to go off for treatment only minutes from full time. At the end Norman went into the treatment room to fetch him, and though Mick was wincing with pain he joined us with his arm in a sling in the walk up to the Royal

163

Box to collect our winners' medals. It was an emotional moment for all of us. We had won the FA Cup at last.

The Monday after the Cup final was my thirty-seventh birthday – but more important, we had to go to Molineux for a crucial League game. We'd been in contention all season, and now we needed to draw or win for the title. Our two rivals were Liverpool, who were playing their last game at Arsenal the same evening, and Brian Clough's Derby County, who'd finished their season.

We couldn't understand why the FA wouldn't let us play the game a few days later. Obviously we'd have liked to celebrate winning the FA Cup after all those attempts, and to make us play only a couple of days later was, I thought, out of order. But we had no friends in the Football Association.

Anyway, we went to Molineux to play Wolves. They went ahead just before half-time, and then in the second half Derek Dougan made it 2–0. Billy Bremner managed to claw one back, but although we pressed them hard, we couldn't get that goal we needed. The final score was 2–1 to Wolves – and with Liverpool losing to Arsenal, Derby County became champions. We were runners-up again.

12

ONE BOOK CLOSES, ANOTHER
OPENS . . .

The leaving of Leeds closed the book on one of the most exciting phases of my life.

Twenty-three years earlier, I'd made that train journey from Ashington with not much more than the clothes on my back. Now I was going home with a tidy bank balance and almost every honour the game had to offer.

To that extent, I'd good reason to thank the club. And yet when I walked out the gates of Elland Road for the last time, I felt just a little bit let down by the club officials. It had to do with my testimonial game against Celtic. They took £40,000 at the turnstiles on the night, which was a nice sum for a man who had never earned more than £175 a week. But then I saw the deductions – £12,000! What really bugged me was that they included a match fee of something like £8,000 to Celtic – and Celtic owed us a game for a match at Parkhead the previous year. Now, the Leeds directors could have insisted on a reciprocal arrangement and requested the Scots to scrap their fee for my game. But they didn't. Instead, they kept it for themselves, an asset to be cashed in at their time of choosing. I mean, it wasn't as if Leeds United was a poor club.

I thought that was just a little unfair. Perhaps they reckoned that I'd made enough during my time at the club and didn't need the extra money. It's true I wasn't strapped for cash. I collected the £28,000, put it in a trust fund for my kids, and haven't seen it from that day to this. That, however, was skirting the issue. I'd been with the club all my playing life, and in the process I'd put in a record number of appearances for Leeds, 629 in the League and 773 overall – a record that stands to this day, that will probably never be broken. I'd scored ninety-six goals for the club, making me the ninth highest Leeds goalscorer of all time. I'd represented Leeds on thirty-five occasions in the England team. But in the end, they still held back on me. And that rankled.

Contrast the way they treated me with the way they treated Brian Clough after his ill-fated sojourn the following year. Though Cloughie was there for only forty-four days in all, he left with a golden handshake of something like £98,000 from the club. Bloody hell!

How they ever came to appoint him in the first place was a mystery. Brian's record in club management was impeccable, but he never had any great love of Leeds United, and he lost no opportunity to publicize the fact.

Towards the end of Don Revie's reign the feeling among the lads was that Johnny Giles would succeed him. He knew the game, he commanded the respect of the other players and what's more, he was already installed as player/manager of the Republic of Ireland team at that time. Giles would probably have been an automatic choice had not Billy Bremner entered the race at a late stage. Now there were two highly respected players in contention for the job – and the only conclusion that makes sense to me is that the Leeds directors ducked the choice. Instead of running with the best man and antagonizing the other, they opted for a compromise.

I had left by the time Cloughie arrived, but some of the stuff coming back to me was hair-raising. Brian is not the most diplomatic man in the world, but even by his standards some of his actions at Elland Road were astounding. Later, he would claim that the players had ganged up against him. This, they vehemently deny, but had they done so, I, for one, would have understood perfectly. Apparently he didn't often speak with them, restricting his team talk on one occasion to just a few terse words: 'If you're so good, it doesn't need me to tell you. So, go out and show me.' Don Revie, the most dedicated man to detail I've ever known, would have been sick at the sound of that.

Maybe it was a kind of shock therapy, but on one of Brian's first days in charge, he told the players, 'Anything you've won at this club, you should throw in the bin, because you won it by cheating.' What a man, what a damn cheek!

I got to know Brian afterwards when we were both members of the ITV panel. We'd go down to London and stay at the Tower Hotel. There was a pub near by, and we used to go there for a couple of pints in the evening – I remember Brian was always very friendly with the lads in the pub. We got on very well. Maybe it's because we're both from the North-East of England, I don't know, but we never seemed to disagree on a point of football. We both looked at the game in the same way. I always admired Brian's teams. His players always seemed to know what they were doing and where they were going. Brian is one of the

167

very few people in the game whose teams I've actually been to watch playing. In fact, there's been very little that Brian has ever done – except while he was at Leeds United – that I've ever disagreed with.

The only thing that used to annoy me about Brian was that he would always turn up late. Like when we were all wired up, sitting round a table ready to do a broadcast, Cloughie would always arrive at the last moment and then there'd be a panic. After a while I got to see that he did it for effect. He'd sit outside in the car listening to the radio, just so he'd make a bigger impact when he came on.

Long before the end of the 1972–73 season, I had already decided to hang up my boots and go into management. I was approaching my thirty-eighth birthday, I had seen it all as a player and, frankly, I didn't fancy the idea of soldiering on for another year. I was no longer an automatic choice in the starting line-up. At the beginning of the season, Don had signed Gordon McQueen as my understudy – a tall guy and a good header of the ball, though he never knew where it was going. Don had taken me aside at the beginning of the season and explained that he would be replacing me in the first team from time to time. 'The problem with you', he said, 'is that you can now only motivate yourself for the big games' – and, on reflection, I had to admit that he was quite correct. I fought to keep my place, but I knew my days were numbered, particularly after a hamstring injury in the FA Cup semi-final against Wolves prevented me from playing towards the end of the season.

When I told Don I wanted to retire, his initial reaction was that I had still something to contribute to the team. He offered me a two-year contract, and I think he had an idea that I might finish up on the staff at Elland Road. But he didn't push it too hard. Typically, he told me that his phone line was always open if I needed any advice after leaving the club. That was an invitation I appreciated. Don was the best in the business, and if anybody could set me right on my new career as a manager, it was him. As it transpired, most of my subsequent conversations with him were purely social – but it was reassuring to know that he was in the background if I needed him. I didn't know then, of course, that Don would be leaving Leeds only a year after I did to become manager of the England team.

By this stage I was known in the game as somebody who was very interested in coaching. As a young pro, I'd had the foresight to go to Lilleshall for my FA coaching badge, and the spin-offs were considerable. Not only did it teach me how to get on my feet and make my point as clearly as I could to an audience, but it took me among people who were respected managers at the time, or in the process of becoming so.

I had a few calls from intermediaries acting on behalf of clubs wanting to know my plans, and then came a direct enquiry from the England team doctor, who happened to be a director of Middlesbrough. Stan Anderson had just quit as manager and the club chairman, Charlie Aymer, was interested to know if I'd take the job. There wasn't a lot I knew about Middlesbrough at the time. They were in the Second Division, and apart from the rare occasions when their path crossed with Leeds United in our Second Division days, I didn't have any particular cause to take an interest in them. But if I didn't know the players, I was aware of the club's great tradition and of the esteem in which it was held in our part of the world. As a boy, I'd heard of great players like Wilf Mannion and George Hardwick and I knew that Middlesbrough used to boast teams capable of matching the best in the country.

It was now twenty years since they had last played in the First Division, but essentially they remained a big club. The infrastructure, if a little shabby, was still in place – and with a big catchment area, the potential of the club was considerable.

I went to see Middlesbrough play, and I remember thinking, they're not bad, these. So I agreed to go and meet the board. They sat me in an annex, and then the members went into the boardroom. After a while they called me in. I sat down, and they started asking me questions, like in an interview. 'Wait a minute,' I said, 'I didn't come here to be interviewed for the job, I came here because I was told that you wanted me to manage the club, and that the job was mine if I wanted it.'

They went, 'Well, we have to find out about you.'

'No, you don't,' I said. 'I'm not prepared to accept that. In fact, all you've gotta do is agree to this – and if you agree to it and still want me to be manager, I'll take the job.' And I got out a sheet of paper that Don Revie had given me. It was a list of manager's responsibilities, making it clear that I was the boss and had a say in everything. It was unusual to ask for such total control – but I knew that there were a lot of clubs interested in me and there was no doubt in my mind that I could get a manager's job elsewhere.

'I'll just go and sit outside while you read it,' I said, 'so we won't need to have a discussion. If you decide that you want me to be manager, OK, and if you don't, just let me know and I'll go.'

So I went outside and I waited for about fifteen minutes. Then I started to get a bit impatient. I knocked on the door and said, 'Excuse me, but you seem to be taking a long time to make up your minds. I'm gonna sit out here for another ten minutes, and if you haven't made your minds up by then, I'm off.'

So I closed the door and sat down again. Five minutes later they asked me to come back into the boardroom again, and when I sat down in there, they said, 'Yeah, you've got the job.'

I told them I wouldn't sign a contract, I'd stay for a maximum of four years – and if either party felt so inclined, our agreement could be terminated earlier with no hard feelings on either side. The money was adequate rather than great, but at that point it wasn't a major consideration. I've never had a contract as a manager, not even with the FAI.

I set off for London to watch Leeds play in the 1973 Cup final against Sunderland in the knowledge that I'd already come to the end of the road with the club. My hamstring injury ruled me out of the game. The Cup final was being played on the Saturday, and my testimonial would be on the following Monday. From then on, the only team I wanted to see in the headlines was Middlesbrough.

But first we had to beat Sunderland. I was working for television at the time, sat up in the gantry watching the game. To be fair, Sunderland were quite a good team. A lot of the players they had then, players like the big centre back Dave Watson, went on to better things afterwards. I thought that Leeds dominated the game from start to finish. But could we score? Could we hell! Their keeper Jim Montgomery made save after save. Then, after half an hour, Ian Porterfield crashed a volley into the net at the other end. It was completely against the run of the play. I said to the television viewers, 'It's written in the stars, this. Leeds can't win this game.' I think I was more frustrated than the players down on the park.

After the game finished the Sunderland players took their manager, Bob Stokoe, on a lap of honour. As he passed the gantry, he looked up at me – and he stuck two fingers up in the air.

Losing to Sunderland for me was the dregs. Because up in Tyneside, you're either a Sunderland fan or a Newcastle fan. It's a bit like Spurs and Arsenal in North London, or Liverpool and Everton. If the word comes through to St James' Park that Sunderland are getting beat, there's a great roar goes up from the crowd.

I always say that there's no way Sunderland would have beaten us if I'd been playing. Now whether that's fair or unfair I don't know, but I feel certain that we'd have won if I'd been playing.

I'd attended the Football Writers' banquet on the Thursday before the game, and it had been my good fortune to be sat beside Jock Stein. I say good fortune, for I left the dinner that night with my team plans for 'Boro already in train. Jock was recognized within the game as one of the shrewdest managers around, a man who six years earlier had proved it by taking Celtic to victory in the European Champions Cup final. When he proffered advice on my new job, I listened.

His first recommendation was to take the team on tour as early as I could. He said that I'd learn more about my players living and sharing with them for a week or ten days away than in an entire season of League football. You'll learn who you can trust, who you can't trust, and the ones to keep an eye on. Afterwards I took up his offer to arrange three pre-season games for me in Scotland. Just as he had predicted, it proved a valuable learning experience. I came back from the trip having identified two or three barrack-room lawyers who had got to go, and very quickly they went.

Jock's other big deed of the night was to give me some advice which I took up later. There will come a time, he told me, when your players become complacent and start taking advantage. They might have done nothing wrong, just become a bit blasé about the results or their performances. It's then that you have to crack the whip. What Jock used to do was to go into the dressing-room and pick on someone for some minor offence. Say he saw a boot on the floor and recognized it as his captain's, Billy McNeill's, he'd say, 'Who's boot's this? Get it out of here, you're the captain, you set an example. Clean it up, this place is like a pit!'

It may seem a little hard at the time, but Jock was absolutely right – you've got to shout at your players now and again, just to stir them up a bit and make them take notice.

I phoned Jock just as the season started and asked him if there were any players in Scotland I should take a look at, that I might want to buy. I told him I needed a player in this position, I needed a player in that position, but most of all I needed a right side midfield player. And Jock said, 'I'll give you Bobby Murdoch.'

Now apart from those occasions when we'd clashed in England–Scotland internationals, I'd good reason to remember Bobby from the two European Cup semi-final games we'd played against Celtic in 1970. Not only did he break our hearts with the winner for Celtic in the return match, but his distribution throughout the tie was uncanny. I have never in my life seen a better passer of the ball than Bobby Murdoch. I mean, when he hit them, the ball appeared to hold up in the air, or alternatively gather speed to find the player running on to it, in precisely the right stride. It was, of course, an optical illusion, but that was the measure of the man's timing. Didn't have a lot of pace, did Bobby. The exception was when an opponent kicked him or when he got annoyed about something or other. Then he'd suddenly discover another yard, and anybody who got in his way soon discovered there was another side to this affable Scot.

Bobby was a player who had given Celtic superb service over the years. Jock said he was available on a free transfer – all I'd have to do was pay him a signing-on fee. He was only twenty-eight, and Jock reckoned that he still had a few good years left in him. He told me that if I could come up with a signing-on fee for him, I wouldn't regret it. Bob had the kind of gait which suggested that even when fit, he was always overweight. But Jock assured me that when it came to preparation, he was as conscientious as anybody. He explained that he had a younger player coming through who he thought was ready to replace Bobby that season in the Celtic side.

I was a bit suspicious. I started thinking, why? What's wrong here? So I phoned up Bobby, told him what Jock had said, and asked him to come and see me. We had one of the most honest and frank talks that I've ever had in my entire life. He admitted he had to diet to keep his weight down. He also told me that he was working hard to get it under control. Thus reassured, I signed him. It was an investment which would be recouped over and over again in the years ahead.

That summer was a long one to kill, for while the contracts of various players needed sorting out, there was nothing much I could do until they reported back for pre-season training. My backroom staff, I already knew. Harold Shepherdson, who was effectively my number two, had been trainer with the England team during the World Cup and I knew that I could trust him implicitly. He was installed as chief scout at Middlesbrough when I got there, and I would come to value his ability to identify emerging players. Harold was a smashing guy who presented a good face for football. But if he had a fault, it was his reluctance to make decisions in my absence. So I took him aside one day and told him that whatever he said or did in my absence, I would back him, even if I didn't agree with it. It took a while to bury the habits of a lifetime, but eventually the penny dropped and we worked happily together for the next four years. Jimmy Greenhoff, not the former Leeds player, but another old pro, was also on the technical staff, as was another man with a lot of experience, Ian McFarland.

In the meantime, I plunged myself into the job of making the place more presentable. Ayresome Park might have seen some great days in the past, but by 1973 it bore all the tell-tale signs of a stadium in decay. The first thing which struck me when I got to the ground was the state of the main gates. Grey and rusty, they looked anything but inviting to people who might otherwise be tempted to go in and watch a game. There and then, I decided that the place would have to be tidied up before the start of the season. I took it upon myself to go to the local ICI offices and ask them if they would make us a pressie of the paint. Together with British Steel, they were the biggest employers on Teesside, so I felt justified in making the approach. To their credit, they responded positively. So long as we didn't publicize the fact and start a queue of clubs looking for free paint, they'd let us have the stuff. So in a matter of days, Ayresome Park had a beautiful new dress of vivid red and white.

Then I made my first mistake. At one of the few board meetings I chose to attend, I happened to mention my little coup with ICI and how it wouldn't cost the club a penny. And the chairman goes, 'I've a good friend in ICI, I'll give him a call.' I tell him as politely as I can not to bother, the deal's already done. But Charlie has to be seen to be discharging the responsibilities of high office, so he puts through the call. The following week, there's a bill in the post for hundreds of gallons of paint, and I've learned my first lesson in management. If you want things done, do them yourself and tell nobody.

Nothing daunted, I had the seats in various sections of the ground painted in different colours, so that when people looked at a map in the outer office, they knew exactly what they were buying. A small point, perhaps, but one which I felt could streamline the marketing side of things.

And then there was the matter of television facilities at the ground. On those occasions when the cameras went to Ayresome, they shot their pictures almost from ground level. And they projected a bloody awful picture of our games. Once again, I had words with a friend, Mac Murray. He put in a new gantry just beneath the roof of the stand and the improvement in the quality of the coverage was enormous.

In fairness, Charlie Aymer is a nice man. But he

Leeds professional, aged 21.

Alf Ramsey. (Allsport)

Celebrating our World Cup victory, 31 July 1966. Next to me are Bobby Moore and George Cohen; behind us are Martin Peters, Ray Wilson, and Bobby Charlton.

West Germany's first goal in the 1966 World Cup final, scored by Helmut Haller. I always felt I could have stopped his shot, but I thought Gordon Banks had it covered. Also visible in the picture are Ray Wilson and Bobby Moore. (P.A. News)

Martin Peters ghosts in to score England's second goal in the 1966 World Cup final. I saw the ball coming out towards me, and I prepared myself to shoot, but Martin got there first.
(Popperfoto)

At home with my mother and Bobby just before the 1966 World
Cup final. (Syndication International)

Ashington reception for the Charlton brothers, August 1966.
(Newcastle Chronicle)

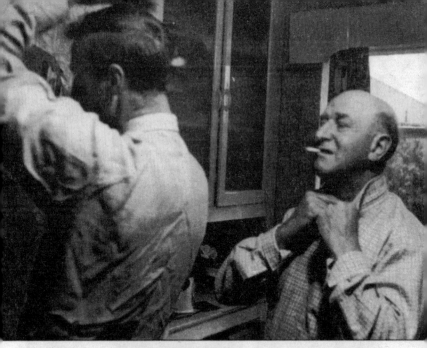

Father and son, just after the 1966 World Cup. (Daily Sketch)

Back at home with Pat and the kids. Son Peter, born only days after the World Cup final, was nicknamed 'World Cup Willie' by the press.
(D.C. Thomson & Co)

Wives and girlfriends (and Norman Hunter's mother) of Leeds United players set off for the 1965 FA Cup final against Liverpool. Don always made sure they were well looked after, but kept them away from us before a game.

(Daily Express)

Hobbling off at half-time in the England-Scotland game, April 1967. Despite the fact that I'd broken bones in my foot, I managed to play on and scored a goal towards the end of the game. Our contests with the Jocks were always very competitive.

(P.A. News)

League champions, 1968-9. Back row, left to right: Revie (manager), Reaney, Hunter, Belfitt, Gray. Middle row: O'Grady, Charlton, Sprake, Harvey, Jones, Madeley. Front row: Clarke, Cooper, Hibbitt, Bremner, Giles, Bater. Peter Lorimer seems to have gone walkabout.

(Colorsport)

The man who made the difference: Bobby Collins leads out the team, 1965.
(S & G Press Agency)

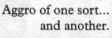

Aggro of one sort...
and another.
(Colorsport/Daily Express)

With Bobby. (Colorsport)

can be pig-headed on occasions. In those early days, I had a few shouting matches with him before he got the message. Like the time when another director went and got angled frames so that the perimeter advertising on the ground could be picked up better by the television cameras. Now Charlie was shrewd enough to know that if an advertiser was good enough to support us, he deserved to have his product properly displayed. But maybe because the idea of the angular frames wasn't his, he didn't support it. And I was not too pleased.

But once the ground rules had been established, I began to enjoy the job. I was manager of a club which I considered had substantial potential and I was going to do everything in my power to tap it. With that in mind, I had our fixture list for the season printed on big sheets. I took them round myself to offices, factories and mills and asked the people in charge to display them in canteens and places like that. Within a matter of weeks, I had people coming to Ayresome looking for them. That done, I approached the bus companies about the possibility of organizing special transport to our home games. The net effect was a dramatic improvement in Middlesbrough's attendance figures in my first season there.

And there was another little idea which I thought would benefit the club – this time on the pitch. Traditionally, Middlesbrough wore red shirts with a white collar and cuffs. Pretty enough in its day, but something which I felt now needed to be changed. When I first joined Leeds United as a young pro, the club colours were blue and gold. And they remained that way until Don Revie, the great innovator, took over as manager. Very soon, he thumbed his nose at tradition and ordered a new, all-white strip for the club. This was the gear Real Madrid played in, and the initial reaction from the local press was that Revie was aping the Spaniards. Not so, explained Don. In his opinion – and he was absolutely right – white is the easiest colour to identify on a pitch. When you have only a split-second to make a pass before the tackle comes in, you're more likely to pick up the right man if he's wearing not red or blue or green but white.

So I went and had 'Boro's strip changed, still pre-dominantly red but now with a broad white band. Old timers thought I was crackers, but I knew my football and the value of being able to spot a team-mate under pressure.

Besides the two potential troublemakers, I had lost another player in pre-season – but in this case, it had nothing to do with indiscipline. Nobby Stiles, my tried and trusted friend from the England team, was already at the club when I arrived, and frankly I was looking to him to do a holding job for me. I thought he would be a valuable old head to guide the younger players around him. Imagine my disappointment, then, when he walks up and informs me that he wants away. I tried to talk him out of it, but he was adamant. His wife wanted to return to the Manchester area, so I arranged for him to join our Robert, who by this time was managing Preston North End. Our Bob had been at the same Football Writers' banquet when I'd sat next to Jock Stein. He'd already taken the Preston job, but he never mentioned it to me, which I found a little strange. The first I knew of it was when I read about it in the Sunday papers a few days later.

Nobby's departure was a blow. But never mind, Bobby Murdoch would soon fill that role for me. The rest of the team was taking shape within weeks of the start of the season. Jim Platt, a Northern Ireland international, was in goal, and at full back we had two solid operators in John Craggs, a former Newcastle player, and Frank Spraggon. Spraggon, a son-in-law of Harold Shepherdson, was a good, strong player, though when it came to passing the ball, he was bloody awful. As a younger pro, he'd been kicked in the head and it left him with impaired vision in one eye. We're stood at a game one day, watching Frank mistime yet another pass, when suddenly Jimmy Greenhoff says, 'I think I've got the answer to Spraggon's problems. We'll get him to close both eyes when he's passing the ball. That way we have a fifty-fifty chance of getting it.'

The two centre backs were Stuart Boam and Willie Maddren. Boam was a big, old-fashioned type of player who discharged the basics perfectly, and, had it not been for knee problems, I reckon Willie Maddren would have played many times for England. Those were the men who minded the shop for me. But like every other manager, I knew that my team would stand or fall on the quality of our midfield play. To that extent, I could have done with Nobby Stiles for at least another season, but if we lost one good player, I soon discovered that we had unearthed another.

Graeme Souness was a young Scot who had been tried and rejected by Tottenham. Harold had signed him at the end of the previous season and it didn't need a genius to deduce that with proper handling, he could become a top-class midfielder. As a footballer, Graeme had a mean streak – in the best sense. When he put his foot in for the ball, he intended to win it. And he spared nothing or nobody in the process of doing so.

Why Tottenham ever let him go is a mystery. Perhaps he didn't settle in London, or it may have been an attitude problem. But within days of meeting him, I had put my mind at rest on this second issue. I took him into my office and confronted him straight away. 'You've a reputation as a bit of wide boy who likes the birds and the booze,' I started. And before I'd said another word, he got in his spoke.

'That's right,' he said. 'I'm fond of the girls and a night out, but I tell you this – I'll not cause you any problems. I want to succeed in football, and neither women nor drink will get in the way. I'll prepare for games as carefully as anybody. I'm annoyed you felt you had to haul me in here in the first place.'

I liked that last bit. The lad had a bit of fire in him, and if his skill was as good as I'd been led to believe, I reckoned young Souness would make out pretty well. In that I was proved right – but only after a period of trial and error.

Graeme, when he started with us, was a left-sided midfield player. To my mind, he didn't have the kind of pace needed to get up and down the flank. But I reckoned he could do the business in the centre and it was there, in fact, that he grew into one of the great talents in British football. As a distributor of the ball, he was already displaying some of the characteristics of Bobby Murdoch. But unlike Bob, he'd often play it backwards or sideways – and that needed urgent correction. Day after day, I preached the necessity of getting it to the front men, of looking up when he got past an opponent, of playing it into the spaces and then supporting. It was alien to his way of thinking, but he worked hard, and eventually he did precisely what I demanded of him.

On the left side of midfield, I had another teenager, David Armstrong, who looked anything but a footballer. He was smallish, had blond hair and to the casual observer didn't impress as a guy who could cope with the pressures of the professional game. So much for appearances! David was a great runner, had a good left peg and very soon developed into a key member of the team. Later, he would go on to represent England and make a fine career for himself in the game.

John Hickton and David Mills played up front, and they complemented each other well. David was the pacier of the two, but Hickton would go where it hurt, a brave player who got a lot of important goals for us.

I've so far omitted to mention one member of the team – and in a very real way, he was the one who made it all work for us. During the summer months, I'd given a lot of thought to the way the game was developing and how we could adapt to that situation. At the time, the implementation of the offside trap was the biggest thing defenders had going for them. They were pushing out at every opportunity and condensing the midfield area to a degree which was becoming ridiculous. So I had this plan. Instead of trying to carry the ball through them, we'd deliver it from further out and employ a midfield runner to get in behind them as they were coming out.

I'd never seen any team use this system. I didn't copy it from anybody. It was purely my idea and my response to the managers who were determined to shut out forwards by the simple expedient of playing them offside. I was convinced I was on the right track, but to make it work I needed a player with real pace.

Enter Alan Foggon. I'd seen him play at Newcastle and I wasn't over-impressed. He wasn't a good player in the sense that he was tricky or clever when the ball was at his feet. But Jesus, could he run! At school he'd been a 220-yards champion, and once I'd convinced him that this was the strong point of his game, he was a different player.

Mind you, it took some time to persuade him that he was no Stanley Matthews. He still wanted the ball to his feet, so much so that I had to introduce a local rule that anybody caught facilitating him would be fined. We wanted the ball played through as the defenders were charging out. With his pace, Foggy was capable of latching on to it before the goalkeeper could react. The timing had to be right, of course. If the ball was struck a split-second too late, he was liable to be caught offside – and then there was the problem of getting the two front men to move out with the defenders. John Hickton was pretty alert, but David's basic instinct was to turn and chase in after the ball. He must have been caught offside a hundred times in our first six games, but gradually he got the message.

It took us until Christmas to get the system right, but once everybody understood what they were about and the timing improved, we were unbeatable. Nothing like it had been tried before, defenders simply couldn't handle it, and we slaughtered teams from then on to the end of the season.

I recall going to Craven Cottage in March on the day Bobby Moore made his début for Fulham. Bob was as astute a player as any I've known, and after we'd hammered them 4–0 he came and sought me out. 'What have you done to that Foggon, then?' he asked. 'If he keeps playing like that, you may even get him a cap.'

Opposing defenders weren't the only ones baffled. The media, for example, branded us as a kick-and-rush team, strong at the back but lacking real flair. But then, they simply didn't know the name of the game we were playing. According to them, we were just booting the ball forward, hoping for the best. What they didn't or couldn't appreciate was that it took skill, real skill, to match the pass to the midfield runner. We had three of the best passers of the ball in England at the time in Murdoch, Souness and Armstrong. And Armstrong could gallop a bit, too, when Bobby and Graeme needed to hit somebody other than Foggy with the ball. I have never played kick-and-rush football, but I love balls played into space.

Promotion was secured with seven games still remaining, when we beat Oxford United with a David Armstrong goal on 23 March, and we went to Luton the following week knowing that a win would give us the championship. No club, to my knowledge, had ever made the winning of the Second Division title look easier – but to be honest, I didn't want to win that game at Kenilworth Road. My plan was to settle for a point and then secure the championship against Notts County in front of a full house at Ayresome Park the following week. Thanks to a strike from David Mills, we led for most of the game, and with time running out, I'm running up and down the line shouting, 'Let 'em have a goal, let 'em have a goal!' Would they hell! They defended that lead as if they were playing in a Cup final, and my grand little plan went up in smoke.

We still finished in style, however, and after trouncing Sheffield Wednesday 8–0, we went and played our final game against Robert's team, Preston, at Deepdale. Preston were already relegated, and the press made much of the fact that I did nothing at all to help our kid by beating them 4–2.

We finished top of the Division by fifteen points.

After all those years, the Ayresome faithful could look forward to First Division football the following season.

The improvement in the space of nine months was such that had it been a horse race, we might have been up before the stewards. But we won the title basically on a system, a method of playing that flummoxed every team we met.

I received an OBE that year, an honour I prized, particularly since Robert had got one before me. We went down to London for the presentation by the Queen.

It's amazing the little things which stay in your mind about occasions like that. We had our kids with us and I remember our Debbie wanting to go to the bathroom when we arrived at Buckingham Palace. When she eventually came back, she couldn't wait to tell us about these strange toilet seats. Later, I had occasion to go into the loo myself – and I couldn't believe how anti-quated the fittings were. The toilet seats were definitely relics of another generation. I wonder if they've ever thought of changing them for something more modern?

There was one more pleasant surprise waiting for me, when I was invited up to Scotland to attend the luncheon for the Bell's Manager of the Year award. Unlike other award schemes, the winner is not notified in advance. When I got there, I discovered I was in the company of Bill Shankly, Malcolm Allison, Lawrie McMenemy, and two or three other top-class managers. Eventually, they opened the envelope containing the slip and a cheque for a thousand pounds, and announced, 'The winner, and the first Second Division manager to take the award, is – Jack Charlton!' Hell's bells, I'd done it! Whereupon Shanks leans across to me and says, 'Well done, Big Man – but that's a thousand pounds you owe me.' That was Bill's way of telling me that he should have won it – and d'ye know something? He was right.

During that first season, I trained with the lads, not with the specific intention of playing but merely to keep myself in reasonable shape in case of emergency. Stuart Boam, I recall, got a bit upset about that, for he thought that I was going to take his place in central defence, but eventually I persuaded him that his fears were ill-founded.

I discouraged the players from addressing me as 'Boss', a word which was beginning to come into vogue in football at the time. I wanted them to feel that I was, in every sense, a part of the team. But there were times, I have to admit, when the dividing line between manager and player became a bit blurred. We were training one morning when John Craggs, just for the hell of it, clipped my heel and I fell flat on my face. Old instincts die hard – and when I got up, I chased him around the bloody field. Then, just as I was catching up on him, I tripped. Then and there I decided, hell, I'm getting too old for this lark.

The lads were having a bit of fun at the expense of the new manager – but I drew the line when I got a bill for sixty-eight pounds for a broken skylight in a hotel we stayed in after playing a game at Grimsby. I confronted the players back at Ayresome Park, and after I had threatened to deduct the money from their wages unless the culprit came forward, a hand eventually went up at the back of the room. The player, who shall be nameless, said that he had succeeded in enticing a young lady back to his room, and once the word was out, his team-mates, in the manner of these things, had climbed out on the roof to look through the skylight.

Unfortunately, one of them got so excited that he fell through the bloody thing.

I'm stood there in mock horror. I turned to the baby of the team, Stan Cummings, a lad of seventeen, and said, 'Hey, I hope you weren't up there on that roof.'

'No, Boss,' he says, 'I were in the cupboard.'

Ian McFarland left after we won promotion, saying that he had not been given enough credit. To be honest, I ran the business, and gave little thought to the staff I left hanging around.

There's a well-known story about a manager who says to his squad towards the end of the season, 'Come on, lads, one more heave – we'll get promoted and then I'll have the money to buy some better players.' That used to be a joke – now it's a fact. That's what plenty of people do nowadays. Sunderland got promoted in 1996, and it's been reported in the press that they will have to spend ten million pounds on players to keep them in the First Division. What happens to the players who got them there?

I totally disagree with this attitude. I believe in giving the players who've won promotion the opportunity to show how they'll perform in a more competitive environment. Once they've had a chance, if they fail to take it, that's the time to buy new players. Don Revie had taken the same line when we got promoted to the First Division. So I didn't spend unnecessarily during the close season to strengthen the squad for First Division football. Instead, I decided we'd do it from our own resources – and we'd change our scouting system to consolidate for the future.

At the time, the club had scouts all over the place. We'd people in Scotland, Ireland, the Midlands, and the South – and I reckoned that was a waste of resources. We'd kids coming down from Scotland at the age of fourteen or fifteen, but when it came to the crunch, they were always picked up by one of the big Scottish clubs like Rangers or Celtic if they were good enough. So I decided, to hell with this. We'll get rid of all the existing scouts, and concentrate on getting the best of the young talent in Northumberland and Durham. This area has produced more footballers than any other in England, and if we did our homework properly, we'd get as many as we needed here. We duly changed the system, and I'm glad to say it worked.

Terry Cooper, a player I had grown to admire when playing alongside him in the Leeds and England teams, was the only notable addition to our squad that season. Yet we fully justified our promotion by finishing in the top six, and eventually came within a hair's breadth of qualifying for Europe. That we failed to do so was down to a bloody stupid mistake by Bobby Murdoch, of all people, in our last game of the season, against Derby County at Ayresome Park.

We're leading by a goal from David Mills going into the last minute when we win a corner on the right. And I'm running down the line, yelling at Bobby, 'Play it short, keep the bloody thing in the corner.' But does he listen? Does he hell.

He knocks the ball across the face of the box – but we're lucky, it goes out for another corner. Surely he can't do the same thing again? But incredibly he does. This time, the ball is played square across our back four on the halfway line. Kevin Hector makes the interception and runs half the length of the bloody pitch to put the ball in the net for an equalizer, with the second to last kick of the game.

That was the difference between us getting to Europe

187

and the prospect of big-time football at Ayresome Park – and I'm afraid I didn't spare Bobby in the dressing-room. It was the last game of the season, so there was no putting it off until Monday. Nobody had done more to put me right at the start of my managerial career, and now he was guilty of the schoolboy error that cost us Europe.

I bought Phil Boersma from Liverpool to replace Murdoch the following season, but unfortunately it didn't really work out. Phil was a tall, rangy lad who had produced some good performances in his time at Anfield. But he lacked the passion I was looking for and seldom fitted into the scheme of things. For some reason he had more pulls and strains in that period with us than I'd had in my whole career.

This was the club's centenary season, but while we again succeeded in impressing as one of the better teams in the First Division, we failed to get into the shake-up for the title. And that disappointed me.

But we won the Anglo-Scottish Cup against Fulham, thanks to an own goal by Les Strong, and reached the semi-final of the League Cup against Manchester City. After winning the first leg 1–0 at Ayresome, we blew our chances, alas, on a disastrous night at Maine Road. The team coach arrived late at the ground, the players never settled when we eventually made it onto the pitch, and we got well and truly stuffed, 4–0. I remember thinking to myself, I can't handle too many more nights like this.

Something else happened that season which troubled me greatly. For the greater part of three seasons we had been trading on a running game which was revolutionary in English football. But eventually other teams cop on to what you're doing and learn how to counter it.

And on a wet, windy night at Birmingham, I discovered that the game was up for us. Instead of pushing out as other teams had done and giving us the space to get in behind them, they posted their two central defenders just outside the box. It closed down the space for Foggy to run into, and on the rare occasion we got the ball in behind them, it just skidded on the damp surface and ran through to the goalkeeper. Birmingham had discovered how to play us, and I knew it was now only a matter of time before the word got out to other clubs. I recall taking Alan aside after the match and telling him, 'You're now redundant as a midfield player – from here on in, your chances of getting into the team depend on your ability to displace one of the wingers.' Foggy had been a man for his time, but coming back on the coach that night, I knew he had outlived his usefulness.

The fact of the matter is that Birmingham weren't the first team to catch us out and cotton on to our system of playing. Back in my first year at Ayresome, we went to Wrexham for a Cup game and against all the odds, they beat us 1–0. They did to us exactly as Birmingham would later do, never pushing out, never giving us space to get Alan or David Armstrong running in behind them. Had we stayed in the Second Division for a second year, it's possible that others would also have found us out. But we won promotion that year and when we went up into the First Division, we were meeting different teams, different defenders who were encountering a running midfield game for the first time. And because of that, we were able to consolidate the club's revival.

My fourth season at Middlesbrough was frustrating in the sense that we didn't progress. We'd a good FA

Cup run before losing to Liverpool, but after a great start to the championship, we lost our way in mid-season and finished off the pace. We needed to change our team pattern, which meant spending some money. That was something I never liked doing. I treated club funds like my own – how naïve can you get?

I'd never really succeeded in replacing Bobby Murdoch, and with John Hickton at the end of his career, I needed a centre forward. I tried to buy David Cross, but I thought the £80,000 Coventry wanted for him was too much and I told Coventry to keep him. This was a mistake, which I very much regretted after-wards. In fact he went to West Ham for £120,000.

And then I got to thinking about some advice my trusted friend Jim Bullock had given me. Jim was a big Labour man, an ex-pit manager who chaired the first mine manager's union. He was also a bit of a phil-osopher, one of the shrewdest men I've known, and I valued what he said. One of his theories held that four years was the optimum with any bunch of players. At the end of that period, they get to know how you think, to anticipate what you're going to say and, frankly, they switch off.

Jim advised me to go while the going was good. Another mediocre season and I might be asked to leave – and that was unacceptable to me. Though I'd had a few rows with the chairman, none of them was par-ticularly serious, and I reckon Charlie Aymer was the most surprised man at the club when I walked up to him in February 1977 and told him I was quitting at the end of the season.

After twenty-six years of non-stop involvement in the game, I felt I needed a break and time to explore life outside football. Yet, if I'm honest, I regret now that I didn't stay another year at Ayresome and take them to a First Division championship. I reckon that I was only two players short of a title-winning team, and I could have got them by spending some of the money I'd amassed for the club in the previous four years. But for better or worse, I chose not to do so.

13

ENGLAND EXPECTS. . .

The only time I ever wrote a letter and applied for a job, I didn't even get an interview.

I had been riding high as manager of Middlesbrough. We'd won the Second Division championship, fifteen points ahead of the runners-up, and finished fifth in our first season in the First Division – despite not buying any new players or spending any money. I'd been named Manager of the Year.

All right, we'd taken a bit of stick from the London press for the way we played, particularly in my second season – you know, 'What kind of team is this that Jack Charlton's put together?' and that sort of thing. It's true that we went to the top of the First Division after twelve games having scored very, very few goals. But I said at the time that by the end of the season we'd score as many goals as anyone else – and we did.

Now I'd quit Middlesbrough, having achieved everything that could be expected of me, and more. I was available. When Don Revie decided to quit the job as England manager, I felt, myself, that I could be the man to succeed him.

I thought that I could do the job – although I didn't like to say it, because people think you're bragging. After all, I'd played international football. I'd worked

192

under two international managers. I was a staff coach for the FA. I'd been part of the FA's coaching system for twenty years. I'd played in Europe. And I'd managed a team very successfully. So I felt I was at least entitled to be given an interview for the England job.

I'd got a phone call from a press guy, who'd said he had been asked by two members of the committee that were picking the England team manager if I would apply. Now I don't know whether the journalist was on the level, because I never heard directly from the committee. But I had been at a talk-in for one of the newspapers with Peter Swales, the chairman of Manchester City who was on the committee, and one of the questions that had been put to me was, 'Would you take on the England job if it was offered to you?' I sort of hedged a bit. I answered, 'Nah, I don't think so. I'm not ready for it' – or something like that. Peter looked at me and said, 'Oh yes you are.'

Somebody shouted out, 'What about Cloughie?' and Swales replied that Brian Clough would never get the England job – over his dead body would he get it. That surprised me. At the time we all thought that Brian Clough was the obvious choice – with what he had achieved in Europe and the teams he had built. He had managed to get the best out of players in a way that nobody else did. I was a great Cloughie fan. The fact that Brian never became England team manager was always – well, it always surprised me – although he had a bit of a bad reputation for the things he would say through the press. Whether the England people thought they wanted someone whom they could control, I just don't know. They could never have controlled Brian.

193

And I suddenly thought to myself, if not Brian, what about me?

So I sent the FA a letter. Then I sat waiting for a reply – even if only to say, you know, well, we're not interested in you, or whatever – but I *never* got a reply to my letter. Not even a phone call, yet my name was mentioned in the papers in connection with the job virtually every day.

They were interviewing people like Lawrie McMenemy, and with all due respect to Lawrie, who's a very good friend of mine, he had no knowledge of international football – he had never been involved in it. He hadn't anything like the experience I had.

I was annoyed. From that moment on, I said to myself, I will never, *ever*, apply for a job again in my life. And I didn't. I didn't apply for the Sheffield Wednesday job, I didn't apply for the Newcastle job, I didn't apply for the Ireland job.

I never even received a reply, and I couldn't understand why. Whether they thought that me being a Revie lad, I would be like Don, I don't know. Don had left under a bit of a cloud, or a bit of a shadow, through no fault of his own. People think that Don walked out on England just because of the money the Arabs were offering him. Well, the story I was told is that at least two other managers had been asked if they would be interested in the job over the phone just before Don was due to take the England squad on a tour of South America. Were they plotting to get rid of him? Don didn't get on very well with Sir Harold Thompson, who was Chairman of the FA at the time. Early on in his career with England, Sir Harold had said to Don, 'When I get to know you better, Revie, I shall call you Don' – to which Don had replied, 'When I get to know

194

you better, Thompson, I shall call you Sir Harold.'

Well, these two managers phoned up Don to say, 'Hey, somebody's just offered me your job.' So of course Don was looking around. He had an idea that they were planning to sack him. He met a Saudi prince at a friend of mine's house, and then he agreed to fly out there, not to take the job but just to have a look at the situation and decide whether he thought Saudi was somewhere he could work. Then he'd join the England team in South America. Only there happened to be a journalist from the *Daily Mail* on the plane. This journalist, seeing Don and knowing that the England team was just off to South America, went over to sit next to Don and asked, 'What's going on here?' Don was caught with his pants down a little bit – so he agreed to give the guy an exclusive later on if he didn't print the story now. That's what they agreed. Then Don goes on to South America where there are big rows, and eventually he says to Sir Harold Thompson, 'Pay me up and I'll leave.' Which was agreed. But when he came back to England Don did exactly as he'd promised and gave the story to the *Daily Mail* guy. Suddenly it appears in one paper that Revie's quitting England and taking up the job in Saudi, and all the other papers are asking, 'How the hell has the *Daily Mail* got this?' Overnight he made an enemy of virtually everyone in the game and in the press – because he kept his word to that journalist.

They never forgave Revie, you know, the press lads. They made out he was money mad, and a lot of stories were printed, allegations of this, allegations of that. A lot of slanderous allegations were made about Don, which I found very hard to believe. In all my dealings with him I found him an honest, straightforward guy.

But the newspapers went to town, printing these stories that were totally out of order. Some Wolves players had alleged that we had tried to fix that last game at Wolves which cost us the 1972 League championship. Billy Bremner took them to court for defamation of character. I went to court and gave evidence, as did Derek Dougan. 'I never knew anything about these allegations,' said Derek, 'and as the senior player at Wolves at the time, I would have known.' Billy got a hundred and fifty thousand quid in damages from that case.

As well as the idea that I might be a Revie lad, there had been the black book incident as well, and that too may have counted against me – although I was proved completely innocent at the time. Maybe they resented me for it, though. Who knows the way people think?

Maybe I was a bit inexperienced. But maybe too I would have brought a few new ideas to the England job. Maybe I would have been a bit of Alf Ramsey, a bit of Don Revie, a bit of Bill Shankly, and a bit of Jock Stein – not a bad foursome to base yourself on, after all. I considered these guys to be friends of mine. And I always felt that they liked me, and thought that I was part of their business. The same was true of the great players, men like Stan Matthews, Billy Wright or Tom Finney – the legends of the game. Even while I was still a young player at Leeds, people like that would make their way to talk to me. These very famous people in the game would stop me to talk. I think they recognized that I knew what I was about. And I knew many of the best current managers as well, from my days at Lilleshall. I felt they all recognized that I had something to offer the game.

Everyone seemed to think well of me, except the FA. So I still feel bitter about it yet.

Much later, after I'd been appointed Ireland team manger, Des Casey, President of the FAI, told me a story. Apparently he'd been to a game in England where he bumped into the FA's new chairman, Bert Millichip. And Millichip had told him, 'You made a mistake, appointing that man.'

Des had great pleasure in telling that man, after we had beaten England in Stuttgart in 1988 and drawn with them at Wembley in 1991, 'It was quite a good mistake, that one, wasn't it?'

14

IN THE DUGOUT

Apart from the disappointment with England, life during that summer of 1977 was relaxed and satisfying. For the first time in my adult life, I didn't have to fret about kicking a football or watching others do so, and I loved it. No contracts, no pre-season training – bliss! Instead, I took the family on holiday, got more involved in television work and, yes, you've guessed it, got my fishing rod out again.

Two or three newspaper people, purporting to represent clubs looking for a manager, contacted me at different times, but I was sincere when I told them I wasn't particularly interested. Then, in October, I had a call from Roy Whitehead, a director of Sheffield Wednesday. With the minimum of preamble, he told me that they wanted me to come and join them as manager. 'But you already have a manager, Len Ashurst,' I said.

'Len's leaving,' he told me, 'and he's recommended you as his successor.'

'Tell him I'm grateful for the vote of confidence,' I replied. 'But when the job is vacant, come back and talk to me.'

And I dived for the nearest newspaper for a quick gen up on Sheffield Wednesday. No wonder Len was thinking of a new job! The season's only a couple of months old and already they're four or five points adrift at the foot of the Third Division.

In that moment, the prospect of a new career with Sheffield Wednesday looked anything but inviting. It would mean going from a job with a First Division club to the Third Division – and with the exception of Tommy Docherty, not too many managers have done that. Fortunately or otherwise, the phone rang before I'd too much time to dwell on it. It was Roy Whitehead again, and this time he started by telling me that Len had quit.

I said I'd think it over, and perhaps go and have a chat with them. So together with Pat, I went and bought two tickets to watch them play Brighton. They won the game 2–1 – but without putting too fine a point on it, they were bloody awful!

One or two of their players could go a bit, but compared to the group I'd left behind at Middlesbrough, the rest were nondescript. After the game we wandered across to meet the club directors and I was introduced to the club chairman, Bert McGee. A nice fellow was Bert, but like everybody else at Hillsborough, I reckoned he was pretty close to his wit's end at that point, trying to save a club that once commanded so much respect.

Oddly enough, I've never been attracted to a club which was at the top of their division or even close to it. Perhaps that's down to the fact that when you inherit success, so much more is expected of you. That kind of pressure certainly didn't apply in this instance. Perhaps it was the realization that we could move only in one direction which attracted me. Anyway, before I left the ground that evening, I'd agreed to take the job and guaranteed them that I'd stabilize their rocky boat.

Before long, I discovered there had been a lot of aggravation at the highest level at the club. Fortunately, there was a change of personnel in the boardroom and I was able to get on with the job of finding myself a coach and organizing the players. I chose to put a call through to Maurice Setters, a man whom I'd known to be a tough competitor as a player, and a football fanatic if ever there was one. I mean, Maurice would think nothing of going to watch three or four games a week, just for the heck of it. It was at Lilleshall that I first got to know him, and despite his abrasive qualities, or perhaps because of them, I liked him. Now he was in a position to offer a lot of help – for unlike me, who knew absolutely nothing about the Third Division, he had already done a stint there as manager of Doncaster Rovers. Unfortunately, things hadn't worked out for him at Doncaster, and eventually he took them to a tribunal hearing for unfair dismissal. When you embark on that course in football, you virtually write yourself out of the game, because no other club will touch you. In that situation, I didn't have a lot of bargaining to do, and the salary I offered him, something like £4,000 a year, was ridiculously low. But I promised there would be more available once the club finances improved and we began to get a few good results. Maurice eventually said yes and I'm glad to say that we went on to work effectively together for many of the next twenty years.

During those first few months, Maurice and I trawled the country looking for players. I remember sitting him down in my room at the end of our first season and asking for his thoughts. What he said made sense. 'The lads in the Third Division may not be the best players around, but they're great workers.

To live with them, we've got to up our work rate.'

That corresponded roughly with my own views. Facing the ball, the majority of the players were quite good – it was when they tried to turn and play that they got themselves into trouble. Here the sophistication of Leeds and, to a lesser extent, Middlesbrough seemed light years away. The gambit, the only gambit that I thought might work, was to throw the ball into the box and play from there.

The challenge was clear. I had to find myself a big goalkeeper who could handle crosses into the penalty box, a big centre half to help him, and a big centre forward who could change the direction of the play from the crosses we would deliver. I would be into my second season at the club before I finally found the men I needed.

From day one, I had warned the directors that the only feasible target in my first season was to keep them in the Division. Given the situation I found when I first went there, they were happy enough to accept that.

To be fair, they didn't meddle unduly, but that was only after I had established the ground rules with Bert McGee within a couple of months of going there. One of the gems of wisdom which Jim Bullock imparted was that you are never stronger in any managerial job than in the first few months of taking it. If you don't assert your authority in that period, you're living with a time bomb.

I've never forgotten that. So when Maurice informed me that McGee had gone into the dressing-room and castigated him and trainer Tony Toms after a 3–0 defeat in a reserve team game against Everton, I decided to act. I marched into a board meeting, and asked McGee to come outside where, with the help of a few expletives, I let him know I was not best pleased.

'You've been down to abuse my staff about results. Don't do it again,' I told him. 'If you have any comments to make about the team, talk to me. And furthermore, it's come to my attention that certain directors are shooting their mouths off in pubs and golf clubs about players and the staff. That stops, right now. Any information relating to the workings of this club stays within these gates or you can stuff your job.'

I could see he was shaken. He started to blurt out something but before he got going, I let him have more stick. I know I can be a bit abrasive at times, and afterwards I felt sorry for upsetting him – but he had to be given the message there and then or not at all.

Within a couple of months of going to Hillsborough, I knew that I had taken on a hell of a job. We were drawn against part-timers Wigan Athletic from the Northern Premier League in the FA Cup, and incredibly they managed to beat us when they scored from a free kick on the edge of our box, shortly before the end. This was humiliation if ever I saw it.

Going out of the FA Cup to a non-League club was bad enough, but the final indignity came when our team coach got stuck in the mud when we tried to leave the bloody place. In vain, twenty strong men tried to shift it and we were forced to stand there, red-faced, until a replacement coach arrived.

That first season at Hillsborough, working with players who, in many instances, had little to offer except commitment, was very trying, but we managed to realize our primary objective of staying in the Division. Deep down, however, I knew the real job hadn't yet begun. Too many of the lads lacked the basic skills to do the job I needed. I remember watching in exasperation one morning as we rehearsed the ploy of putting one of our players into the opposition's wall when we had a free kick around their eighteen-yard area. This was a move I had learned at Lilleshall from Jack Rowley. Jack's theory was that if a player joined the wall at precisely the moment the ball was struck, there was no way the opposing goalkeeper could re-adjust in time to cover the gap. And he was right, of course.

I was watching a lad called David Grant taking the kicks at Sheffield and despite all the instructions I was shouting at him, he just couldn't get the timing right. I've always believed it's better to show than talk. So I walked on, brogues and all, put the ball down and then walloped it into the net, at the angle of the post and the crossbar. And he's stood there looking at me as if I'd two heads!

We spent hours going over dead-ball situations, so that every member of the team knew his responsibilities when the kick was taken. With the way the game was develop-ing, more and more goals were coming from set-pieces. The players responded well to the training, and David Grant's left foot got better once he knew what he was at.

I'd had a full season to assess the strengths and weaknesses of the players at my disposal, and it was apparent that we needed to buy replacements in key positions. Up front we'd a pretty good goalscorer in Tommy Tynan, but during that first season, he'd had nobody to play off.

I was on the look-out for a big, strong target man, and after much searching, I found him in Andy McCulloch. I'd seen Andy play for Brentford and, while he wasn't the most skilful when the ball was at his feet, he was a good brave competitor in the air, just the kind of player to upset defenders. Eventually, I got him for a fee of £70,000 – the deal, I remember, was struck on a gantry at Wembley where I was working for television during the FA Cup final between Ipswich and Arsenal. It proved one of my better investments.

Brian Hornsby, a tremendous striker of the ball, had arrived at the club the previous season, and then we got Terry Curran, who turned out to be one of the most important acquisitions of all. I signed Curran from Southampton as a winger, but more by accident than design I moved him to centre forward, where he was a revelation. All his career, he was accustomed to turning quickly on the ball and taking on defenders, as wingers do. He played the same way after I'd moved him inside, and central defenders, unused to that kind of situation, were wrong-footed over and over again. Then he started to play like an orthodox centre forward and, suddenly, his impact on games began to wane. Terry, in his naïvety, thought he was progressing, but I wanted him to play like a winger in a centre forward role. After many a long discussion, he saw the light and went on to get more important goals for us.

By selling Chris Turner to Sunderland and replacing him with Bob Bolder, I not only ended up with a bigger goalkeeper but improved the club's finances considerably, and then I strengthened the defence still further by signing Mike Pickering, a centre half who didn't believe in taking prisoners. In the space of a couple of weeks, I had reshaped the spine of the team with big men and as I mentioned previously, this was an essential part of the survival game in the Third Division.

Pre-season training that year was like nothing I'd ever known. The trainer at the club was a lad called

Tony Toms, an ex-marine who had been brought to the club by Len Ashurst. Now Tony had never kicked a ball in anger in his life, but when it came to conditioning players, his methods were, to say the least, a bit unusual. He took us down to Limpstone, the marine headquarters on the south coast, and there, for the greater part of a fortnight, subjected the players to a commando-type course which included things like scaling walls and crossing rivers on ropes. What this had to do with football, God only knows, but by the time we left our barrack headquarters we were ready to take on the world.

Tony was a real character, a big good-looking guy, and the ladies loved him. And hell, did it get me into trouble with some of the more strait-laced of the club directors! I remember one occasion when he was chatting up the hotel receptionist, a well-endowed young lady who wasn't shy about showing off her attributes. It wasn't serious and we all stood there, directors included, having a good laugh. But when I got back to the club, I was ticked off by those self-same directors, who considered that his behaviour was not that expected of a club member.

So I let them have it straight from the hip. 'How the hell can you say that now?' I asked. 'If you thought it offensive, why didn't you have words with him there and then?' There was no answer to that, for the very good reason that they had enjoyed the little cameo just as much as the rest of us.

On another occasion I was summoned to Bert McGee's office, where one of the directors alleged that Tony had been seen with the wife of a director of another club. And he wanted to know what I intended to do about it.

'Nothing,' I replied. 'Until such time as it becomes a public issue, it has nothing whatever to do with me.' And that particular story never did reach the tabloids.

A real character was our Tony, but there was at least one occasion when I was vaguely tempted to chin him. Doubling up on the last game of cards on a coach journey back from a game, he scooped the pool by producing four kings. I didn't have enough money to settle up then, but the following Tuesday I sought him out and handed over the six pounds I owed him. He duly pocketed it and then, cool as you like, admitted that he had cheated by holding back the four kings from a previous game. I promptly demanded my money back – but would he give it? 'Fine, so I cheated,' he answered. 'But you didn't find me out then, did you?' And to this day, Tony Toms owes me six quid.

Things were a lot better in that second season at Hillsborough. We didn't win the championship but we'd a good run in the FA Cup and it provided me with the evidence that we were indeed on the right track in our team-building programme. After requiring replays to beat Scunthorpe and Tranmere, we were drawn against Arsenal in the fifth round. And that developed into one of the most fascinating ties in which I've ever been involved.

We drew 1–1 at Hillsborough, came out with the same scoreline at Highbury, and then settled into a long war of attrition with the team which went on to win the trophy. Two further replays at Filbert Street failed to provide a conclusive result, and when we went back to Leicester the following week for a fourth replay, the press were tagging it the tie of the decade.

In each of the earlier games, Liam Brady had played from the back and we handled him without too many problems. Now he began taking the ball off the front two, and instantly we were in trouble. Thanks mainly to Brady, Arsenal went on to beat us 2–0. I'd learned a lesson about how Liam could play most effectively which would stand me in good stead on other days.

One of the few things which impressed me when I first arrived at Sheffield Wednesday was the club's catchment area. Hillsborough was a fine stadium set in a densely populated area, but unfortunately the results at the time weren't nearly good enough to bring in the uncommitted. It was the prospect of exploiting that potential which drove me for my first two years there. By the start of the 1979–80 season I felt we were at last getting somewhere. The marathon Arsenal tie had the effect of getting Sheffield folk talking about football again and attendance figures for our home games climbed accordingly.

Even as the gates improved, however, the club began to acquire an unwanted reputation for the behaviour of some of its supporters at away games. They'd cause trouble in bars and cafés, and generally projected a bad image for the club in the towns and cities we visited. To be fair, the troublemakers were a small minority, but in the manner of these things they got all the publicity for the wrong reasons. Ever since my Leeds days, I'd been aware of the dangers posed by hooligans masquerading as supporters. For a while, it had got out of hand at Elland Road. The FA had closed down the ground temporarily, and by ordering us to play home games on a neutral ground, had effectively cost us a First Division championship.

I didn't want this happening at our ground, so I devised a plan. After we'd played away, I'd go and see the head of the local police authority and enquire how many arrests had been made. He might say five or six, and I'd then offer to make a pact with him. If he undertook not to publicize the fact, I'd sort out the troublemakers when I got back to Sheffield. The plan was simple. In every match programme at Hillsborough, I'd make a point of saying how pleased the police authorities had been about the conduct of our supporters the previous week at, say, Stoke or Birmingham, and that we would always be welcome back there. The psychology was that if I gave people responsibility, in this case of upholding the club's good name, they would invariably try to live up to it. Go the other way and brand them as thugs, and they will act accordingly.

It didn't happen overnight, but gradually this collective thing about making fans ambassadors of the club grew and grew to the point where we didn't have a single incident when we played away from home. And I think I'm right in saying that to this day, Sheffield Wednesday's supporters enjoy the reputation of being some of the best behaved in Britain.

That summer, I made my one and only big investment, buying the Yugoslav, Ante Mirocevic, for £200,000. Ante had played for the Yugoslav Olympic team and I thought that he could give us the little bit of quality which we lacked.

I still reckon that Ante was a good signing, but there are those at Hillsborough who would dispute that to this day. In my book, he was different to anything we ever had at Sheffield. For three seasons, we'd huffed and puffed our way in the Third Division, matching the best in work rate but lacking real flair. Ante filled that void, and what's more, he gradually got those around him to play a bit more. The only problem was that he couldn't bear the cold weather. Tony Toms's commando courses were simply anathema to him. There was one day when Tony demanded that the players wade through a stream – but would Mirocevic do it? Not on your life. He pretended he couldn't understand English when it suited him not to, but as I recall he never had many problems when the talk got round to money.

For the first couple of months of the season, while there was still a lot of grass on the pitches, he was brilliant. Then the winter came and Ante would turn up for training with gloves, a balaclava, two shirts, two sweaters and a track suit. I've never known a man who hated the cold more, but once spring rolled around, he was on his bike again.

We finally got out of the Third Division in my third season and that thrilled me. Ideally, I would like to have done it a year earlier – but take it from me, it's an awful lot harder to get promotion from the Third than from the Second Division.

By the start of my fourth season, I was quite comfortable with the way the team was developing. Second Division football demanded new priorities, but youngsters like Mark Smith, Kevin Taylor, Peter Shirtliff and Mel Sterland had by now come into the squad and were settling well.

We did well enough to finish comfortably in the top half of the championship table, and then the following season we missed out on promotion by a single point. It was a bitter pill to swallow, the more so since in one of our last games against Luton at Hillsborough, the referee played seven minutes' injury time and they scored an equalizer with almost the last kick of the game. It was enough to cost us a place in the First Division the following season – and that hurt. It was even harder to accept when I learnt from one of the press lads that had the points system not been changed that year (to giving three points for a win rather than two), we'd have been promoted.

I had now been at Hillsborough for almost four years, and I sensed the time was right to start preparing for my exit. I decided to give it one more season. In the event, it proved the most exciting of all my time in Sheffield. Mick Lyons had arrived from Everton to give us extra experience at the back and by Christmas, we were top of the table and looking good for promotion. Unfortunately – and I repeat unfortunately – we then got involved in more Cup marathons, and they cost us dearly.

We weren't eliminated from the League Cup until January. I remember saying to the chairman, 'We don't have the resources to handle this situation. We've only got fourteen or fifteen professionals at the club, and we're playing far too many games. I reckon it's in our best interests to go out of the FA Cup early.'

That didn't mean 'throwing' games, but by resting a couple of players in Cup matches we could improve our championship prospects. But Bert McGee blew the suggestion out of the water, arguing that it would do the club a lot of good, financially and otherwise, if we gave the competition our best shot. In my heart of hearts, I knew it was the wrong decision, and it turned out to be just that. We lost Andy McCulloch and Brian Hornsby with long-term injuries, and gradually we drifted out of contention in the championship.

I'd set my heart on taking Wednesday from the Third to the First Division. To have come so close and failed was one of the bitterest experiences of my career. Eventually, we got to the semi-finals of the FA Cup, but alas, there was no joy here either. A day which began badly when we set off for the game against Brighton at Highbury without Gary Megson, one of our key players – we didn't discover he wasn't on the coach until we were almost at the ground – was to end in frustration. Brighton opened the scoring, and after Ante Mirocevic had equalized, Jimmy Case sank a free kick in the back of our net. We were on our way home to Hillsborough with nothing to show for a season's graft except a bundle of hard luck stories.

Before we went to Highbury I'd informed Bert McGee of my intention to leave. Imagine my surprise, then, when within days of the Cup semi-final, I had a letter from him offering me new, improved terms for the following season!

Each of the club directors in turn came to my house, asking me to stay, but all to no avail. Jim Bullock's advice was to leave while they still want you – and, for all the happy times I had experienced in Sheffield, I knew this was the time to go.

I had come to see football from a different perspective after my dear friend Jock Stein had collapsed and died of a heart attack during a Wales-Scotland international at Ninian Park. I'd been watching the match on the television, and I was deeply shocked when they announced the news. Then and there I said to myself that I wasn't going to die in the dugout. There are more important things in life than football. If I can choose the way I will leave this world, it will be clutching a rod, with a forty-pound salmon on the other end of the line dragging me down the river!

There were more offers in the run-up to the 1983–84 season, but this time I was determined to stand my ground and not be pressurized into doing

211

something which didn't really appeal to me. Between after-dinner speaking and television work, I was earning a good living. I could face every day in the knowledge that I didn't have to go to a football field or a training ground. For once I was a free spirit, and I could pretty well go and come as I pleased.

That lasted until the January or February of the following year. Then I received a frantic call from an old friend, Mike McCullagh, who at that stage was chairman of Middlesbrough. Malcolm Allison had just left Ayresome Park, the club was dangerously close to the foot of the Second Division table, and on top of that they were having money problems. The way Mike put it, they were in desperate trouble. There weren't too many fixtures left and having been to the First Division just a couple of years earlier, they didn't want to slip back into the drudgery of Third Division football again.

Now the last thing I needed was a situation like that, but out of loyalty to Mike, I said I'd come and try to keep them in the Division. When I say that McCullagh was a friend of mine, it's a bit of an understatement. For example, when I left Middlesbrough for Sheffield Wednesday and bought a house in Barnsley, I needed bridging finance of around £20,000. Apart from the first house I bought in Leeds, I've never had a mortgage, but now, with my house in Middlesbrough still unsold, there was a shortfall. I happened to mention this to Mike, and in the post next day I had a cheque from him from £20,000, which fortunately I was able to repay within a matter of weeks. That is the type of man he is – and when he came to me in desperation, I wouldn't, I couldn't, turn him away.

So I said, 'I'll do it for you as a favour. I don't want

a wage, I'll pay my own expenses, but I'll do the job you ask of me. I'll make sure you don't go down.' And I did.

The sequel to it was that I almost fell out with Malcolm Allison. Now, Malcolm and I had been friends for many, many years, but somehow he got the impression that I was responsible for him losing his job. I met him at the FA Cup final at Wembley that year, and it was clear that he wasn't particularly happy to see me. So I marched right up to him and said, 'You've got the wrong end of the stick, Mal. I didn't want your bloody job at any cost. As a matter of fact, now that 'Boro have finished their programme, I'm out of it.'

I'm not sure if he believed me – certainly Mike McCullagh didn't. As soon as the club was safe from the drop, he called me in and started talking about buying players for the new season. So I told him in no uncertain terms that since the rescue job was now over, I was through with them.

Mike and I remain the best of pals and, hopefully, I'm also still in Big Mal's good books. I've always had a soft spot for Allison, bold, brash and bigger than life. To a large extent he was the author of his own misfortunes, but as a football man, he had the respect of all of us.

Mind you, Mal got me into a bit of hot water with Pat on one occasion. He and I were regulars on the ITV football panel, and one Saturday morning we were in London together trying to kill time before a game. Mal suggested that we go to a lunch-time reception for the the singer Sammy Davis Jnr at the Playboy Club. Anyway, we went down there, where we posed for a picture with David Frost. I didn't notice this woman appearing and putting her arm round Mal – I only learnt later that she was his girlfriend at the time. Then the camera's snapping and next day my picture's in the *Sunday People* with Mal and this woman, 'relaxing at the Playboy Club in the early hours of the morning'. Pat gave me one of her looks when she saw that – I'm still not sure if she believes my explanation!

There was a much more serious side to that summer of 1984 that had nothing at all to do with football. The National Union of Mineworkers tried to take on the Conservative government of Margaret Thatcher – and found themselves badly beaten.

I was then living in Barnsley, a great mining town surrounded by dozens of villages in which mining was a way of life. To that extent, I was very sympathetic towards the miners' strike. I came from a mining family, I had been down the pit myself for a couple of awful months. I knew the hardships of the job and how the miners felt about it. I also knew the sacrifices the families of miners were having to make, the dreadful insecurity of not knowing how they were going to meet mortgage repayments, or how they were going to put food on the table for their families.

The miners' welfare centre, where families went to be fed each day, was directly behind our house. My contribution, such as it was, was to sponsor a few of the lunches. I had bought a farmhouse in the Yorkshire Dales, and for a period I was able to give two or three of the strikers some work renovating the place.

But the thing which got my name linked publicly with the strikers was the loan of my car to a friend of mine, Jim Exley, who worked in the mines. I never asked him why he wanted it or where he was going, but the reality was I didn't have to be told. Then one day it was reported in the papers that my car had been spotted on the picket lines. The press were going round taking details of the car registration numbers, and it gave them a story when they discovered that mine was one of those being used by the strikers. I never admitted that I knew where the car was – but deep down, it gave me a lot of satisfaction to know that I was indirectly involved.

I lived close to Arthur Scargill, and had got to know him quite well. Together with his wife, he had been in our house socially on two or three occasions. I have always admired him as an intelligent man, one who worries about his industry and those who earn a living from it. People laughed at him when he trotted out figures listing the number of mines which would be closed by Margaret Thatcher's government. They thought he was exaggerating wildly – but regrettably, he was proved 100 per cent right in his predictions.

Unfortunately, I think Arthur did himself and the miners a disservice when he went on television, pointing fingers at people and yelling, 'No, no, no!' This was not the Scargill I knew and admired, and I didn't like what I saw. All negotiators must leave themselves a back door, an escape route – but Arthur never seemed to be able to comprehend this.

I recall being a guest at a miners' picnic and Arthur telling me the story of the day he thought the strike had been settled in a hotel on the way to Selby. Everything was agreed on the Friday, and the parties went away contentedly to leave the lawyers to thrash out the deal over the weekend. They came back on the Monday in the belief that all it needed was a pair of signatures on a piece of paper. And I still remember the look on his face as he recounted how the Coal Board official at the top of the table was asked to leave the meeting and take

215

a phone call before the document was signed. When he came back into the room, the official promptly announced that the deal was off, there was no room for compromise. They were as close to settling the strike as that – and while the official refused to disclose who was on the other end of the line, the union representatives had no doubt it was Margaret Thatcher.

To be truthful, it didn't greatly surprise me to hear that. My politics and those of my parents were always Labour. Indeed, I recall our Bob making a speech one night and saying that his grandfather would turn in his grave if he knew that one of his family was seated beside a Tory Prime Minister, Edward Heath, as Bob was that night. To be fair, however, Mr Heath sent me a very nice personal letter after I had got my OBE, in spite of the fact that, in his words, I was 'on the other side'.

I don't think the ordinary English person understood to any great degree what was involved in the strike. They didn't know the mines or those who worked in them. Perhaps if they had, it would have been settled a lot earlier, to everybody's satisfaction.

People in our area had seen the great steel industry in Sheffield disappear before their eyes, and the great fear among the miners was the uncertainty of the future – that was, if they had a future at all. But as in the case of those who worked in the steel industry, the miners have readjusted well. If you were to talk to some of them now, they would tell you that the closing of the mines was the best thing that ever happened to them. They have found a new lifestyle, and, more importantly, new hope. And that was something which was thin on the ground when the strike was in its darkest hours.

15

ON THE TOON

Apart from that brief second spell with Middlesbrough, I'd had a year out of football. And that was just fine.

To those on the fringes, the game seems so glamorous: the publicity, the travel, the excitement, the adulation – when you get it. But talk to those who make their living from football and you will very often get a different picture. It's a seven-day-a-week job, and you never get away from it.

From where I stood, it was all getting a little boring. And I – didn't like the practices which by now were starting to creep into the game.

Take, for example, the signing of a player. In the old days if you fancied a player, you went and saw him, had a cup of tea, offered him a deal and if he liked it, the business was done there and then. By the 1980s, however, things had changed considerably – and changed for the worse. Now, if you went to sign someone, you were met by an entourage of doctors, accountants, agents, even bank managers – you name it, they were there.

I could appreciate the need for doctors and accoutants, I suppose, but agents were out as far as I was concerned. The only agents I ever dealt with in my career were Alf Darcy and Tommy Lawrence, two

217

former players who were responsible for bringing Ante Mirocevic to my notice at Sheffield Wednesday. I had no hesitation in doing business on that occasion because I knew they were all right. The rest I left well alone.

By my reckoning, there are too many middlemen in the game these days – and it's none the better for it! Apart from pushing up fees, they make little or no contribution to football.

Now I was released from all that kind of hassle, I felt free. I'd done almost ten years in club management, and with my outside interests expanding, I would gladly have kept it that way.

We went on holiday to Spain, took the family up to our house in the Dales, and while other managers were fretting about pre-season training, I was a million miles from it all on a riverbank.

Then some time around the end of July, I had this phone call from Jackie Milburn, asking me if I'd take the job at Newcastle United. Arthur Cox, who had led them to promotion to the First Division the previous season, had just left to join Derby County, and they urgently needed a new manager. My name, it seems, was the first on their shopping list, although I subsequently got the impression that people weren't exactly falling over each other to get the job.

My first words to Jackie were, 'Nay, I'm not having any of that.' But Jackie was nothing if not persistent. He went on and on about the family ties with the club and how he had taken Robert and myself there as boys. As a Charlton, as a Milburn, aye as a Geordie, I couldn't turn down an opportunity like this – the family would never forgive me. So at last I said, 'OK, I'll come and talk, but I'm not going to St James' Park.

I'm opening a double-glazing firm in Consett in Durham tomorrow, and if you want to talk to me you can do it there.'

Eventually it was agreed that we'd meet in a golf club just outside Darlington. As soon as we did I sensed immediately that they were pretty desperate. They offered me £30,000, which was more than I got at Wednesday – but when I asked what kind of money was available to buy players, the mood of optimism soon changed. Come September, they told me, I would have £200,000 to spend, and any fees we got from the sale of players would be ploughed back into the kitty. Big deal. Even in those days, £200,000 wouldn't buy you a lot of talent. I could see instantly why nobody wanted the bloody job.

The club doesn't own St James' Park, so that couldn't be utilized as collateral in any deal. Neither could the players be used in that context. One of the great clubs in England was being run on a shoestring.

I again said no – and I wasn't bluffing. I didn't know a lot about the players at Newcastle at the time, but experience taught me that there wasn't a lot you could do with £200,000 if the squad needed strengthening. But once they had got me talking they weren't in the frame of mind to let me go. Eventually, for better or for worse, I decided to take the job.

I've never been one to go about prying, seeking out hidden dangers. In football, I've always tended to accept things at their face value, but in retrospect I should have smelt a rat when I discovered the depth of their desperation to find a new manager.

Arthur Cox had just upped and left after winning them promotion to the First Division – and that was, to say the least, unusual. More than that, Kevin Keegan, who had done so much to get them out of the Second Division, had announced his retirement as a player. I didn't seek out either Arthur or Kevin for explanations but I could draw my own conclusions.

After Kevin, Terry McDermott, the old England and Liverpool player, was the most senior member of the staff during their promotion season. I soon discovered that he had turned down Arthur Cox's offer of a new contract just before the manager left.

My first action on arriving at St James' Park was to call Terry and ask him to come and see me. 'I don't know if you're coming to the end of your career,' I told him, 'but I'll give you the same terms as Arthur offered you. And if you are what I want, I'll see that you get more within a couple of months.'

The look on his face told me all I wanted to know. 'You didn't drag me all the way up here from Liverpool just to tell me that,' he said angrily, in the kind of tone that suggested he had already made up his mind to leave.

He was demanding a contract with all kinds of guarantees. I said, 'No, you're not having that. I'm a man of my word and if you stay and show me what you can do, I'll honour it.'

He didn't seem very happy about my proposal. So I asked him, 'Do you want a release? Here – you can have it.' And in five minutes flat, Terry McDermott had taken his leave of Newcastle United.

I took a bit of stick for that, but no other Football League club came in to sign him, and in my heart of hearts I knew I had done the right thing.

I didn't know a lot about Newcastle. Sure, I was aware of the club's great tradition, but many of the current players were unknown quantities to me. I did know, however, about Chris Waddle, Peter Beardsley, and Glenn Roeder, the team captain. Waddle was a young emerging player with a lot of skill, good pace and great shooting power. He was one of the lads who had shone in Newcastle's promotion year, and as I soon discovered, the word was out about his tremendous talent.

Beardsley was also there when I arrived, and like Chris, he had a lot going for him. Here were two players who would grace any team – but my immediate problem was to fit players in around them who would complement their talent. Easier said than done. With so little money to spend, I realized that there would be no quick solutions.

Still, we started the season promisingly enough. We went to Leicester and won 3–2, beat Sheffield Wednesday 2–1 at home, and then, thanks to a couple of goals by Chris Waddle and another from Peter Beardsley, fairly hammered Aston Villa in our next home game. So far, so good. But then we went to Arsenal and got stuffed 2–0. Much of what I saw that day worried me, and my worst fears were realized at Old Trafford the following week, when Manchester United ran all over us in the second half and won 5–0. As an old centre back, I was appalled by the way we had defended. There was a lad playing at left back, John Ryan, whom they had paid a lot of money for. I can't vouch for his performances before I arrived at the club, but watching him that afternoon, I thought he was very overrated, and he was on his way almost immediately.

Gary Megson, a player I greatly admired in my time at Hillsborough, came to join us soon afterwards, and then I signed a big centre forward named George

Reilly. At the time, Waddle and Beardsley were playing up front and they kept telling me they needed a big guy to take some of the weight off them. George did a reasonable job for us, but he was never a goalscorer on a regular basis.

My relationship with Peter Beardsley was, at times, very tindery. We went to play at Queens Park Rangers one day and were leading 4–2 well into the second half. Chris Waddle then had a great drive tipped over, but instead of playing the corner short, Peter directs it straight at the goalkeeper. Now, the opposing player you cannot afford to give the ball to in those situations is the keeper. He's the one player who can change the flow of a game in an instant and, sure enough, the lad humps the ball upfield and QPR are in for a goal. Eventually, it ended 4–4. Near the end of the game I had tried to get through to Peter: 'When we are ahead, keep possession, kill time, be negative.' To be fair, players very seldom do listen to the manager while they are concentrating on what they are at. But maybe shouting at them helps us managers.

Now Peter is a good player, he takes up good positions, and when he's running at defenders, he's at his most dangerous. But in my experience, he just doesn't listen or if he does, he chooses to ignore what you say.

Years after I'd left Newcastle, travelling up by train from London, I met a schoolteacher who had taught Peter Beardsley, among others. He told me that Peter was never one who absorbed information easily. And I said to him, 'I wish I'd met you earlier!'

All of which is by way of introducing a second incident later in the season, another example of Peter's failure to listen and learn. My philosophy on the game

222

is that the first objective is to win it – the margin is merely of secondary importance. If you're leading 1–0 with time almost up, forget about a second goal. Play the ball in negative areas, keep possession and never let the opposing goalkeeper get it into his hands. As I've said, the keeper is the one player who can change the play from one end to the other instantly. I must have said that a hundred times in our dressing-room talks – but does Peter take the slightest bit of notice?

We're leading by the only goal of the game against Luton, when in a repeat of the earlier incident, Peter lashes a corner into the six-yard area, directly into the keeper's arms. We get away with it in that instance, but almost immediately he goes and does it again. He picks up the ball in our half and instead of playing it into one of the corners, he sets off straight down the middle of the pitch. On this occasion, he overruns the ball, the goalkeeper collects it, and, but for a goal-line clearance by John Anderson, we would have dropped two points. The full-time whistle goes almost immediately, we've got an important win that keeps us comfortably in mid-table, well away from the relegation zone, and by rights, I should be leaping and dancing about with joy. But I'm not. Beardsley has put the game at risk, not once but twice, and he's going to have a piece of my mind.

My second-in-command, Willie McFaul, is pleading with me to say nothing until we get back into the dressing-room, but I tell him, 'No bloody way, Willie, that silly bugger has almost cost us the game and I'm going to let him know it.' So as the players are coming off the pitch, I give Peter the bollocking of a lifetime. I put my arm around his neck or his shoulder and he shrugs me off. 'I nearly scored,' he protests.

'You nearly cost us the fucking game,' I told him, 'why don't you ever listen?'

The reporters sat up in the press box soon cottoned on to what was happening, and next day the incident became bigger than the game itself. Some of them said I was wrong to have done what I did, but I was determined to have it out with him while it was still fresh in my mind and, more important, still fresh in his mind.

I'm not sure if the relationship between the two of us was ever the same again. Peter kept telling the press that he was staying at Newcastle – but surprise, surprise, the following season he was off to Liverpool.

Chris Waddle was a better listener. Not only could he play, but he had the football sense to know when to open up a game and when to kill it. You wouldn't find him giving the ball away too easily in situations in which we needed to keep possession.

Waddle's performances were, without doubt, the highpoint of my time with Newcastle. The lad was playing out of his skin. I remember taking Bobby Robson aside after one particular game – Lawrie McMenemy was also in on the conversation – and convincing him that he had to cap Chris.

Bobby did just that – and I lived to regret it. Chris went off to Belfast to play for England against Northern Ireland, and from that day, I had lost him. I don't know where it happened or how it happened, but after that trip, Chris was never the same player for Newcastle. Sure, he turned out, but from where I sat, he was obviously just going through the motions. His mind was elsewhere. And with the certainty of night following day, he was gone to Tottenham within a matter of months . . .

From relatively early on in the season, I had sus-

Liverpool's manager Bill Shankly congratulates Billy Bremner and me after our goalless draw at Anfield clinched the 1968-9 First Division championship for Leeds.

(Syndication International)

Celebrating our FA Cup semi-final victory over Wolves, 7 April 1973. I had been taken off injured after half an hour, and the injury meant I missed the final, which we lost 1-0 to Sunderland.

(Syndication International)

Celebrating our 1972 Cup final win over Arsenal.

(S & G Press Agency)

Keeping Chelsea's Peter Houseman at arms' length, 27 March 1971. (Syndication International)

Scoring the only goal of our penultimate game of the 1970-1 season against Arsenal. But Arsenal had the last laugh, winning their final game against Spurs to clinch the championship, leaving Leeds runners-up for the fourth time in seven seasons.
(Syndication International)

Farewell to Elland Road after twenty-three years with Leeds United, 7 May 1973.
(Syndication International)

(Top) In action against Spurs's Pat Jennings, 18 January 1969 and (above) 14 February 1970. My tactic of standing at the near post in front of the keeper for corner kicks caused consternation in opposition defences and became a standard ploy in the game. In these two games, Spurs are in white and we are wearing the unfamiliar darker shirts.
(Hulton Getty/P.A. News)

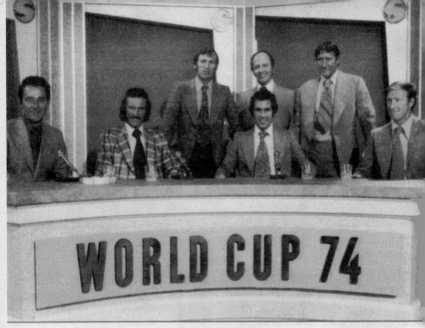

The ITV World Cup panel, 1974. Left to right: Brian Clough, Derek Dougan, Pat Crerand, Bobby Moncur (seated), Brian Moore, Malcolm Allison and me.

Coaching youngsters in 1976. (Tyne Tees Television)

Outside Buckingham Palace with the family after collecting my
OBE, November 1974. (Hulton Getty)

Charlton family gathering at the Box Tree in Ilkley, some time in
the 1960s. Brothers Gordon, Bobby and Jack sit with my mother
Cissie in front; behind is my father Bob, flanked by Pat and
Bobby's wife, Norma. (Newcastle Chronicle)

Collecting the Middlesbrough team's track suits before the game in my first few months as manager, 1974. This gave me an opportunity to have a last word with the players before the game started.
(Syndication International)

In the dugout at Ayresome Park. Ian McFarland sits at my left. (Hulton Getty)

Moving in to keep the peace at Oldham, 1980. With my encouragement, the Sheffield Wednesday fans later won a reputation for good behaviour.

(Syndication International)

Unhappy exit from St James' Park at the beginning of the 1985-6 season. The Newcastle fans had become restless when Lawrie McMenemy signed Eric Gates, and yobbos in the crowd had begun to chant 'Charlton must go.' I planned to leave anyway, and I've never been one to hang around when I'm not wanted. (Newcastle Chronicle)

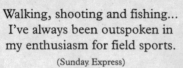

Walking, shooting and fishing...
I've always been outspoken in
my enthusiasm for field sports.
(Sunday Express)

pected that I'd do well to hold on to Waddle. And I wasn't helped by the local press. Every so often they'd run stories that clubs like Real Madrid or Barcelona or Bayern Munich were getting ready to bid for him. I knew that was rubbish, because in all that time I'd never had a direct enquiry from a European club wanting to sign him. So, I'd spoken to the fellow who had written the piece and asked him if the club had been in contact with him. No, the club hadn't contacted him, but he'd made contact with the club. And, of course, they gave him the standard answer to such enquiries: 'We're always interested in good players.'

In anybody's book, Waddle was a good player. But that was a long way from saying that they were going to sign him. And despite my protests, they kept running the stories at a time when I was desperately trying to hang on to Chris. I don't know if press people realize the damage they do in such situations. So long as they fill space they don't appear to give a damn about the consequences of their 'flyers'.

By and large, I enjoyed a good relationship with the press people at the club. There were times, however, when my patience with them ran a little thin. Football is big news in the North-East and like Liverpool and Manchester, they have their specialist football writers, who concentrate almost exclusively on the club.

I inherited a practice whereby they would turn up every morning at nine-thirty sharp for a press conference. There might be bugger all happening, but they still insisted on going through with the ritual. And when I failed to show on the odd occasion, there would be the usual complaint: 'Aye, Jack's gone fishing again.'

Fishing be damned! Maurice Setters and I would

have been up half the night, travelling back from some game or other in which we had an interest in a player. During that year at Newcastle, we both worked our butts off – but try telling that to the press!

Anyway, I did what I said I'd do. I kept Newcastle in the First Division. We finished fourteenth in the table, scoring 63 times but conceding the bloody awful total of 78 goals. For somebody who prided himself on being able to organize a defence, that was a sickening statistic.

Towards the end of the season, I was beginning to sense the futility of it all. At the start of the season I had two exceptional players, Waddle and Beardsley, players around whom I hoped to construct my team. Now one of them was off to Spurs and the other, I suspected, was merely biding his time at the club.

But if Newcastle were about to lose their two most precious assets, another, even more gifted youngster was beginning to surface. Paul Gascoigne was only a small, podgy boy at the time and apart from a couple of brief substitutions, I didn't use him in my year at St James' Park. But even then, he revealed glimpses of an enormous talent.

Paul, at the age of sixteen, looked anything but a footballer. I think he was reared by his grandmother and, apart from being into junk food, he liked his Mars bars. Conscious of that, I arranged for him to have lunch every day at a restaurant away from the ground where he could have a high-protein meal of steak or anything he fancied and the club picked up the tab. It has to be said that it didn't do anything to take the fat off him, but that didn't worry me. In the case of most fit players, it is possible to pick out every stomach muscle in them when they strip. But there are others, people like Alan Foggon, who can train six hours a day and they'll always look podgy. When they make it through to the top these players are normally very strong, however, and Gazza is a classic case in point.

I signed him as a pro at the age of seventeen on a wage of £200 a week, which was good money at the time. Now, Paul is a very generous lad and if he went into a pub with money in his pocket, he was liable to buy drinks all round. So I arranged that he be given £100, and that the other £100 be paid into a bank account for him to collect at the end of his contract.

Leopards never change their spots and even as a kid, Gazza was a prankster, a fun lad who got up to all kinds of devilment like tying together the laces of players' shoes. There was one day when Glenn Roeder stormed into my office fuming. If I didn't stop one fat sixteen-year-old apprentice messing him about, he said, 'I'm going to chin him.'

So I marched Paul to the back of the building, stood him up against a wall, and told him with as much sincerity as I could muster, 'If you don't start treating the senior pros around here with a little respect, you're out the frigging door and I'll see that you never get another club.'

To be honest, I don't think it changed him one iota. He didn't get caught after that, but I suspect it was because he was getting a little cuter. Gazza was never a nasty or vindictive lad, and he isn't to this day. But I must confess that I was surprised when he turned out to be a bit of a rebel. He was never that as a kid.

His appearances as a first-team player were too brief to suggest anything other than a useful talent, but I remember to this day the way he played in the Youth Cup final against Watford. Paul got the second of the goals with an orthodox header and then, late in the game, produced a stroke of genius which is still as fresh in my mind as if were only yesterday. He went for a throw-in on the right, and as he ran for the ball, he checked and ducked and the ball went over the player who was marking him. Then he started running diagonally towards the corner flag on the other side of the pitch, before suddenly stopping at the angle of the penalty area. His chaser slid past him, and now the ball was between his feet. Your ordinary player would at that point have shifted it to one or other foot and tried the shot. But Paul looked up, saw the keeper off his line, and with the ball still lodged between his feet, swung his leg and with the outside of his right boot, got it up, over the keeper and down just beneath the crossbar.

The ball was struck while he was totally off-balance. To do it, he had to produce the kind of intuitive skill that you see perhaps once in a lifetime. I remember turning to Maurice Setters who was stood beside me and saying, 'If you live to be a hundred, Maurice, you'll never see a better goal than that.'

Chris Waddle may be gone and Peter Beardsley may soon be leaving, I told Setters, but if that lad goes on improving, we have found ourselves a nugget. In fact, I was jumping ahead of myself with that statement, for I'd only agreed to take the job for one year to keep them in the First Division. But the Newcastle directors didn't come looking for me, nor did I go to them, and more by default than anything else, I found myself back at St James' Park for pre-season training. We had a couple of games in the Isle of Man against Leicester City and Blackburn Rovers, and two more when we got back against Wigan and Carlisle. We were to finish our pre-season programme with a home game against Sheffield United.

In the run-up to the match I opened transfer talks with the Ipswich player, Eric Gates. I'd always fancied Eric as a lad who could do a job for us, and after agreeing a fee with Ipswich, I invited him up to Newcastle for talks. Unfortunately the terms he was seeking were over the top and I told him so. But Eric wouldn't budge and we eventually parted, agreeing to differ. Unknown to me, Lawrie McMenemy was also interested in bringing the player to Sunderland, and when I lost interest, he promptly stepped in and signed him on the morning of our game with Sheffield United.

Newcastle folk interpreted that angrily, as the old enemy putting one over their club. I was disappointed, too, but no way was I going to be held to ransom by any player, however much I liked him.

When I went to St James' Park in the afternoon, the story had already broken in the local papers, and the mood among a section of our supporters was obviously hostile. The game itself was a nothing affair – I think it ended in a 1–1 draw – but soon the chants began: 'Jack out, Charlton must go.'

Bloody hell! We're not yet into the new season, but the yobbos are already after me. So without as much as a second thought, I march up to the directors' room. Stan Seymour and a few others are there and I tell them, 'I'm off, I'm having none of that kind of nonsense from so-called supporters.'

They try to dissuade me, but I'm so incensed, so goddam upset that I'm in no mood to listen. Resignation was the last thing on my mind when I walked into the ground that afternoon, but once I heard the hooligans, I decided, 'To hell with it.' I didn't need that kind of hassle. I spent the following day with the family in the Dales and then returned to St James' Park to collect my belongings on the Monday. And when I got to the ground, there must have been four or five hundred people outside, cheering and telling me not to resign.

Once inside, I sought out Joe Harvey, the chief scout, an old Newcastle player who knows the scene there better than anybody. I asked Joe if I'd done the right thing. I still remember his response: 'Once that crowd get after you, they're never going to stop.' If I'd any doubts about my decision, that settled them. By the time I'd got my stuff sorted and left the ground, the word had filtered through to the crowd outside that I hadn't changed my mind. And the transformation was remarkable. Now they were shouting, 'Good riddance, who the hell needs you anyway?'

I didn't make many friends in Newcastle by doing what I did. Some interpreted it as a snub to the club, and it was a long time before Jackie Milburn and myself got back on friendly terms. Even when I got home the reception from Pat wasn't particularly warm. The thing that annoyed her was not that I had quit my job but we'd bought a new house in the area, and only recently moved in and had it decorated. I told her not to worry. 'I may have left Newcastle United, but we're not leaving this house.' And we're still there to this day.

16

IN THE FIELD

Over the years I've had to put up with quite a bit of flak about my love of fishing. I can't really understand why. After all, fishing is the most popular sport in the country, so I'm not that unusual. If I played golf, like so many sporting so-called celebrities, no-one would ever mention it. Everyone in football thinks fishing is crazy – but it's the best sport, because you do it alone, you don't need anyone to go with.

I did in fact play golf for a while. Back in my early twenties, in the days when I was a young pro with Leeds United, I joined the South Leeds Golf Club. I didn't have a car in those days, so I used to walk up to the club on a Sunday morning and carry my clubs back again afterwards. It was about a four-mile walk.

I got into the Leeds United golf championship, which was known as the Braithwaite Cup. We used to go to a different venue every year. I remember playing at Wetherby one spring day with Johnny Giles, Peter Lorimer and Billy Bremner. I was playing really well, when we reached a hole which was only about one hundred yards. I took a wedge and I pitched the ball up. It dropped behind the bunker, down by the river. I thought, if I putt that from the edge of the bunker, it will leave me a putt of about twelve feet for my par three. But as I went and got my putter out, Gilesy said to me, 'You're never gonna use a putter, the way you're playing?' And I said, 'Nah, you're right.' So I put the putter back and took out a wedge instead. The ball bounced on top of the bunker, it rolled back, and – I can see it yet – it sort of stopped still. If it had run on another couple of inches, it would have gone right down to the hole. But it didn't, and it came back down into the bunker.

Now, at that time of year there was no sand in the bunkers, because when the river rose it washed all the sand out. It was all ridges. I came out and into the far bunker, took two or three shots to extricate the ball, and then back into the other bunker. I finished up with twelve on a short hole!

That was it as far as I was concerned. I threw my putter into the river, then I got my bag and started to walk back to the clubhouse. 'What are you doing?' the others asked. 'I'm finished,' I said. 'That's me over, I'm done, finished!' I walked off the course, got in the car and drove home – and I virtually never played golf again for more than twenty years.

I'd met some ex-rugby league players who liked to shoot, and I started to go shooting with them. We rented some woods in the Selby area, and we put a few pheasants down. Or we'd build hides and shoot pigeons. Later we found some ponds near Castleford, where we'd go to shoot the ducks at night. In winter we used to go up to Scotland, after the geese. We did a bit of ferreting as well. Over the years it's got more sophisticated – we now have our own shoots, syndicates and other things – but those were the days we enjoyed most, when it was what you call rough shooting. We used to have a grouse moor, but we lost it last year – and it's been a big loss to me. It's not the shooting so much, it's the camaraderie of meeting all your pals once a week or so. It's part of my life that has disappeared.

To be fair, I don't do as much as I used to because the shooting interferes with the fishing, and I much prefer fishing to shooting. I've always fished from being a boy. I didn't do much fishing while I was a young pro at Leeds, but from the age of about twenty-five or twenty-six I started again, doing some coarse fishing with my brother-in-law. When I went to Middlesbrough, Jimmy Greenhoff got me back into trout fishing. Then I got an invitation from Ivor Broadis, the former Sunderland player, to go fishing for salmon at Carlisle. 'There's a lovely river there I can get you on,' he told me – the River Eden. So I took my young son Peter with me. It was the first time I ever went salmon fishing, a red-hot day in the middle of summer, bright sunshine, totally wrong – and I caught a salmon!

It weighed fourteen pounds. I'd never caught anything that big in my life. The gillie couldn't believe it when he came and found us with a salmon on the bank. I mean, some people go salmon fishing for years and never catch anything!

That's what started me salmon fishing. And I really got into it when I moved back up to Newcastle, because there's plenty of salmon fishing nearby. The Tweed is only about an hour's drive away, and there's the Coquet, and now there's the Tyne, which has been cleaned up and stocked, and has really come back as a salmon river. I've been fishing for salmon ever since.

I still go trout fishing. I like to fish for sea trout when I get a chance, and I fish in the sea at Filey or in Ireland – I like all kinds of fishing, really. Fishing has become very much part of my life. I mean, I play a bit of golf now and then, but fishing is my main form of relaxation. People smile about my fishing, but it's the most relaxing sport in the world. Mind you, it's sometimes hard to get away from people. I was fishing in the middle of a river in Ireland the other day, and this girl took her shoes and socks off and waded out to me for my autograph!

When Charlie Flynn, a friend at Yorkshire Television, approached me to do a series of programmes on field sports early in the 1980s, I thought twice about it. It was a time when the anti-blood sports campaigners, as they liked to style themselves, were very militant. Protest demonstrations were common up and down the country, and I knew I would be putting myself in the firing-line. But controversy has never fazed me and it certainly wasn't the reason why I didn't accept Charlie's invitation for a couple of weeks.

No, my reluctance had more to do with the futility of trying to convince people who didn't want to be convinced. In my experience, the anti-blood sports militants have never bothered to investigate the sports which upset them so much.

Eventually, I got back to Yorkshire Television and told them that I was prepared to present the programmes. And as we discussed the series, Charlie said, 'We've got to kill something in every programme. Otherwise we'll be shirking the central issue of what field sports are all about.'

That didn't appeal to me at all. Now the series would be more provocative than ever to a section of the public – but I went along with it all the same. I remember discussing the programme with a friend, who wanted to know how I would answer the question, 'But how do you feel when somebody kills something?' And I was absolutely honest when I told him that to somebody like me, questions like that were very difficult, almost impossible, to answer. To those who don't know the countryside and the ways of the countryside, it may appear cruel to kill an animal. But it all depends on the way you've been brought up. I've always done it, always been able to do it. Some people can't do it – some people can't do all sorts of things. But that doesn't necessarily make them wrong.

I've shot lots of partridges, pheasants and grouse. I've done a bit of stalking. I've never got involved in fox hunting, but I like to think I understand people who do. But with my hand on my heart I can honestly say that I've never been cruel to anything in my life – except possibly on a football field!

For me, it all goes back to my boyhood and that incident in the garden with Old Witton when he showed me how to wring a chicken's neck. As long as it's done humanely, there is no cruelty involved.

The first programme, about wild hare coursing on foot, took us up to the moors near Huddersfield. To be honest, I didn't know much about it beforehand, but I did a lot of interviews with the people involved. And I remember going up to two old fellows who were chatting in the middle of a field. When I asked them why they weren't following the hunt, they blandly told me they didn't need to follow it. Hares run in circles, I was informed, the one now being chased had been 'lifted' in the spot where they were stood – and it would soon be back.

I thought they were having me on. But sure enough, some ten minutes later, the hare came through a gate at the bottom of the field, ran across the field within fifty yards of where we were stood and out the other side.

In the course of the interview, I asked them if they had seen many hares killed. They told me that they had been going to hunts for twenty-odd years, and in all that time they had never seen a single kill. And I simply couldn't credit that. They explained, however, that the quarry invariably led the hounds a merry dance, and that in most cases the dogs eventually lost the scent.

Unfortunately, there was an added bit inserted into the programme in the cause of realism which showed a kill. But this was not the hare being chased. It was one which had been lying doggo and the hounds just happened to stumble on it.

Like fox hunting, all the songs they sing, all the stories they tell about hare coursing are not about the kill but the chase. I mean, who wants to kill a hare? It's about exercise, people and dogs running across fields, and everybody enjoying it. It was a lovely day out and it gave me a different perspective on the sport.

I didn't do a programme on fox hunting because I don't understand it, even though I've followed it a few times. But I know that the animal is rarely killed in sight and that the only people who generally witness a kill are the lads with shovels who dig it out of a hole before shooting it and feeding it to the dogs.

It gets bad publicity in the media because from time to time, you see pictures of all kinds of atrocities with a fox hanging by its neck. The reality, of course, is that this publicity is very often contrived and set up by the newspaper and television people involved.

As I've said, my experience of the sport is very limited. But I know enough about it to believe that the image portrayed is very often misleading. And I'm convinced that if the 'anti' people ever succeeded in having it banned, they would quickly move on to something else – like fishing.

After that, I went deer stalking up in Scotland and spent the best part of two days trudging up and down hills so that we could get a camera crew into position to film the shooting of a stag – not any old stag, but one which the gillie had seen limping and which in his opinion had to be taken out of the herd. We came across plenty of stags on the way, but as I've said, it was nearly two days before we found the one which needed shooting.

There were 5,000 deer, he explained, on the hill, which really was a range of mountains. There was enough food to sustain all of them in summertime, but not in the winter. So their numbers needed to be controlled, otherwise they would die of hunger or else be down in people's gardens, chewing up trees and shrubbery.

You can't round up wild deer like cattle and take them to an abbatoir to be killed humanely. But by controlling the numbers in an ordered way, you can ensure that the herd survives all the year round. And that made sound sense to me.

On another occasion I was invited to Sheffield, where the local Labour Council had banned all shooting on their lands. They had one of the most beautiful laid-out shoots I had ever seen, but there was absolutely nothing on it – I think I saw one hare and the odd flock of blackbirds and crows, but other than that, nothing. And that, for me, was the classic example of what can happen if the sport is not controlled. If you banned shooting, you wouldn't stop shooting. But you'd get all the wrong people doing it for all the wrong reasons. That shoot at Sheffield made the point perfectly.

I've always derived immense pleasure from pheasant shooting, but here again the misconceptions among the public are remarkable. In my experience, although I don't say it happens all the time, you select only the birds which are a test of skill, the fastest ones, the highest ones. You don't take the easy ones, those who come out of a wood at a height of something like ten feet; if you did you would blow them to bits. There is no sense of achievement in that – but there is when you pick off a bird which demands both accuracy and swift reaction. There is nothing more beautiful than the sight of a pheasant; but I tell you something, there wouldn't be too many of them about if it weren't for the people who spend small fortunes on shooting days. People think that the pheasants they see walking about are wild. They're not. They'd last no time and an industry employing vast numbers would be lost, were it not for the care and protection of those who rear them.

Likewise, there would be no fish in our rivers were it not for fishermen. The fishermen are the people who police the rivers, who patrol and protect them from those who would destroy our fisheries almost overnight.

Our purpose in doing the series was to educate people, to illustrate the organization and control that goes into field sports, and to point up the number of people who earn their living from them. And when it was filmed and in the can, I was gratified to learn that three of the camera crew, who had been definitely 'anti' before we started, had now come round to a different way of thinking. Unfortunately, the militants aren't really interested in listening to the counter-argument.

I never received any direct threats when I presented the series, but on three or four occasions when I travelled to London with Sheffield Wednesday, detectives insisted in coming on the coach and staying in the team hotel overnight. That action was well intended, but it annoyed me. I didn't need protection from detectives. I was capable of looking after myself. If I needed any support, I had fifteen strong footballers with me.

On another occasion, when I went to Coventry with Newcastle United, we discovered that the pitch had been littered with broken glass overnight. Presumably, the culprits were of the same mind as those who had earlier released mink from private farms, and in so doing created a whole new hazard for the wildlife they professed to care about.

Now what kind of people would deliberately spread broken glass on a pitch and put twenty-two innocent players at risk – all because Jack Charlton liked shooting? They weren't going to harm me – I wasn't playing – but they could have seriously injured the lads, were it not for the efforts of the ground staff in removing the stuff.

Needless to say, their actions didn't change my thinking one iota. The people who campaign against field sports generally live in towns or big cities and have little or no knowledge of the subject. But I do know that if a referendum were held in urban areas on banning sports like shooting or even fishing, it would be carried.

I have always argued, however, that the only people qualified to speak on the countryside are those who live there and police it. I'm a great traditionalist, and I happen to believe that the right people have been

17

ACROSS THE WATER

Early in December 1985, the phone rang in my office at home. The voice on the other end of the line was, unmistakably, Irish.

'Is that Jack Charlton?'

'It is,' I replied.

'This is Des Casey, President of the Football Association of Ireland. Would you be interested in doing the job?'

'What job?' I enquired.

'Managing the Ireland team.'

'Yes,' I said – and with that, the line goes dead. Not another word, nothing. Bloody hell!

That got me to thinking. I remembered an evening about two months earlier when I was sat at home, flicking through the television channels. They were showing highlights of Ireland's game against Denmark in Dublin, and I remember wondering how a team with so many good players could be stuffed 4–1 at home.

The Danes were then emerging as one of Europe's better sides, but even so, that was a crazy result. The Irish had some good players at the time but their organization didn't seem to be the best. I think they had about six centre backs in the team. There were centre backs playing at full back and in midfield, and

241

I'd said to myself – this surely can't be right.

But the point I remembered most vividly of all from that first televised encounter with the Irish was the length of the grass on the pitch. I mean it was so long that at times you couldn't see the players' boots. No wonder they couldn't get a result!

Most, if not all, of the Irish team of the period were playing in England, on pitches which in many cases had little or no grass. And they simply didn't adapt as readily as the Danes to conditions which were totally foreign to international football.

I like Ireland. I like the Irish people, I like a pint of Guinness, I like the crack. I like the fishing in Ireland – in fact, I like it so much that I've bought a house on the west coast there with a friend, to serve as a base when we go fishing. And I wanted to be an international team manager. If the Welsh had offered me the job, or the Scots, or even the English, I'd have taken it, because I felt that's what I wanted to do. So, yes, of course I was interested. But I have to say it didn't seem at that stage very likely to happen.

I went off with Pat to a holiday home we have in Altea, just outside Benidorm, without giving the Ireland proposition too much consideration. Within days of our return, I'd another phone call from Dublin.

'This is Des Casey. Are you still interested in the job?'

'Yes, I am,' I answered – and the conversation dies a second time on me. And I'm still asking Pat if all this is for real when he phones back within the hour and asks me to meet him.

As it happened, I was doing a 'gig' in Manchester the next evening, so we arranged a meeting at a hotel just beside Ringway Airport. There were three FAI people there to meet me: Des Casey, Dr Tony O'Neill and Joe Delaney.

The talks were short and to the point. They wanted to know what I thought of the way international football was evolving, how I would go about organizing a team, and – pointedly – if there was a risk of me doing another 'Newcastle' on them.

Now that upset me more than a little. In all my football career, I'd never been a quitter. I'd stood and fought my corner wherever I'd been. And I would have done the same at St James' Park, had it not been for the louts who were more interested in trouble than football.

I got the impression that the FAI trio were on their way to interview more people, and since I had a function to attend, the talks ended pretty smartly with a handshake – and no promises either way.

After that I didn't give it a second thought, so you can imagine my surprise when I'm away doing a job in Birmingham a fortnight later and I get a call from Jimmy Armfield, the former England player who I'd worked with on the *Daily Express*.

'Congratulations, you've got the job,' he starts off.

'What job?'

'Managing Ireland.' And I swear I'd forgotten all about it!

I didn't know they were making an appointment on that evening. Nobody had bothered to get in touch after our brief interview and with no contact number, the only way they could reach me to convey the good news was through Jimmy Armfield.

And it was Jim who asked me the first embarrassing question. 'What do you know about them?'

243

'Nothing,' I replied, 'absolutely nothing.' I was never more sincere.

My initial reaction was one of astonishment. I'm an Englishman, not an Irishman. I learnt later that they'd never before appointed a non-Irishman to the job.

I was still fairly shocked by the suddenness of it all when I was asked to go to Dublin to meet the rest of the FAI hierarchy and to introduce myself to the Irish journalists. In no time at all I was sat there in this big hotel room with few familiar faces around me for reassurance.

It was then that I began to doubt whether I had done the right thing. Almost immediately, I'm into my first row with the press people. They're going on about Bob Paisley and how he didn't get the job, and the way my appointment was made. Now this is all news to me. Apart from the phone conversations I'd had with Des Casey, such as they were, and that meeting with Casey, O'Neill and Delaney in Manchester, I had no dealings, good, bad or indifferent, with the FAI before they appointed me. Apparently, there had been some controversy in Ireland about the way the thing had been handled – but when Bob Paisley's name was introduced that evening, it was genuinely the first occasion that I was made aware that he'd been a candidate. And I wasn't particularly interested anyway.

So when this guy is rabbiting on, I stop him and tell him some basic facts. I don't give a damn how I got the job. The pertinent thing is that now I have it – and for better or worse, he'd better get used to the idea.

That put a few of them off their stride, and they were still working out the supplementary questions when I upped and left the room. Leaving like that probably didn't impress them, but I felt I had to make my point right at the start.

Clarification point number two was only minutes away. We went to another room in the hotel for a social drink with some of the FAI officers, and there I was introduced to Peadar O'Driscoll, a somewhat portly man who, at the time, was General Secretary of the Association.

And we're talking about the various members of the existing technical team, the physio, Mick Byrne, in particular, when O'Driscoll says, 'He's on his way, we're not having him any longer.'

To me, that was like a red flag to a bull. In each of the three clubs I'd served as manager, I'd never started out by bringing in my own people. I'd always made a point of giving the existing staff, players and technical people alike, the opportunity to show me that they could perform. If they didn't, they were soon looking for new employers.

It was with some force, therefore, that I told Peadar, 'I'm now the manager here, I decide who goes and who stays. There will be no changes in personnel without my say-so.'

I don't imagine he was used to that kind of treatment by my predecessors – but again, harking back to Jim Bullock's advice, if points have to be made, they are more effectively made on day one.

As it turned out, Mick Byrne stayed with us. And in time, he emerged as a very influential member of the back-up team, a person who in addition to doing his specialist job was remarkably effective in lifting the morale of players.

Up to this point, there hadn't been a mention of money or the conditions under which I would work. When the subject was eventually broached, I told them I'd be happy to have the same as my immediate

245

predecessor Eoin Hand had been getting – and then asked how much that was. When they told me, I nearly fell off my chair! Eoin was on something like £16,000 a year. 'Hell, I'll need a bit more than that!' I said. Eventually, we agreed a figure of £20,000, which, in relation to the going rate at the time, was still only a pittance.

But I've never argued over money, and I certainly wasn't inclined to do so in this instance. I informed them I didn't want a contract. I would stay for three years, which would take us through the 1988 European championship and into the qualifying rounds for the 1990 World Cup. If either party was dissatisfied at that point, the agreement would end with a handshake.

There was an interesting sequel to the business of the night some years later, when I had an unexpected visit from a member of Her Majesty's Inland Revenue staff. That surprised me, for I had never previously been singled out for special attention. I informed the taxman that I had always paid my taxes and that my books were invariably accurate. 'Yes, Mr Charlton,' he explained, 'but there was such a sharp decrease in your returns for the year 1986–87, that we thought it proper to call on you.'

The fact of the matter was that I had taken a big drop in earnings to get the job I wanted. I think I earned something over £30,000 in my year at Newcastle, and then there was the supplementary income from speaking and television engagements. All that went out the door in my first couple of years with Ireland, because I was so busy.

Considering the circumstances of my appointment and the fact that I was the first Englishman to take charge of an Ireland team, I was mildly apprehensive about the way it would be received by the Irish public. In fact, their reaction was remarkably enthusiastic. Everywhere I went, I was showered with good wishes. People genuinely wanted me to succeed and that was a great source of encouragement in those early, uncertain weeks in Dublin.

I recall going to a race meeting in Phoenix Park the day after I was appointed and meeting a disgruntled punter, who quickly forgot his last losing bet to engage me in a conversation about football. 'It's a tough job you've taken, Jack,' he told me. 'But I know you'll succeed. You've some good players in the squad – but I hope to God you get them running a bit faster than some of them bloody horses out there!'

My first game in charge of the Ireland team – a friendly against Wales at Lansdowne Road in March 1986 – was notable for three things. Ian Rush got the only goal for Wales, their keeper Neville Southall got a broken ankle, and I got a reputation for forgetting the names of my own players.

As I've said, I knew little about the players I was about to manage before I arrived in Dublin. John Anderson had been with me at Newcastle and I had gone and spoken with Ray Houghton and John Aldridge just a couple of weeks earlier. But I knew players like Liam Brady, David O'Leary and Frank Stapleton only by reputation. Sure, I had seen them play many times for their clubs, but I'd seen very few of them perform in green shirts.

So I said to Mick Byrne, 'You've been with this lot seven or eight years. You know the form, you pick the team. I'll just sit back and watch and I'll take it from there.'

One of those he chose in the squad was a local lad,

Pat Byrne of Shamrock Rovers. Pat was the best League of Ireland player I've ever seen, not the quickest but a superb striker of a pass of anything up to twenty or thirty yards – just the kind of operator I admired.

I mention his name because some time afterwards, a player I'd got rid of called Michael Robinson wrote a piece in one of the Sunday tabloids, sending me up for confusing Pat with a supporter when I first arrived in the team hotel. Michael, by this stage, had long since disappeared from my plans, and in return for a hundred pounds or whatever they paid him, he put his name to this piece in which he alleged that I didn't know the players' names when I took the job and that I couldn't distinguish between players and fans. He instanced the Pat Byrne case, and then said that I kept referring to Liam Brady as Ian Brady. Well I am a Geordie and it sounded right to me. Robinson just wasn't good enough to stay in the squad and when I got rid of him pretty smartly, I think he chose this as his way of trying to get back at me.

It's possible that I may have called Liam Brady Ian on a couple of occasions. All my life I'd been accustomed to dealing with Ians and Tommys and Bobbys, and suddenly I've got Irish names like Liam and Niall and Pat! And when you think of it, it's not that difficult to confuse Liam with Ian when you meet a person for the first time.

Robinson's article helped to fan the myth that memory-wise I was a bit dodgy. But as those who know me well will testify, nothing could be further from the truth. In the old days, I would listen to the football results on the radio travelling home from games, and if you asked me later, I could rattle off the scorelines of all forty-six games in the Football League – and the Scottish First Division – not in sequence, but correct in every other detail.

Watching games in which I've an involvement, my recall is total. And if you doubt me, just ask some of the players who were taken to task for small incidents which, more than likely, had escaped the notice of others. The fact is that I remember what I want to remember. Over the years, I must have come in contact with hundreds and hundreds of newspaper people. But I could probably identify no more than a dozen of them by their names. The reason is that I wasn't particularly interested in the rest.

But I was stuck with this reputation for forgetfulness. And rather like the fags bit, it became a bit of a party piece with me. Announcing the Irish team to the press after training, I'd go, 'Bonner, Morris, Houghton, Moran – and the big lad, what d'you call him . . .' And someone would prompt me – 'McCarthy!' – without realizing that I was taking the mickey yet again.

Mind you, Mick McCarthy, one of the most loyal, trusted players I've ever managed, also had the occasional jocular swipe at me. I recall him writing about the team talk I gave before the World Cup game against Holland in Palermo, in which he alleged I said the two Dutch players to watch were 'Ceulemans' and 'Van Cleeve'. And Mick, as captain, is supposed to have said, 'Hold on a minute, Boss – Ceulemans plays for Belgium and the other fellow, I think, is a movie star!' Hell, I never said that – at least, I don't think so. After all, I knew Ronald Koeman and Wim Kieft as well as the rest.

Anyway, our next fixture was against Uruguay which we drew 1–1, and then . . . nothing. I needed a few games to sort out the team before we started our qualifying programme for the European championship just four months later – but when I talked with the FAI, I couldn't believe how disorganized they had been. They told me we might be going on tour to South America, there was a possibility of a tournament in Iceland, or there might even be a game in Europe. This was in the late spring, the last realistic chance to get the players together before the end of the football season!

I recall meeting Franz Beckenbauer, my old German adversary, who by that stage was managing the national team. He said how pleased he was that I'd got the job, and told me he thought I'd make a success of it. That seemed as good a time as any to get in my spoke, so I enquired if they'd come and play us. He asked 'When?' – and I could see the look of astonishment on his face when I said, 'Next month.'

'Jackie, my friend,' he answered, 'we in Germany know where we'll be playing in the year 2000.' Suitably chastened, I quickly changed the subject.

In the event, we went to Reykjavik for a three-nation tournament involving Iceland, Czechoslovakia and ourselves. And it turned out to be an illuminating exercise in more ways than one.

I'd been around the various clubs, checking on our players' form, and eventually I named a squad of eighteen for the tour. It didn't include David O'Leary at first, but when Mark Lawrenson and his two Liverpool team-mates, Ronnie Whelan and Jim Beglin, pulled out because of a club trip to Spain, I found myself short of cover at centre back. David was the obvious man to fill the vacancy, so I made contact and asked him to join us. He told me he couldn't, that he'd gone and booked a family holiday when I left him out of the original squad. So I said, 'Postpone the holiday. This is an important tour for us and I want to see you play.'

But he refused, and it would be near enough to three years before he got another invitation to come and play for us. Before long, the media had interpreted that as a sign of bloody-mindedness on my part. Now, I've never held a grudge against anybody in my life. Rows? Yes. But when I said my piece or the other party had a go at me, I closed the book and forgot it. In football, you simply can't afford to hold grudges. You pick the best players you have, irrespective of personal relationships, otherwise you're deliberately handicapping yourself.

I never, at any point, doubted David's ability as a player. Whether he turned out for Arsenal or Ireland, he would guarantee managers a level of performance in keeping with his reputation as one of the better centre backs in the game. But essentially he was a drop-off defender. He didn't believe in getting tight on his opponent, preferring instead to rely on his pace to pick up the bits and pieces. I'd been to see his brother Pierce play at Celtic, and he was exactly the same. And to be brutally frank, they didn't fit my game plan. I needed centre backs who would compete with the players in front of them, push them out, deny them time and space to turn with the ball. David O'Leary didn't do that, at least not consistently – so I left him out.

Some of those who branded me as petty pointed to the fact I used Lawrenson, Whelan and subsequently Beglin, even though they, too, had absented themselves from the Icelandic assignment. At the time, Mark was possibly the best centre back in Europe, and it would

251

have been the height of stupidity not to have played him when he became available again. The same went for Whelan and Beglin, and I had no hesitation in including them when the occasion demanded it.

David had the opportunity to press his claims in Iceland, and he chose not to take it. That was his business. But I always maintained that I'd play him when I needed him. And I did.

The other pertinent fact in the O'Leary episode was that in Mick McCarthy and Kevin Moran, I had two players who fitted my thinking on centre backs perfectly. Here were two guys in their prime, strong, aggressive, exceptionally competitive, who would prove their ability over and over again in the years ahead.

I'm not sure if David ever fully forgave me. For my part, I can genuinely say that there were no hard feelings and I was happy to co-operate with him in the organization of his testimonial game at the close of his international career.

By the time we got ready to go to Iceland, I'd already determined which way we would play. My philosophy of football is that it is better to do the simple things well, rather than get involved in complicated patterns which are foreign to our game. At the time, most European teams were playing a sweeper system, but it wasn't the old-fashioned type of sweeper who stayed behind the back four and soaked up everything which fell behind the centre backs. Franz Beckenbauer was the prototype of the new breed, a player who in addition to discharging his defensive duties, came to play in midfield when the occasion demanded. And by so doing, caused chaos in opposing defences.

With few exceptions, the Europeans played the same way. They worked the ball from the back to midfield, with the primary aim of getting their playmaker free. He was the one who did the damage, the one who sorted out the final ball that got the opposition into trouble.

We couldn't operate like that, not because we didn't have the players, but because most of our players played in England, and the British 4-4-2 style of game was fundamentally different in its concept. Here, the primary aim was to get the ball into the box at the earliest opportunity, and the best player in the team wasn't always the guy who played in central midfield.

It would have been nonsense for me to try to emulate the European way of playing. They had a twenty- or twenty-five-year start on us in that kind of game, and there was simply no way we could hope to beat them at it. No, we'd go at it in a different way. We'd take the better part of the British game, marry it to our own particular style, and impose a pattern of play on the opposition which would prevent them from playing their possession, knockabout football . . .

If our midfielders had the ball, they gave it to the full backs. These would then drop off as far as they liked, before delivering the ball into the corners behind the opposing full backs, and immediately we'd push forward to condense the area. John Aldridge would be on his way into the corner for the ball even as it was struck and almost by definition, his marker followed him. That meant that one of their three centre backs was already drawn out of position and a space opened up in front of goal. If Aldo got there first, Ray Houghton would push up to support him – but I would say to John, 'Don't worry if the centre back gets to it first, just stay on top of him. That way he has to play the ball out of the corner and if we've enough bodies in there, he'll find that difficult.'

253

When John won the ball, our other front runner Frank Stapleton would go to the back post, a midfielder, Paul McGrath or Mark Lawrenson, would take the near post, and now we had people in position to converge on the cross when it came in. The vogue in Europe at the time was that every one of the outfield players should use the ball constructively. If a full back hoofed the ball into touch he was booed – and soon they all fancied themselves as playmakers. That was fine as long as nobody pressurized them, and in general, nobody did. But we were about to do just that, and the effect was immediate. Suddenly, the elegance disappeared and the assured defenders I had seen on television now began to look a lot less composed.

Only when the ball was in the last third of the field were our players allowed to decide for themselves how to play. You cannot legislate for situations which may arise in that area. People then have to react instinctively, to judge for themselves the kind of ball that is on and go for it.

The tenets of our game plan were as simple and as basic as that. So simple, in fact, that the opposition couldn't handle them. And when they eventually stumbled on the answer many years later, it was more by accident than design.

Iceland, never the most pretentious of international teams, were the first to encounter our new way of playing, and they were flummoxed, absolutely flummoxed. With the kind of players I had, I would have expected to beat Iceland anyway, but it was not so much the victory as the way it was achieved which delighted me. We played the ball in behind them, got on top of them when they had it, and, throughout the entire ninety minutes, prevented them from developing any kind of pattern. That was the day the slogan 'Keep them under pressure, Jack' was born – and the Icelanders were the unwitting first victims.

Paul McGrath and Gerry Daly were our goalscorers, and it was only an elementary mistake by Packie Bonner in allowing the ball to drop over his head which enabled the home team to escape with just a 2–1 defeat.

Iceland, as I've said, were no great shakes, but Czechoslovakia would present a truer test of what we were about. The Czechs had always turned out strong, technically proficient teams, and I couldn't wait to see how they handled our new way of playing.

I needn't have worried. As in the first fixture, we imposed ourselves on them from the start, and in the end won the game more comfortably than the 1–0 scoreline suggested.

For the first time in their history, Ireland had won a tournament, albeit a small one, and the lads, who had known nothing but disappointment in the past, celebrated accordingly.

But the more important thing for me, by far, was the fact that I now knew I was on the right track in our game plan. It would be some time yet before we perfected it, but I was encouraged by the way players, accustomed to a different type of game with their clubs, had adjusted. The spirit was willing, and all we needed now was more practice before we started making ripples in Europe.

There was one other aspect of that tournament which stays in my mind – the short-lived international career of Mick Kennedy, the Bradford City player whom I had watched on a number of occasions. Kennedy had a reputation of being a wild boy – some of his tackles had to be seen to be believed – but he could also play a bit. And when I found myself short of left-sided players, I had no hesitation in putting him in at full back.

I reckoned he was doing quite well in the game against the Czechs until he put in this ferocious tackle, which on a bigger occasion might well have led to a riot. The ball was there to be won, but Kennedy, not holding back, went in with his elbow to catch the Czech player right in the mouth. Surprisingly, the lad stayed on the pitch, but when I visited the Czech dressing-room after the game, their manager was enraged. And he calls over this player who is in a right mess, with his teeth all knocked. The guy wants to know what action I'm going to take against Kennedy.

Instinct tells me to defend my own player, but I've just seen something which I didn't like. Kennedy never played for Ireland again. Occasionally, people have accused me of ending his international career on the evidence of just one tackle. Well, that's only half true. I didn't call him up again because, in Tony Galvin and Kevin Sheedy, who weren't available for that particular assignment, I considered I had two players who could do a better job for me down the left side. If I'm honest, however, I have to admit that I didn't like what I saw that day. As player and manager, I've always been a tough competitor. But there's a thin line between toughness and meanness. And I thought Mick Kennedy transgressed it in Iceland.

Another person I felt was out of order in those early days was Liam Tuohy. I remembered him from his playing days at Newcastle, but I didn't get to know the guy personally until after I had taken my new job. By the time we were through, I wished I hadn't.

Liam was a respected figure in Irish football – in fact, he had been one of the first people to manage the national team. He had resigned from the position in 1973, when he was replaced by John Giles, but he subsequently returned to manage the Irish Under-18 and Under-21 teams. And it was in that role that he crossed my path for the one and only time, before an Under-18 game against England at Leeds. The team was based in Sheffield, and I had lunch with Tuohy before travelling on behind them in my own car to Elland Road.

I went into the dressing-room before the kick-off just to wish them luck, and I returned at half-time, when they were already 2–0 down. Tuohy asked me then if I wished to say anything to the players. Now, it had been apparent to me that the midfielders had not supported the front runners during those opening forty-five minutes, and I lectured them on the futility of just humping the ball forward if they didn't push up after it. Perhaps I went on too long, but I don't remember having a go at any individual in particular. We still lost the game 2–0, but I thought the lads did a lot better in the second half.

Imagine my surprise when some Irish journalists rang me the following day and told me that Tuohy had resigned, alleging that I had interfered with his job! Absolute nonsense! I said my piece at half-time only after he had invited me to do so. And in any event, as national team manager with overall responsibility for the national sides, I was entitled to say my piece if I so chose. In fact, that was a prerogative which I rarely used at any time in the job.

Tuohy's resignation was a serious setback to me. I was only a matter of weeks in charge and didn't know anybody in Ireland. There were two or three under-age

18

GREEN SHOOTS

After just four games in charge of Ireland, I was already pretty certain that I'd made the right decision in backing my instincts and risking the pressures of international team management at the age of fifty.

The FA authorities in London might have ignored me, but the people in Dublin had enough faith to give me a chance to show what I could do at this level. In a sense, one merely had the effect of making me more determined to succeed in the other.

The Irish might not command the same respect as an England team travelling abroad, but now I had the opportunity to redress that situation, and I was determined, fiercely determined, to grasp it.

By and large, the reaction of people I met in England to my new appointment was favourable. Folk in the North-East of England have a rapport with the Irish, in that both are naturally friendly people, curious about strangers in a nice way – and to that extent, I was on sound ground locally. The media, too, reacted well, although their interest was probably motivated more by curiosity than anything else. An Englishman managing Ireland was a good source of copy – and almost from day one, the number of English journalists covering our games began to increase.

Television? Now that was interesting. For years I'd been involved in television work, mainly for ITV. I was a regular member of the panels for big football events like the World Cup and European championships. And in the spring and early summer of 1986, I waited patiently for the word that I would be involved in ITV's coverage of the World Cup finals in Mexico. Did I get it? Not a dicky-bird. No letters, no phone calls, no contact whatever from the people in London who had been in touch on a regular basis over the years. And I found that strange, to say the least.

Since three of our European championship opponents – Scotland, Belgium and Bulgaria – were playing in the finals, I had my own reasons for wanting to be in Mexico. So, having ratified the trip with the FAI, Pat and I went there to join the ordinary rank and file in the stands.

Mexico City had just been hit by a massive earthquake, and when the hotel lift stopped a good foot or so short of the eleventh floor where we were housed, I began to worry. And on discovering huge cracks in the wall when we eventually got to our room, I decided to find myself a new hotel.

Within hours of arriving, I'd a call from a BBC Television crew asking me if I'd do a piece with them. Sure, no problem. I was a free agent, I'd help them out. And then one of the crew members says, 'We were surprised to discover you weren't working for ITV.' I tell him he's not half as surprised as I am. Then he says, 'As a matter of fact, we had a call from ITV, informing us that they didn't intend using you in Mexico and asking us if we'd follow suit.' Bloody hell!

To this day, I've never discovered the reason for this strange behaviour. Was it down to the controversy over the field sports series I'd done for ITV, or had it some-thing to do with my taking the Ireland job? As I say, I don't know the answer. But I have my suspicions.

The ITV boycott, if that's what it was, lasted for some time, but then I was contacted by their office in London who informed me that the old regime had now gone. The new people in charge appreciated what I did, and if I was agreeable, they would like to have me on their programmes. That was an offer I gladly accepted. I'd always got on well with the ITV people before Mexico and by working with them, I got to see a lot of big games which I would otherwise never have attended. To me, as a manager, that was vitally import-ant. You get to see the way the game is developing, how new patterns are being introduced, when you watch the World Cup finals, and I benefited accord-ingly.

Those finals in Mexico reinforced my belief that the only way we could hope to make an impact was by imposing our kind of pressurized football on our op-ponents. They all did exactly the same thing, all con-formed to a pattern which was foreign to the British game. Everything went through midfield, every move had the primary objective of getting the playmaker free to do his thing. The phrase I entered in my notebook was 'peas in a pod'.

The exceptions, curiously, were the Belgians, and seeing that we were due to open our European cham-pionship programme against them just two months later, that interested me no end. Yes, they too had good midfield players, but unlike the rest, they varied it. The ball would be played through the midfield to the forwards and then back out again to the full backs. The object of the exercise in this instance was to get their best player, Jan Ceulemans, running in behind the defence when the cross came over.

It was a variation of the theme which I had used to such good effect with Alan Foggon at Middlesbrough. I knew already that it would present us with our biggest threat when we got to Brussels in September.

Some time after we returned from Mexico I had a call from Alan Wade, an old friend from my Lilleshall days who, I gather, was one of those responsible for recommending me to the FAI. Alan was going to watch the Belgians play a friendly game and I took him up on his offer to do a match analysis for me. One line from Alan's report still sticks in my mind. 'The only ball which will get you into trouble against Belgium', he wrote, 'is the one they play to release Jan Ceulemans.' That coincided exactly with my own reading of their game, and, in the belief that forewarned is forearmed, I knew that I already had a psychological advantage on my Belgian counterpart, Guy Thys.

The Heysel Stadium, when our coach arrived there, was like nothing I'd ever seen in football. It was the first big game to be played there since the disaster of the Liverpool–Juventus European Cup final a year earlier – and clearly, the authorities were taking no chances. There were tanks and armoured cars everywhere. Armed soldiers and police encircled the stadium. It was literally a ring of steel. And to have to go in there and play an important game – the biggest since I'd joined Ireland – was as much a test of character as skill.

I had mentioned the name of Ceulemans so often in the preceding two days that our players must have dreamt about him when they went to their beds. And one of the key players in our attempt to frustrate him was Liam Brady. Both the Belgian full backs were excellent strikers of the ball, but of the two, Eric Gerets on the right was probably the better. And since Brady would be one of those in closest proximity to him, it was imperative that he change his normal game and go to the full back every time he had the ball.

Liam was probably the player I had most problems with in our early days. And in a sense, I understood perfectly why. After all, he was one of the most gifted ball players in Europe at the time, every bit as good as Maradona or Platini when it came to sorting out the last pass. I was asking him to do a job that was totally alien to him. All his life, he'd been accustomed to taking balls off the back four and then playing through midfield. Now, our defenders were banned from giving it to him in those situations – and given the talent of the man in front of him, that must have been as hard for them as it was for Liam.

I wanted him to operate in a much more advanced position for us, and I kept reminding him of the problems he had given Sheffield Wednesday when he eventually moved up to play off the front two in that famous FA Cup marathon with Arsenal.

I spent most of that game against Belgium running up and down the line, yelling at Brady, 'Get close to him, get close to him.' Never once did he acknowledge my presence. But good professional that he was, Liam went and did what was required of him. Gerets, denied the space to knock the ball into the box, found himself having to move the ball square to his centre backs; and Ceulemans, already on the run, arrived in our penalty area only to discover that the wide pass hadn't been delivered.

Mind you, we weren't so clever in defending set-pieces, and both their goals, from Claesen and Scifo, came from corner kicks. But Stapleton and Brady scored for us, and a 2–2 away draw, against the team which had finished fourth in the World Cup, represented a good start to the competition for us.

The next game, against Scotland at Lansdowne Road, was memorable more for the state of the pitch than the result, a disappointing scoreless draw. The Irish Rugby Football Union leased the ground to the FAI for big soccer games, and all too often, in those early days, they got their money under false pretences. As I saw it, the ground was never prepared properly, and people ended up having to play soccer on a rugby pitch. That was clearly unacceptable, but in time things improved considerably.

The loss of a home point to the Scots was not a particularly good result for us. We had battered them for most of the match without ever finding the skill to break down a heavily massed defence. Still, I had seen little to unnerve me for the return game at Hampden Park some four months later. That said, I couldn't have legislated at that point for a situation in which I would have to replace both the full backs who had played in the first game, David Langan and Ray Houghton. With no specialist cover available, I was forced to withdraw Paul McGrath and Ronnie Whelan from midfield and play them on either side of Mick McCarthy and Kevin Moran.

A section of the press found that quaint to say the least – but even if I say so myself, it proved a masterstroke. Against the bulk of our back four the Scots chose to go with three comparative lightweights, Mo Johnston, Davy Cooper and Pat Nevin, and it proved the mismatch it looked. By the time they decided to rectify things and bring in a fourth midfielder, Paul

McStay, to bolster up their midfield, we had grabbed the lead with an opportunist goal from Mark Lawrenson, and it stayed that way to the finish.

The earlier Brussels expedition had proved enlightening, but it was that evening in Hampden Park when I sensed that, with luck, we could now go all the way. From my England days, I knew that Scotland at home were a good test for any team. We had just gone and beaten them at Hampden – and now with four points from three games, three of them earned away from home, we were in good shape.

Apart from the result, there was one other aspect of the Glasgow trip which fascinated me – the readiness of the Irish to party. During my long playing career, I'd been involved in some big wins with both England and Leeds United. But the celebrations were seldom excessive, rarely more than a few beers for the players. With Ireland it was vastly different. Here, the team hotel was accessible to the supporters after games – and heck, did they avail themselves of the facility! With the help of a few professional musicians who joined the fans travelling to the game, they had the mother of all parties in Glasgow that night. It was in full swing when I retired to bed at 2 a.m., and it still hadn't finished by the time I got up to catch an early flight back to Newcastle the following morning.

That was the first occasion I'd really heard Irish music. In time, it would form an important part in moulding the morale of the squad.

Yes, that was the night I got to know the travelling Irish and their special way of celebrating. And all on the back of a 1–0 win over Scotland! What would happen, I wondered, if we ever made it into the big time?

Our game in Bulgaria the following month was

notorious for two bad refereeing decisions, and they cost us a 2–1 defeat. I've always lectured players on the futility of arguing with the man in the middle. I've watched hundreds of people do it and I've never yet seen them convince a referee to overturn a decision. The only effect it has is to get them booked – and bookings are a costly thing these days in football. But in the Vasil Levski Stadium in Sofia that evening, I broke my own precept and went for a Portuguese ref named Valente, with more passion than tact. I told him that he was guilty of two disgraceful decisions, but, of course, he merely waved me away with contempt.

In the first instance, the Bulgarian centre forward Sirakov blatantly pushed Mick McCarthy in the back during the build-up to the first goal; and then with just minutes remaining, the same player slid into the box, after being tackled two yards outside it by Kevin Moran. At that point the referee was a good twenty yards behind the play, but without any hesitation, he ran up, pointed to the penalty spot – and we'd lost a precious point.

Note that name, Sirakov, well. A nasty piece of work, he compounded our anger by spitting in the faces of both McCarthy and Moran. Another name had gone into the black book, and he might find himself paying for it when he came to Dublin at the end of the year.

The game against Belgium at Lansdowne Road wasn't in the same class as the earlier one in Brussels. They came for a point, and for all the frantic action in their goalmouth, they got it from a scoreless draw.

I borrowed a phrase from Don Revie's book for our next two games, home and away to Luxemburg. On those occasions when we needed to be geed up against a bottom-of-the-table club, Don would say, 'Remember Cowdenbeath once beat the Rangers.' In other words, never underestimate the opposition, however small their reputation. The first match, away, was won conclusively enough, 2–0; but we were bloody awful in the return. After going a goal down, we were grateful to scrape a 2–1 victory.

And so on to the big one, the return with Bulgaria. This was the one we had to win, and we did – thanks to second-half goals from Paul McGrath and Kevin Moran. And Mr Sirakov? He got his come-uppance, too, but all within the rules, you'll understand.

That was a day when quality and passion came together in an unbeatable formula. Brady was brilliant, just brilliant. He was playing off the front two, taking on defenders, going to them when they had the ball, doing everything I had entreated of him for more than a year. I remember turning to Maurice Setters and remarking, 'The penny has at last dropped.'

And then this gifted man, who can calculate a pass to the last roll of the ball, goes and destroys it all. We're leading 2–0, there's only a couple of minutes left, and as he turns away from an opponent with the ball, he's kicked. What does he do? He spins around and kicks the guy back, straight in front of the referee. Off! My heart sinks. Whatever happens now, whether we get to the finals or not, he's going to pick up a minimum two-match suspension.

Normally, I would blow my top at such stupidity, but in a peculiar kind of way I empathized with Liam in that moment. He had just produced one of the great international performances of the year, had lumps kicked off him in the process, and then with time almost up, he had suffered one foul too many. What he did was purely reactive – but his reaction threatened to prove expensive.

With just one team to qualify from Group 7, it was now all down to Scotland's ability to beat Bulgaria in the last game in Sofia to get us through. A draw would be good enough to qualify the Bulgarians on goal difference, and to be honest, I reckoned that was the very least they would get. Not only were they a good technical team when playing at home, but the Scots, already out of contention, had nothing but their self-respect to play for.

The day of the game, I went duck shooting with a pal of mine just outside Shrewsbury, timing our return to his house so that we'd get to see the match on television. We're sat there watching, with the game still scoreless, when I get a phone call. A Birmingham journalist whom I don't know is on the other end.

'Congratulations, Jack,' he says, 'you've qualified.'

'Qualified for what?'

'The European finals,' he tells me, 'Scotland have won in Bulgaria, you're through.'

I think the bugger is winding me up. 'Hold on a minute, I'm sat here looking at the game the same as you, and it's still scoreless.'

Then he tells me that it's a delayed transmission. The game is already over, and Scotland have won 1–0. I'm still not fully convinced until I watch it through and see Gordon Durie set up the goal for Gary Mackay with just a couple of minutes left.

Hell's bells, we've done it! We've made it into the finals of a major championship for the first time – and a Scot, of all people, has worked the miracle for us.

Then the press calls started flooding in, and suddenly the Ireland team was big news. And the question most of them posed was if I'd send Gary Mackay a crate of champagne for his good deed.

Well, the answer to that in the end was, 'No.' I promised the lad in print that I'd do it, but when I contacted the Scottish FA, they informed me that it wouldn't be appropriate and so I dropped the idea. I met him many years later, however, at a function in Scotland, and thanked him suitably for putting us on the road to the big time. 'Yeah,' he said, 'it might have helped you, but it didn't do much for my international career.'

Afterwards, people would say that we owed our place in the last eight to young Gary. Rubbish! He may have scored the winner in Sofia, but we had done our business in Brussels, in Glasgow, and, not least, in Dublin against the Bulgarians. No, the breakthrough had been achieved on merit, and now I couldn't wait for the summer of 1988, and the chance to test our style of play against the very best in Europe.

19

INTO THE BIG TIME

Success invites scrutiny, and our achievement in qualifying for the finals of the 1988 European championship suddenly began to occupy the attention of journalists who had taken only a cursory interest in our progress over the previous two years. And some of what I read in the British press irritated me.

I had no problem at all with the English-based reporters who accompanied us on our trips abroad on a regular basis. From a very early stage, they identified with what we were trying to do, wrote their copy fairly and accurately – and, in time, some even had a greater sense of belonging than many of their Irish counterparts.

There were others, however, who set out to take the mickey, to demean the team with snide remarks about the number of British-born players we had in our squad. And that both annoyed and hurt me.

Firstly, Ireland was not the first country to claim players under FIFA's ancestry rule. England had done it, not just in football but in rugby and cricket as well. Virtually every country, European and South American, took advantage of a rule which, the critics tended to forget, was introduced by popular demand in the 1960s.

But the bigger point by far was that every player we brought into the squad considered himself Irish. Every one of them prided himself in his roots – and who could deny him that? Had it not been for the economic circumstances which forced their parents or grandparents to emigrate, they would have been born and reared in Ireland. Should they now be victimized and denied their heritage because of the whims of journalists? I think not.

Oh yes, they might speak with different accents to those of the Irish-born lads in the squad. But scratch the surface and they were every bit as loyal, every bit as proud to pull on a green shirt.

Never once did I have occasion to question the commitment of anybody in the team, never once did I have to say, 'Well, an Irish-born lad might have done that job better for me.' On the contrary, these lads would run through a brick wall if they considered the situation warranted it – and that, for me, was as important as skill.

Without the slightest trace of doubt, Ireland has been well served by the 'Anglos', as the cynics liked to label them. Having said that, it worked both ways. By giving lads the platform of international football on a regular basis, we helped them to become better players.

In this way we were able to give something back to the clubs. I had words about this with some of the Irish officials when I first went there. They didn't seem to realize that we only borrowed the players – the players didn't belong to us, they belonged to the clubs. Their managers might not want them to play for us if they had big games coming up. I had this problem with Roy Keane in particular, who was an important player both for Brian Clough at Nottingham Forest and for Alex Ferguson at Manchester United.

You couldn't discipline players like you could as a club manager. You couldn't fine them – not that I believed in fining players anyway. My attitude was a Don Revie attitude: you look after the players, you make sure everything is done for them, you treat them right – and then you expect them to toe the line and obey the rules. But we had no way of punishing them except not playing them, and when you've got as small a group as we had to chose from, you're cutting off your nose to spite your face if you leave your best players out. So you've got to make them want to come and play for the national team. The only way you can do that is to make them enjoy the experience – and of course it helps to get the results. The players came to play for us because they wanted to – even if their managers weren't always particularly keen.

Because we operated from such a limited pool, without the foundation of a strong national league as in Germany, Italy or England, people tended to stay in our squad a lot longer than was the case in many other countries. The up-side of that situation was that we became more and more like a good club team, in which everybody is aware of both his own responsibilities and those of the players around him.

I often think that the English and, to a lesser extent, the Scots resented the fact that we spotted people they had ignored, and developed them into outstanding international players. Players like John Aldridge, Andy Townsend and Ray Houghton were good examples of trust repaid to Maurice and myself, over and over again.

In time, the English FA moved to close off what they

perceived to be a loophole. By offering dually qualified players the chance of caps at Under-18 or Under-21 level, purely to tie them to England, they did the lads concerned no favours.

On one occasion we went to look at Stephen Froggatt, a young midfielder at Aston Villa who we thought could develop into a decent player. But Graham Taylor and Lawrie McMenemy got wind of it, and by putting him in their Under-21 team, ensured that he could never come to us. And, of course, that was as far as the boy got. I'm not saying he would have made the grade with us, but common sense suggested that he had a bloody sight better chance of doing so than by involving himself in the infinitely more competitive scene with England.

The reaction of the Irish public to the fact that more and more players born outside the country were coming into the side was interesting. There were occasions early on when I got the impression that they were preoccupied with the locally born lads. If a person hadn't played Gaelic football or hurling, he was in some way inferior to the others. Nobody ever said as much – but if that was the case, they soon changed their minds. As success bred success, the whole country united behind the team – and that at a time when there were so many divisions in other areas of life.

The one thing some of them could never understand, however, was why the players didn't sing the Irish national anthem during the pre-match ceremonies. And I recall on one occasion getting this shoal of sheets one day with the words of the anthem written on them. Fine. But when I looked closer I discovered that the words were written in Gaelic. Now, whatever chance I had of teaching them the words in English, there was no chance of them learning Gaelic! Bad enough having to listen to John Aldridge and Andy Townsend sing. But in Gaelic? Never!

One of those players born outside the country whom I inherited from Eoin Hand's team was Mark Lawrenson. And when it came to 'the cause', he illustrated perfectly much of what I've just said.

Lawrenson, at his prime in the mid-1980s, was probably one of the best players around. He was strong in the air, fast on the ground, and he had the kind of skills which enabled him to go past opponents when he chose. Liverpool used him mainly as a full back or central defender, but our needs demanded that we slot him into a kind of sweeper role, playing in front of the back four. His primary task was to stop anybody coming down the middle. When one of our centre backs was taken out of position, he'd drift back and fill the hole. That was an essential element of our match plan and, again, we were well ahead of the posse when others became aware of the value of such a player.

But, of course, there was much more to his game than that. He was just as effective going forward, and while Liverpool usually deployed him as a defender, I always reckoned that he was too good a player to put at the back. That would have bordered on football heresy, and in any event, as I've said, I now had two good centre backs in Mick McCarthy and Kevin Moran.

That was Mark Lawrenson, the perfect all-rounder, probably the most complete player in Britain in his time. I felt sure that the European finals in Germany would provide him with the stage to bring his talent to an even bigger audience. And then – disaster! Playing in a club game for Liverpool early in 1988, he 'did' his Achilles tendon, and, sadly, the word from the specialists was that there was no way back. That was a huge loss to football in general, and Irish football in particular.

Even the bigger countries would have struggled to replace such a gifted player, but in an Irish context, it was quite impossible. We'd lost a player who in ordinary circumstances would have been one of the bedrocks of the team for another three or four years. And to suffer it just a matter of months before the European finals was to twist the knife in the wound.

That was just one of the setbacks we suffered in the months before Germany. Liam Brady was on a two-match ban after that sending-off against Bulgaria, but any hope he had of appearing in the finals disappeared when he suffered a bad knee injury, playing for West Ham at Derby. Effectively that injury ended his career, for while he came back briefly, he was never again the player who once commanded the respect of Europe. No less than Lawrenson, I rued Brady's absence – and yet, in a way, it skirted what might have been a very delicate problem for me. Assuming he missed our first two games in Germany because of the suspension, it could have been difficult putting him back into a settled team. On balance, of course, I would gladly have gone with that problem, but it was not to be.

We lost Mark Kelly, too, in early spring, and unlike either Brady or, to a lesser extent, Lawrenson, he was just at the start of a career which promised much for Portsmouth and Ireland. He was one of those players who qualified for both England and ourselves, and I thought I was on to a winner when he chose Ireland. I was even more convinced of it after he had played in the warm-up game against Yugoslavia in Dublin. He was absolutely brilliant that night. The opposing full back was reduced to kicking him so often that he was eventually sent off.

We were not to know it then, but that set the pattern for Kelly's ill-fated career. He was a brave little fellow who would take the ball past people on the inside, and when you do that, you're running into big trouble. Had he survived until he was twenty-one or twenty-two and got a bit cuter, he could have been a fine player. But by that stage he had already been kicked to pieces and was never able to deliver on a great talent.

And then there was Davy Langan. He had first played for Ireland under John Giles and was coming close to the end of his career when I took over the team. In his time, he had been an excellent full back and a good crosser of the ball. But injury problems had robbed him of his pace, and by now Chris Morris was settling into the team at right back. Whereas Langan struggled for pace, Chris had plenty. He was brilliant in getting to the dead-ball line, though once there, he was frequently awful. I mean, he couldn't cross the ball for nuts – but in every other respect he was an exception-ally gifted full back. And curiously enough, there were more enquiries from Europeans about Morris after the finals than about any other Irish player.

I hadn't seen Davy for months when I bumped into him at a reception after one of our last warm-up games against Poland. I reckon he had a few drinks on board and he started giving me a bit of stick about leaving him out of the squad. More than that, he was going on about me not phoning to tell him that he was out of the squad. When a player had an injury problem and he fitted into my plans, I never hesitated to make contact. But I never felt the need to call players and tell them they were out. What was the point? Even if you did

276

phone, they wouldn't listen to the reasons. No, my philosophy was to concentrate on those I had picked in the squad rather than those I left out, and I reckon it's hard to argue about the logic of that.

Aggravation was the last thing I needed at that particular time. We had just won a game 3–1, and I wasn't going to go yelling and screaming at him. So I told him I'd have a talk with him at a more convenient time. As things worked out, however, I don't think I ever saw him again, and that was a pity. He was a good lad whom I would probably have taken with us to Germany had he been fully match fit. But with only twenty places in the squad, somebody had to be disappointed.

We set up our pre-championship training base at Lucan outside Dublin. It was there that we did the hard work, sweating off the extra pounds that had been put on since the end of the club season. By the time we broke camp, I was happy that fitness-wise, we could live with the best in the finals.

But if there was sweat, there had to be a corresponding intake of liquid – and some of it was alcoholic. There was one occasion when we went to Phoenix Park races and I went through the card – backed seven winners and still ended up with just £50. And hell, did the lads give me stick over that!

We were returning from the races when I decided that the coach would stop at a pub and we'd have just a couple of drinks. Note I said just a couple. And we're just back on the coach when they started singing, 'We love you, Jackie, we do.' That was their way of telling me they needed another drink. So, we stopped again . . . and again until we eventually hit base, when a happy bunch of warriors hit the sack.

I've always believed in the maxim that all work and no play is a dangerous formula in any trade or profession. But we knew when to relax and when to do the business. There was simply no way that socializing was tolerated in the approach to games, and the players accepted it. They could sing, 'We love you, Jackie' all they liked, but when the time was wrong, those coach wheels just kept on rolling.

If Langan didn't travel, there were sufficient of his fellow Irishmen in Germany to ensure that Europe at large was made aware of the arrival of a new force in football. There must have been anything up to 15,000 fans with us, and they rewrote the rules in terms of good behaviour. Those of us who had been away to World Cup finals were aware of the reputation of Brazilian fans as carefree, happy people. Now the Irish were about to become the Brazilians of Europe, and the German people loved them for it. They sang, they danced and they drank. They even composed their own songs for the occasion. And throughout the championship finals, they never once, to my knowledge, came into conflict with the law. All this at a time when the game worldwide was being plagued by violence on the terraces.

It was a new experience for them and a new experience for me. As a player with England, I remembered how Alf Ramsey would disappear after a training session to meet the press, and how we would sit and fume on the team coach as we wondered what the hell was keeping him. Now, twenty years on, I discovered the answer. Managing a team in the finals of a major championship is not just about football. It also has to do with communications and the capacity to handle a never-ending series of press conferences. Because of my work in television, I was aware of journalists' need for good copy. So even on those days when little was happening, I tried to stimulate news for them. That way, I would keep them on my side and minimize the danger of the sleazy kind of journalism which surfaces on a regular basis on big occasions.

It is ironic now to recall that our first game in the finals was against England in Stuttgart. Events would show that the other two teams in the group, Holland and the Soviet Union, were stronger than Bobby Robson's team, but the Irish still had this fascination about playing England.

Over the years, I had seen how easily the Scots were motivated at the thought of beating England. And I'm certain the same was equally true for Wales and Northern Ireland. The Republic of Ireland didn't play in the home championship, of course, and because of that, any meeting with the English was special, very special.

They had once beaten England at Goodison Park, but that was almost forty years earlier. I discovered that they still talked about that win when I first became involved with the FAI, but for a whole generation of Irish people, victory over the English was something they had only read about in history books.

Against that background, the build-up to the game in Stuttgart was exceptional. Most of the English players had been in action in the World Cup finals in Mexico two years earlier and, as such, Germany was no big deal for them.

We, of course, were in a different situation. It was all new territory for us, and my biggest job in the days before the game was to try to take the pressure off the players and get them relaxed. Some of our training sessions were so laid-back that they must have sent out reassuring messages to my old friend, Bobby Robson, in the England camp. And that suited me just fine.

The one thing that bothered me about Bobby's team was that he played two specialist wingers, Chris Waddle and John Barnes. Given any kind of latitude, I knew they could destroy us, so I decided to modify our game plan just for this one occasion. Usually, we pressurized people, got on top of them as soon as they had the ball. But not this time. I told the lads, 'Move towards their back four when they have it, make them feel comfortable on the ball but not comfortable enough to look up and deliver it. Get close enough to persuade them that, far from delivering the wide ball, their best option is to play it across the back four.'

That way, their build-up from the back would become even slower, the wingers would be forced to drop back to take the ball, and we would then be able to handle them better. It worked like a treat. Their two full backs, Gary Stevens and Kenny Sansom, could never get Waddle and Barnes into the game, and eventually the wingers ended up having to come back to the halfway line for any scrap of possession.

Ray Houghton had given us the lead after only a couple of minutes, and it wasn't until relatively late in the game that they got us into any kind of trouble. And that was down directly to the fact that Bobby introduced Glenn Hoddle to his team on the hour.

He had set out to beat us by playing through the middle, gradually realized it was getting him nowhere, and then brought on Glenn to start dropping balls over our back four from midfield. Thank God he didn't do it earlier. We struggled to contain the new situation – and Gary Lineker in particular – and but for a couple of marvellous saves by Packie Bonner, we might well have lost the game. But we didn't, we won it. We'd done what we'd set out to do, and given Ireland the win the country demanded.

I had a bit of a go at Packie Bonner after the game, and that was ironic, for according to the press, he was the man of the match. It's true that he produced a couple of superb saves – one from Lineker was simply breathtaking – but from where I was sat, he'd never have had to perform his heroics if he'd done the job right in the first place. When it came to the Bonner fan club, I was up there with the best of them. At the time, I rated him among the top three goalkeepers in Europe, a big, agile man who could grow even taller when it was required. But like most Scottish-based keepers, he had a tendency to stay on his line, and it nearly cost us dear that day. I wanted him to be our sweeper, to get to the ball first when our back four pushed up to the halfway line. Packie was a bright enough fellow, but it took long hours of persuasion to convince him that as long as he concentrated on the play, there was no chance of him being caught out by a long shot, even if he stood on the edge of the penalty area. To prove the point, I devoted much of the next day's training session to Packie. I stood him on the eighteen-yard line, let Frank Stapleton have the ball at his feet some forty yards out, and told him to try to chip Packie before he got back. At the sound of a whistle, both men moved simultaneously. Invariably, Bonner was able to scramble back in time to prevent it going over the line.

The night of the England game, we celebrated suitably. We also introduced a new word to the players – curfew. Some of them wanted to know if it meant a flightless, long-beaked bird, but they got the message soon enough. We'd another big game coming up against the Soviet Union in Hanover three days later and we needed the batteries recharged.

Paul McGrath was a non-starter because of a knee problem, and that worried me no end. With Mark Lawrenson already gone, it meant that we went into a big game for the first time without a central defender in midfield, and that shook the very base of our game plan.

I reckoned we needed that extra cover for the back four. Now, with both Paul and Mark missing, I was forced to gamble in giving the role to Ronnie Whelan and bringing in Kevin Sheedy to central midfield. In the sense that Ronnie had played centre back on a couple of occasions for Liverpool, I felt reasonably confident that he could cope, but I worried how Kevin, an out-and-out flanker, would adapt to a central role.

Happily, my fears proved misplaced. The new formation fitted like a glove, and the 1–1 scoreline at the finish did not do justice to the way we played. It was probably as good a performance as any Ireland has produced away from home. The memorable points for me were Whelan's strike, the goal we gave away, and the reaction of the Soviet manager after the game.

Although Ronnie's score wasn't as flamboyant as it looked on television, it was still a superb opportunist effort as he volleyed Mick McCarthy's throw-in from thirty yards. The Soviet equalizer, sixteen minutes from the end of a game in which we frequently played them off the park, reminded me of a conversation I'd had with Terry Venables some time earlier.

Terry's theory – and I support it 100 per cent – is that centre backs are never more vulnerable than when their team is attacking. Perhaps they lose concentration. In any case, when the return ball is played over their heads, they're in big trouble. And that is precisely what happened when Protasov got through to score for the Soviet Union.

In every respect other than the scoreline, we had won hands down – and the Soviet manager knew it. A couple of days earlier, he had done what he probably considered the hard bit by beating the Dutch. Now, he knew more than most that his team had been second best against us. He shook hands without even looking at me, but I'd never seen a more disappointed, down-in-the-mouth expression on the face of any manager in my life.

The result meant that we now needed only a point from our last game against Holland at Gelsenkirchen to reach the semi-finals. With Paul McGrath fit for action again, I was pretty confident we'd get it. That was until we got to the stadium on match day and discovered that the temperature was in the high nineties for the afternoon kick-off.

Ours was a pressure style, involving an inordinate amount of running. After two hard games in the preceding six days, I feared that legs would go in that kind of heat. To combat it, we devised a plan under which the ball would be played back to Bonner at every opportunity. He would then hold it and bounce it for ten or fifteen seconds, giving our players a brief respite. What Packie was doing was perfectly legal. There was no rule in the book which prohibited a keeper from bouncing the ball. But I noticed the referee was getting increasingly annoyed with him in the second half and I feared that he was about to lose his patience. The plan, regrettably, had to be ditched – and with it went our chance of getting to the last four. Now there were no rest periods, everybody had to chase and run, and suddenly the Dutch were in control of a game in which we had gone closest to scoring with McGrath's header against a post. But with only seven minutes to go, we were still holding them, when disaster struck.

Ronald Koeman's mishit shot looked to be going well wide until Wim Kieft, only in the game as a replacement, got his head to it, and the ball, getting something akin to a leg break in cricket, sneaked in at the far post.

Of all the ways to lose a game! We had competed like Spartans for three games, played well enough to have won all three, and yet we were out of the championship – all because of the biggest fluke of the year.

Holland, of course, went on to beat the Soviet Union in the final, and that made Kieft's goal even harder to accept. Ever since, people have posed the question of how much better we might have done had both Brady and Lawrenson been available to us in Germany. I don't claim to have the definitive answer on that. All I know is that even though we were forced to go without our two principal playmakers in midfield, we weren't a million miles from taking the championship in the end.

Would Liam and Mark have made the difference between winning and losing the title? Who knows? But we had done ourselves proud on our first venture into the game at the highest level – and when we got back to Dublin the following day a welcoming crowd of almost 200,000 people roared their appreciation.

20

ONTO THE WORLD STAGE

On the first occasion I was invited over to meet the FAI, there was an incident on the taxi journey from Dublin airport into the city which convinced me, if I needed any convincing, that I shouldn't get involved in the Irish political situation.

The Northern Ireland problems were at their height at the time, and here was I, an Englishman, on my way to take up the post of manager of the Republic of Ireland team. We were passing under a bridge and I noticed some graffiti about Bobby Sands, the IRA man who had starved himself to death. I made some remark about it to the taxi-driver, and the fellow almost went spare.

'There were eight guys who went on that hunger strike,' he fumed, 'but do the Irish people remember or give a damn about the other seven?' I said to myself, hell, you've made a boob here, Jack. Keep your mouth shut on subjects you know nothing about.

In the ten years that followed, I never forgot that pledge. In that time, I must have been quoted thousands and thousands of times in the press, but never once did I get myself drawn into a situation in which people on either side of the Irish border could point the finger at me and say, 'Hey, he's all for the other crowd.'

There was one occasion when my old friend, Derek Dougan, tried to involve me in a hands-across-the-border movement – but I refused point blank. It was one thing for Derek, an Ulsterman living in England, to lend his name to it, but as a high-profile person working in Ireland, I simply couldn't afford to get involved.

And then, unwittingly, I became embroiled in an incident which the MP Teddy Taylor threatened to raise in Parliament. I don't know if he ever did, but I tell you, it upset me no end.

It was our custom to play tapes on the team coach taking us to games, and one of them was a song called 'Sean South From Garryowen'. I never listened closely to the words, but I vaguely understood that it was a Republican song which dealt with the Black and Tan period in Ireland in the 1920s.

To me, that was unimportant. It had a stirring, singalong air, just the kind to fire up the players, and we made a point of putting it on just as we were about to enter the stadium. That was fine – or so we thought, until the day we ill-advisedly invited some journalists to join us on the coach.

These, as it turned out, were people who would sell their own mothers for a half-page story, and the next day there were screaming headlines in the British tabloids about Jack Charlton, 'the English traitor', playing IRA songs on the coach. Worse than that, they phoned unfortunate parents who had sons killed while serving in the army in Northern Ireland and asked them for their reaction. Naturally, the parents were very angry – and so would I be, if I'd been in their position.

I had a letter from a mother in England, informing me that as a former member of the British army and an

OBE to boot, it was despicable for me to associate in any way with the people who had murdered her son. Now, what do you say to a distressed woman like that?

The song was immediately removed from the tape: soon we had our own World Cup ballads, but the so-called journalists tried to rehash the story once or twice subsequently before it died a death. These 'journalists' were of the same ilk as those who condemned me for jumping up and down with delight after we'd scored against England in Stuttgart. They wrote that it was unbecoming of a former England player to do so. What did they expect me to do – bury my head in my hands and cry? We had just secured the goal that gave us an important win.

I've always enjoyed good relations with the people in Northern Ireland, but I was apprehensive when the Sean South story received splash coverage in the papers. Taking the advice of Jackie Fullerton, a local television journalist who is a good friend of mine, I cancelled a book signing session in Belfast because I feared my appearance might lead to some kind of protest.

I had a second engagement later that day, speaking at a function promoted by the Coleraine club, where my successor at Newcastle, Willie McFaul, was now in charge. I dithered about whether I should attend, but Willie assured me that everything would be fine. As the guest speaker, I was told to stand outside the room until they introduced me. The noise told me there were hundreds of people inside, and as I waited for my cue to walk through the door, a dozen thoughts went through my mind as to how I would be received.

I needn't have worried. As soon as I entered, three or four hundred people got to their feet and started singing, 'We're all part of Jackie's army,' which was by now something of a team anthem.

And as I stood there for thirty seconds or more listening to them, I thought, if only those bloody English journalists could be here to see this. My reception proved that people in Northern Ireland didn't believe the garbage they produced.

Mind you, it was a bit different when we arrived at Windsor Park to start our qualifying programme for the 1990 World Cup, in what was our first big game since the 1988 European finals. Because of the security situation in Northern Ireland, no tickets had been made available to our fans, and as I walked down the line before the start, the abuse was something else. They were calling me 'traitor', 'turncoat', every insult they could pour out. I didn't condone it – but in a way, I could understand. They wanted to see their team win the game, and anything they could do in that cause, including attempts to intimidate us, was open season.

Fair enough. I just smiled at the hostile supporters, and when I put my head through the wire barrier and asked one of them for a light, I think it helped defuse the situation marginally. In fact, there wasn't much in the game to match their passion. It was tough and tense, just like an English club derby. We probably had the edge in scoring chances, but it still took a couple of good saves by Gerry Peyton, deputizing in goal for Packie Bonner, to earn us a point from a scoreless draw.

Apart from Northern Ireland, Spain and Hungary were the danger teams in the group, and when the meeting to arrange dates and venues for the games was held earlier in the year, I took a calculated risk. I decided to open our programme by playing the three hardest games away from home, in the hope that the competition wouldn't yet have developed a fine edge at that point.

When they came to Dublin for the return games, we would have home advantage to deliver what I hoped would be a decisive late charge. It was, of course, a gamble, and by the time we reached Seville for the Spanish game in October, I was wishing that I hadn't been so bold.

That was the trip in which Murphy's Law ruled. Simply everything that could go wrong, did go wrong. For a start, we were based thirty miles away, on the wrong side of the city from either the match venue or the training-ground, and to reach them meant long hours of bumper-to-bumper traffic.

The bigger consideration by far, however, was the fact that I had to take a skeleton team to Seville, a city in which the Spaniards had never lost a big game to that point. Paul McGrath, Ray Houghton, Ronnie Whelan and Kevin Sheedy were all injured. My greatest worry was how I would fill McGrath's place. Eventually, I chose to play Kevin Moran in midfield, and recalled David O'Leary to partner Mick McCarthy at centre half. I was glad to have David back, if only for the fact that it disproved the theory that I held a grudge against him. I'd always said I'd pick him if the need arose, but I wish I could have done so in more favourable circumstances.

As an admirer of Kevin Moran, I bowed to nobody. Like McCarthy, he had limitations in pace. But he read the game so well, and took up such good positions that this weakness was very rarely exposed. As a competitor he was brave to a fault – just look at how much stitching he needed in his time – but for all his attributes, he just wasn't a midfield player. And it soon showed.

The Spaniards fairly took us apart that night. I was pelted with oranges by the crowd when I stood up and tried to correct things – but I can assure you, that was the least of my worries. The team was springing leaks all over the place. At one point, I remember turning to Liam Brady beside me on the bench and asking, 'What do I do now, Liam?'

When he suggested I bring on Liam O'Brien, I readily agreed. At that point, we were already two goals down – it might well have been five – and past the point of no return. It was one of the heaviest drubbings we'd ever had in international football and it proved that we still had a lot of work to do in building up the strength of our shadow team.

Fortunately, we had a full-strength squad when we went to Budapest for our next game, but in spite of dominating the Hungarians, we still had to content ourselves with just one point from a scoreless draw. A couple of years earlier, a draw in Hungary would have been interpreted as a smashing result. Now the Irish press were complaining that we didn't take our chances and that we should have won the game! I agreed with that assessment, but the criticism served to remind me that expectation in Ireland was now reaching a disturbing level.

Still, that was the price of the job I'd taken on board – and when we met Spain in Dublin in April 1989, I knew that our margin of error was zero. This was the game we had to win to stay competitive in the group, and the fact that the Spaniards had made our improvised team look so inadequate in Seville had the effect of focusing minds. They'd had their hour of glory. Now it was time for us to show them that, with a full-strength side, they were only second best.

A month or so earlier, we'd had the Hillsborough disaster, and that, for me, was one of the saddest days of my football life. Ever since my days with Sheffield Wednesday, I'd had a special affinity with the place. I'd seen at first hand how hard the club directors had worked to make the stadium the best it could be. Perhaps ironically, it was because Hillsborough was so well equipped in terms of safety control, with crush barriers and the like, that the tragedy reached the terrible scale it did.

I'd flown into Leeds airport from Dublin for the game, and was delayed getting away because it turned out they'd lost my bag on the flight. I couldn't wait around because I had to drive to Hillsborough, so I said I'd come back afterwards. Even so, I was late arriving at the ground. It was a bad start to a day that was to get much worse.

I ran into the ground, and found my seat just as they were kicking off. Then, after a few minutes, we began to notice something was happening in the stands. A policeman ran onto the field to speak to the referee, who stopped the game. People were beginning to climb the barriers. Spectators spilled onto the ground, and the police started to drag people out. Then they began ripping down the advertising hoardings to use as stretchers. I saw a policeman giving a lad mouth-to-mouth resuscitation, then he started banging away on his chest. He suddenly stopped – and he pulled his coat over the lad's face. And I thought, bloody hell, I've gotta get out of here.

I remember running out of the ground and driving away as fast as I could. I was listening to the car radio as I drove back to Leeds, and as I tuned in they announced that five people had died. By the time I got to the airport the figure had increased to nine.

I went in to get my bag, but before they let me have it, the customs man said he wanted to search it. I had a bottle of whiskey and three hundred cigarettes with me. The customs man said, 'You've got three hundred cigarettes here' – and I said, 'So what?'

'Well, you're only allowed two hundred.'

I was so angry, I just ripped open the packet and threw a hundred cigarettes at him. I couldn't help it. All this tragedy was going on, and the bloody man was worrying about a hundred cigarettes.

I got back in the car and I drove off up the motorway. I had the radio on all the way. The figure kept on rising, and by the time I got to Filey, where I was meeting Pat and the kids for the weekend, it had reached twenty-four.

Over the weekend the death-toll kept getting bigger and bigger, until it reached ninety-six. I don't know why, I just felt I had to go back. A few days later I pulled off the motorway, bought some flowers and went into the ground. I sort of sneaked in, because there were camera crews and photographers about. I walked out onto the field, to the area behind the goal where all those poor people had died. I couldn't believe what I saw. The barriers were all bent into unbelievable shapes. I stood there for five or six minutes, the tears rolling down my face. Then I put my flowers down and walked out through the tunnel.

John Aldridge had been on the field for Liverpool on that terrible day. When I contacted him some time afterwards about the upcoming game against Spain, he told me that he was too upset, far too upset, even to think about playing. I understood perfectly. When you've lived through a disaster like that, football, even World Cup football, seems totally irrelevant.

In any event, it gave me the chance of bringing Frank Stapleton back into the team. Frank was one of the great warriors of Irish football, a fine header of the ball and never less than a great competitor. Fully fit, he was my first-choice target man, but that hadn't been the case since our return from Germany.

Part of our strategy involved one of our two front men dropping back into midfield when the opposition had the ball. It's not a role which comes easily to attackers, but Stapleton did the job for me better than anybody else.

As such, I was glad to have him in my side again, for even with home advantage, we were going to have to work hard to prevent the Spaniards settling into the kind of pattern which can make them world-beaters on their day. But we did what we needed to do, and a 1–0 win put us back on track to qualify for the 1990 World Cup finals. Officially, it was credited as an own goal, but Stapleton was waiting to knock Ray Houghton's cross into the net when Michel's outstretched foot saved him the trouble.

Before we played our remaining qualifying games, I had an appointment I could not miss up in Edinburgh.

A few years earlier, Don Revie's wife, Elsie, had noticed that he seemed to be limping as they walked round the golf course together. Don was suffering no pain, but they decided to get it checked out. The doctor revealed the terrible truth: Don was suffering from motor neurone disease, an incurable illness which attacks the muscles. Don and Elsie were living near Leeds at the time, but they decided to move up to Kinross, on the banks of Loch Leven, and there this once active man steadily decayed. I visited him quite regularly, calling in to see him every three or four months when I was up there fishing – and each time I saw him, he was worse and worse. The terrible thing was that though his body was disintegrating, his mind remained as active as ever. There came a time when Elsie said to me, 'You should leave – you're making him laugh' – and I realized that the poor man couldn't even laugh any longer.

Don was only sixty-two when he died in May 1989. There was a funeral service for him in Edinburgh – and I was amazed to see how people had come from all over the country to pay their respects. Everyone who was any-one in football seemed to be there. Don Revie, the man who had once been reviled, was coming home at last.

Don had been, without question, the most im-portant influence on my football career. He'd been more of an influence on me than all the rest of them put together. He'd taught me how to conduct myself as a player, at a time when there had been a danger I might go off the rails, perhaps even leave football al-together. Just as important, he'd been a model for me as a manager. Many of the practices I later adopted with Ireland and the clubs I managed, I first learnt from Don.

The Spanish result also vindicated me, I believe, in my decision to take the difficult part of our programme at the beginning. By now we were pretty well unbeat-able at home – and with Hungary, Northern Ireland and Malta still to play at Lansdowne Road, we were in good shape approaching the end of the season.

Before we broke for our summer holidays, however, we had to take care of the Maltese and Hungarians, and this was achieved without too much bother. Both games were won with 2–0 scorelines, and against the Hungarians in particular, we played some good football.

Now only Northern Ireland (home) and Malta (away) stood between us and the dream of playing in the World Cup finals – but before we got there, we had an appointment with West Germany for a warm-up game at Lansdowne Road in September. I've never put too much store on friendly fixtures at international level, for the simple reason that managers rarely, if ever, show their hand on such occasions. They use them primarily to experiment, either with players or tactics, and as such, results can frequently be false.

Meetings with West Germany, however, are different. For one thing, the Germans are seldom less than competitive, and with so many good players to call on, they can be guaranteed to put out a strong team in almost any circumstance.

For me, that fixture was ideal. Not only would it help sharpen minds and bodies for the end of our qualifying programme, but it would give me an opportunity of looking at three players who were coming close to the end of their careers, Liam Brady, Frank Stapleton and Tony Galvin.

To be honest, I had already more or less made up my mind that Brady and Stapleton had little to contribute if we reached the World Cup finals. But I still thought I'd have a look at them and, equally important, give the Irish public a chance of looking at them, before I took any precipitate action.

Liam wasn't the same player that he had been. He had never got over his knee injury – and I suspect that deep down, nobody realized that more than the player himself.

Frank, too, had never recovered from his injury

problems. In his prime, he'd been one of the pivotal people in the team, but at this stage of his career, he was living on borrowed time.

Tony Galvin was a very aggressive runner, a lad who took on full backs and went for the back line. He was a one-off as far as Ireland was concerned for, in my time, he was the only one who did that job perfectly – but for some reason or other, he never attracted the same attention as the others. The critics went on and on about Brady and Stapleton, but in many respects Tony, who still had a lot to give when injury ended his career, was the most expensive loss of all to me.

Anyway, I decided to put all three of them in the showcase. Thanks to Stapleton's opportunism in getting on to a German back pass, we were a goal to the good after only ten minutes. Then a German player waltzed past Brady who didn't get within two yards of him, pulled the ball back, and the boy Dorfner buried it in the net from twenty yards. From a situation in which we were in uneasy control of the game, we were now really struggling, and Liam was being run all over the place. So I turned to Maurice and said, 'I've got to get him off, otherwise we're going to lose this bloody match.'

So, with just eight minutes to go to the interval, I pulled him off – and landed myself in one hell of a row. I don't remember the crowd being too upset at the time, but Liam certainly was. In his view, I had humiliated him. When we got in at half-time, he had a real go at me. He insisted that if I was going to substitute him, I should have left it until the interval. And I said, 'No, no. My job is to save this game – not to pander to your pride.'

There was no reasoning with him, however, and at

the end of the game, he announced to all and sundry that he was through with Jack Charlton, that he'd never play another game for Ireland. And by the time the press had finished, I was seen by some as the villain of the piece.

I wasn't happy about having to take him off. And I did think about leaving him on the pitch until half-time. But the thought which went through my mind was if you're going to do it, do it now.

In retrospect, I would have saved myself a lot of flak by leaving him on. But I've never been one for people patting me on the head and telling me that I'm the most popular manager in the world. If I'm popular, it's not because I pander to people, but do my job as I judge it needs to be done. And by replacing Brady with Andy Townsend that night, I ensured that Ireland got out with a 1–1 draw instead of a bad beating.

When Brady became manager of Celtic years later, I like to think he then realized that what I did was right. Players and managers often see a game from different perspectives, but when it's over, it's the manager who carries the responsibility for the result. Anyway, Liam and I are now on speaking terms. Like me, he remains passionate about the performances of Ireland teams.

The return meeting with Northern Ireland in Dublin was a high-profile one. This was not just tribal warfare perpetrated in the name of sport, but a game which offered us the chance of putting our names on one of those twenty-four places on offer for the World Cup finals in Italy. True, we still had to go to Malta, but I reckoned that if we beat Billy Bingham's team, we would be almost there.

For half an hour or more, it didn't look as if we would do it. We just weren't playing our normal game.

Instead of moving the ball into the corners and playing from there, we were thumping it up the middle – and every time it was being returned with interest.

Northern Ireland, in fact, had the better chances early on, and we might have been at least one down before Ronnie Whelan put us in the lead just before the interval. Our dressing-room that day wasn't the quietest place on earth. I lashed the players for the way that they had put the game at risk in the first half. With our game plan back in place, we ran the show in the second half, when Tony Cascarino and Ray Houghton scored to quicken the countdown to Malta.

If the Northern Ireland game taught us anything, it was that we could quickly get ourselves into trouble by deviating from our normal pattern of play. On the face of it, the Maltese didn't pose any real threat. Unless we took leave of our senses, we would get the point needed to qualify us for the finals. Still, football can be a great leveller, and the fear, the nagging fear, in my mind was that somehow the occasion would take over from the game itself and that we could get ourselves into a spot of bother.

That appointment in Valetta was always going to be a big one for the Irish. After all, they had waited nearly sixty years for this day, the day when they would at last come of age and prove their right to play at the highest level. Sure enough, they travelled in their thousands to the match, perhaps as many as 15,000 of them, to be there when it happened. Unfortunately, all flights from Dublin for the twenty-four hours before the game were disrupted by fog, and to make it to Valetta supporters had to fly out of places as far apart as Belfast, Manchester and Glasgow.

My abiding memory of the pre-match warm-up is

looking up and seeing all these planes overhead, presumably carrying our supporters, and wondering how on earth they would get to the game in time. In fact, some of them only made it into the stadium at half-time, and afterwards the Maltese officials delighted in telling us stories of how the Irish fans just parked their luggage outside the ground and rushed in to see what was left of the match.

The latecomers missed John Aldridge's fine strike to open the scoring after half an hour, and then Aldo, the man who failed to hit the target in his first twenty games for Ireland, slotted a penalty to make certain of our place in the finals. In less than four years in the job, I'd taken the team to the finals of two major championships.

Hell, did the beer taste nice that night! I must have signed a thousand autographs after the match, but none to compare with the one the team captain, Mick McCarthy, deigned to give at an advanced stage of the night's revelries. On being asked for the umpteenth time to sign his name, Mick patiently informed one fan that he'd sign anything he produced. Whereupon the fellow dropped his trousers and asked him to autograph his backside. Now, there's a thought to come between a man and his night's sleep!

21

ITALIA '90

I don't admit to having made too many mistakes in my time in charge of the Ireland team – and I think the record book supports that as a statement of fact rather than a show of big-headedness.

But I blundered in my choice of the last of the twenty-two players I took to the World Cup finals in Italy in 1990. Nothing serious, but a gaffe nonetheless.

To the media and the public in general, it was a straight choice between gambling on the fitness of Gary Waddock or opting for the emerging talent of Swindon's Alan McLoughlin, a player who had caught my eye in a 'B' international earlier in the year.

Waddock had won nineteen caps between 1980 and 1985, but then suffered a horrific injury which would have ended the career of a less brave man. Nothing daunted, he went to Belgium to rebuild his career, and having paid back the insurance settlement he received, returned to English football with Millwall.

That kind of character impressed me, and having watched him on a couple of occasions, I brought him back after a five-year absence from international football for the warm-up games against the Soviet Union and Turkey.

McLoughlin had never played a full international

game to that point, and as one who always believed in bedding players into the system before playing them, that went against the grain. He never had the legs to do the kind of job I needed across midfield, but against that he was always capable of sorting things out on the edge of the box.

That was the choice – or so the media thought. But they were wrong. A third player entered the equation. And I acknowledge now that the player I ought to have left out was not the unfortunate Waddock but former team captain, Frank Stapleton.

Frank's attitude during Italia '90 was at times disgraceful. He never really got involved in training – and equally damning, he made little attempt to help others. I believe that when a player of his experience goes on a major trip, he has as much to give in terms of coaching others as in working on his own game.

In Italy, he did neither adequately. He sensed at an early stage that he wasn't going to figure in my team plans, and he was absolutely right. But he still had something to contribute in helping people like Niall Quinn, John Aldridge and Tony Cascarino. He chose not to do so, and that disappointed me greatly. His thinking, I reckon, was that if I wasn't going to play him, why should he bother to put himself about? Underpinning it all seemed to be a sense of resentment and bitterness.

Two incidents typified his behaviour. Like Alf Ramsey when he took us to Mexico in 1970, I had specifically forbidden players to lie about in the sun. They could have an hour or so in the sunshine, providing they wore a hat and were supervised, but after that it was strictly indoors.

And I'm sat on the balcony in the team hotel one

afternoon when I notice Frank and John Byrne going off in a boat on the sea outside. The rest of the lads are indoors playing cards, but here are these two, bare-headed and in short shirtsleeves, cocking a snook at the system.

When they finally got back, I gave them a piece of my mind. John was mildly apologetic and I formed the impression that he had gone only at Stapleton's behest. But from Frank, nothing. He seemed to feel that if he wasn't involved in the team plan, he could get as much sun as he liked.

Now that was out of order. Sure, he didn't figure in my plans. But I didn't know and he didn't know if a circumstance might arise in which I would have to play him. And he was not preparing himself for that eventuality.

The other thing which annoyed me was an incident in the hotel after our game against England. Before we left Dublin, I had issued an order that players' wives came to the team hotel only by invitation – and then just for a few drinks. And that applied to me as much as everybody else.

As a former player, I know how much it means to a guy to be able to meet his wife occasionally when he's involved in a competition which takes him away from home for five or six weeks. That's natural. But generally, lads on tour are happy enough to know that wives will be well looked after, albeit in a different hotel. And I made a point of insisting to the FAI that they take care of this important detail.

After the England game, the instruction was that the women were to be out of the team hotel by half-past midnight, but when I arrive an hour or so later, Frank is still there with his wife. And again it embroils me in aggravation I can do without. I tell him that when I make rules, they are intended to apply to all twenty-two players, not twenty-one. But if he's listening, he certainly doesn't show it.

Why did I go against my better judgement and take him in the first place? Two reasons. As a player who had given Ireland tremendous service over the years, he commanded a debt of gratitude which I felt had to be repaid.

Equally, I was aware of the row which would follow if I dropped him. Journalists form attachments with players. They think they can go on for ever and moan like hell when the manager reckons otherwise. Frank had a lot of friends in the press, and I wasn't going to give them the chance of undermining the morale of the squad by writing knocking stories right at the start. So I chose to keep Frank, and lived to regret it.

That sense of having done the wrong thing was, if anything, heightened by Gary Waddock's exemplary behaviour in the whole affair. I had taken him with us to Izmir for a game against Turkey before travelling on to set up our pre-World Cup camp in Malta. Now I had to tell him that he wouldn't be in the list of twenty-two for the finals – and for a guy who had gone through agony to get back into top-class football, that news must have been shattering. I could see the disappointment in his eyes – and that hurt me almost as much as it did him.

Players have this idea that managers are insensitive buggers. They think we can dish out disappointment without batting an eyelid. My feelings at the airport in Izmir that morning told a vastly different story.

Gary took it like a man, however, and after turning down our invitation to join us as a guest in Italy, he returned to London the next day. I don't think Stapleton would have reacted in quite the same way had he been given that kind of news.

Yes, I was proud of the way Waddock handled the biggest let-down of his life, even prouder when I learned subsequently that on his return to England, he turned down a lot of money from one of the tabloids to write about the episode. He could have made a financial killing by throwing mud at me, but he refused. And I shall remember him for that.

Ireland's participation in Italia '90 would prove a lot of things to a lot of people. Our performances in the European finals two years earlier had made many of our peers sit up and take notice. Now we would show that it was no flash in the pan – that we deserved to rank among the better teams in the game.

Then there were the Irish fans. In Germany they had stolen the hearts of Europe with their humour, their warmth and the sheer exuberance of their support every time we played. Now they were back in even greater numbers, as many as 20,000 of them arriving by air, sea and road. In Sardinia, just as we had done in Germany, we were to open our programme against England – and then we would move to Sicily for the remaining first phase games with Egypt and Holland. Months earlier, our people had been to Sardinia to look at hotels, and subsequently forwarded a list in order of preference to FIFA. Imagine our surprise, then, when we discovered that they had ignored our choice and stuck us in a hotel on top of a mountain, miles from anywhere! The England party, of course, was based in a nice plush place, just a couple of miles from the ground.

Now whether that was because England was a big

My irritating first press conference on being appointed manager of the Republic of Ireland in 1986. The press wanted me to answer questions about my appointment, but I had no idea about the shenanigans behind the scenes.

(Sportsfile)

Celebrating Ray Houghton's winning goal against England during the 1988 European championship, with my assistant Maurice Setters. (Sportsfile)

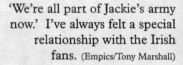

'We're all part of Jackie's army now.' I've always felt a special relationship with the Irish fans. (Empics/Tony Marshall)

Frustration. We'd been 3-1 up against Poland in our European championship qualifier in October 1991, but they came back with two late goals. (Inpho)

Liam Brady is substituted in a friendly against West Germany, 6 September 1989. He didn't like it one bit, and announced afterwards that he never wanted to play for Ireland again.
(Sportsfile)

'Packie' Bonner saves a penalty against Romania to take Ireland into the World Cup quarter-finals, Italia 90. (Sportsfile)

The Republic of Ireland team meet the Pope in Rome, June 1990. During the earlier lesson I must confess I nearly dozed off. (Empics/Phil O'Brien)

'Up yours, Billy.' Exchanging words with Billy Bingham after an ill-tempered World Cup qualifying match against Northern Ireland at Windsor Park, Belfast, 17 November 1993. Afterwards I regretted what I'd said. (Inpho/Billy Stickland)

The key man, Paul McGrath. (Sportsfile/Ray McManus)

Training with the Ireland team in Orlando during the 1994
World Cup. (Empics/Laurence Griffiths)

I'd been banned from the touchline after some aggro with the
FIFA bureaucracy, so I had to sit out our 1994 World Cup game
against Norway in the press box. (Inpho)

Happy times: (above) celebrating our great victory over Italy in the 1994 World Cup (Sportsfile/Ray McManus); and (below) welcomed home by Taoiseach Albert Reynolds and deputy Dick Spring after the 1994 World Cup. (Inpho)

Sad times: (above) facing defeat against Holland and elimination from the 1996 championships (Inpho); and (below) arriving in Dublin for the meeting with the FAI when I announced my resignation. (Sportsfile/Ray McManus)

With Princess Diana and other members of the 1966 World Cup winning team at the celebrations to mark the fortieth year of the Queen's reign. (Syndication International)

Brothers Bobby, Gordon, Jack and Tommy (not visible in picture) carry my mother's coffin at her funeral, 2 April 1996. (Syndication International)

country in a football sense or because they thought that Ireland, taking part in the World Cup for the first time, would settle for any old place, I don't know. But I soon read the riot act – and after a spate of fax messages, we were eventually relocated to the hotel we had originally chosen. Lesson one: you've got to fight your corner off the pitch as well as on it, on these occasions.

I don't know how Bobby Robson's lot chose to spend the day before the game, but we went to an open-air mass on the beach – that is, everybody except Maurice and me. As the only non-Catholics in the party, it probably wouldn't have done us much good anyway to attend, but we had other duties to perform. The press had got wind of the event, and if our people wanted to go to mass, I was determined that they should do so in privacy. So while the rest prayed, the two of us went on sentry duty, determined that the reporters and television cameras would be kept well away. Shades of my days on army duty at Windsor!

I was looking forward to pitting my wits against Bobby Robson for a second time. In Germany, I felt he could have done us a lot of damage by bringing on Glenn Hoddle much earlier and playing balls into the corners rather than through the middle. Now I wondered if he'd change tack – though I doubted it.

I'd known Bob since our days at Lilleshall together. Generally speaking, I considered him a pal of mine. We'd sometimes have a drink together; and if I needed information, I'd give him a ring and he was always forthcoming.

Although we hold different views on the way the game should be played, I have great respect for Bobby. But I always felt that he talked too much to the press. I would listen to his press conferences or watch him on television answering questions, and I would say to myself, 'That's enough, Bob – don't go on and on.' But he always did.

Not that he got any thanks for it. I shall always remember the hurt look on his face when, over a drink in Berlin, he told me how journalists had raked up a story about a woman in Sheffield who he had known fourteen years earlier. I couldn't believe that they could be so nasty.

In a way, that said it all about the attitude of the press towards the England team manager. They campaign for an individual, and then can't wait to find out as much crap as they can about him and use it to undermine his position. As far as they're concerned, you simply cannot pick the right team.

Those were the kind of pressures weighing on Bob in the run-up to our game in Cagliari, but I have to say that I was annoyed with him on being told that he intended to wait until the mandatory fifty minutes before the game to announce his team. And I sent back a message to him through the journalists: 'If you want to play silly buggers, I'll play silly buggers.'

It was all so stupid. In my team talk, I went over the way England would play, the pattern they would adopt and how we would cope with it. Individual players simply didn't come into it. In any event, I still had fifty minutes to dwell on any surprise choices in his team – but as it turned out, I had guessed correctly who he would choose.

John Barnes and Chris Waddle were still there, but the point which reassured me most was Bob's choice of Bryan Robson and Paul Gascoigne in central midfield. Bryan was one of the best midfielders England ever had, but they never seemed to be able to find the right player to complement him. And that was because he was so good at so many things. It would have been fine if Bobby had left him to anchor midfield, but Bryan was also expected to get forward and get the odd goal or two. And because of that dual responsibility, it was never easy for them to find the right partner for him.

Gascoigne certainly didn't meet that requirement. Gazza, a strong runner and a superb passer of the ball, is at his best on the edge of the opposition's box. But at the other end of the pitch, he can be as much of a liability as an asset. He tries to be too clever, aiming to nutmeg people or to pull the ball down, when a specialist defender would just hoof it. I reckoned the more pressure we put on him, the better.

Neither Barnes nor Waddle was particularly good defensively – Chris couldn't tackle his own mother in a cupboard – and in that situation, I reckoned Bobby didn't have enough ball-winners to prevent us getting at his back four. As it turned out, I was right.

We gave away a silly goal to Gary Lineker, but got no more than we deserved when Kevin Sheedy, whose mistake had led to Lineker's score, equalized in the second half. After that, I felt we were always the more likely team, though we never managed another goal. I couldn't believe my ears after the game when Bob told the press that England deserved to win. Talk about rose-tinted spectacles!

The scoreless draw which followed against Egypt was notable from my point of view for the fact that I got myself into trouble with the press in both Cairo and Dublin. I lashed the Egyptians' attitude to the game for the simple reason that I couldn't understand how players which had battled their way through the qualifying rounds could be so negative when they arrived in the finals.

Our performance didn't please the people in Ireland – and it didn't please me either. And I saw red at a press conference the following day when Eamon Dunphy, who was working for one of the Irish papers, sought to question me about it. Dunphy, a former Millwall player who had won a number of Irish caps, was the original contrary journalist. If you said black, he'd call white. He seemed to agree with nothing or nobody.

In Germany two years earlier, I had taken him into the players' lounge because he wanted to do an article with me. Frank Stapleton immediately left the room and then Mick McCarthy came up and told me he wanted him out. So I took him out.

My feeling at the time was that it was better to have him with us than against us and I tried to get along with him. But all that changed on the flight back to Dublin when I read a scurrilous piece he had done on McCarthy. There and then I said, 'You can stick it up your arse, you little prat, there is no way I want anything more to do with you!'

I don't know whether it was because I was English and he was Irish, but no matter what I did or what I wanted to achieve, he always tried to undermine me. I'm a professional who has been appointed to do a job and the last thing I need is a journalist trying to tell me how to do it. I promptly dismissed him to the point where I never read his stuff.

The mistake I made in Palermo that morning was to acknowledge his presence in the room. After listening to his question, I ought to have invited somebody else to speak. But I didn't, and after telling him that he was not a proper journalist and that he should have known I wouldn't answer his question, I packed up and left the conference. That was an error of judgement which I subsequently regretted, because it gave him a degree of notoriety with the international press.

A couple of days later, we were due to play Holland. I knew that a draw would probably be good enough to achieve our basic goal in Italy, to reach the knock-out stages of the competition.

Earlier in the competition, Bobby Robson had out-witted the Dutch by playing a sweeper, Mark Wright, behind Terry Butcher and Des Walker. I thought I'd have a look at the idea of duplicating Bobby's tactic. In training the following day, I positioned David O'Leary at the back of Kevin Moran and McCarthy. And it was bloody terrifying to see the way they were being pulled all over the place! So I promptly scrapped the idea. The next day, the papers were full of the story of Jack being forced to change his mind. Nonsense! I never really intended to use a sweeper in the game. It was just a thought in my mind, and it didn't take long to convince me that we were incapable of playing that system. But I did make a change up front, Niall Quinn replacing Tony Cascarino, and it was Quinny who eventually got us back into the game after Ruud Gullit had put them in front.

Minutes after that equalizer, word got through to the players that England were leading Egypt 1–0 in the other game in the group. If that scoreline stayed intact, a draw would suffice to get both Holland and ourselves into the last sixteen. There and then, the teams made a pact among themselves that they wouldn't bother each other for the rest of the game.

The problem was that nobody told either me or Tony Cascarino. I can't believe the stuff I'm watching, and Cascarino is charging about like a maniac while everybody else is strolling. Eventually, the penny drops with me and Tony gets the message from the Dutch.

In fairness, it's a bit ridiculous. Our back four are passing the ball among themselves without the slightest threat of a challenge coming in. Eventually, the referee, exasperated, runs up to McCarthy, and after pointing an admonishing finger in his face, tells him, 'This is the World Cup – you must play football.'

'But we are playing football,' says Mick with his captain's armband, 'and it's the first bloody time in four years that we have been allowed to play football!'

I brought on Ronnie Whelan for the last quarter of an hour or so of the game against Holland. But at that stage, both teams had settled for stalemate, and in any event, he didn't greatly impress me in what he did. As such, there was no place for him among the final sixteen players we took to Genoa to face Romania in the knock-out stages of the competition.

There had been a time when Ronnie Whelan's name was the first down on my sheet of paper whenever I selected the team. He was that good: a midfield player who could graft and tackle and sort out the final pass when it needed doing. But I fell out with Ronnie – or rather he fell out with me – because he wasn't fit enough to do the job I needed in Italy. Unfortunately, he had picked up an injury in March, and hadn't played for ten weeks before the World Cup finals. But I kept hoping against hope that somehow he could recover his old form.

That, in hindsight, was just wishful thinking. He struggled in training in Malta, and before we ever got to Italy, I knew that he would take little or no part in the action. But players don't often see eye to eye with managers in such situations, and when I left Ronnie

310

out of the sixteen for the game against Egypt, he was furious. In training later that day, I saw him deliberately hoof the ball over the stand. 'What's he gone and done that for?' I say to Maurice – and he tells me that the player is unhappy about being left out. My response to that is to tell Maurice to go and work him even harder, but he's back within minutes to say that Ronnie doesn't want to train.

Somebody suggests that I should go and have a word with him, but I say, 'Nah, I'm not having that. I don't have to explain anything to him. He can stew in his own juice.'

That night I notice Whelan walking around the foyer of the hotel, clearly waiting for the chance to say his piece. Eventually, he came over to where Maurice and I and a few others were sat and asked if he could have a word in private. I refused. If he'd anything to say, he could spurt it out there and then. He tells me that he's not happy at being left out, and I tell him I'm not over the moon with his attitude. It's not that I don't understand his disappointment, but I've a responsibility to pick the best team I can and he doesn't fit in. I know how desperate he is to get a start, but I'm not prepared to put my midfield at risk just to give him the satisfaction of being able to say that he's played in the World Cup finals.

Conditions in Genoa for our game against Romania were absolutely gruelling. The stadium was totally enclosed, there wasn't a breath of air in the place, and with a capacity crowd ringing the pitch, the heat was unbelievable. Both teams suffered, but I saw enough of the Romanians' class in the opening twenty minutes to convince me that they were a very dangerous team.

Gheorghe Hagi had a tremendous left foot, and

twice almost scored before we had settled. It was in moments like those that I was glad I had a player like Packie Bonner in goal. We gradually got back into the game in the second half, without ever breaking down a strong defence. It was all very taut and tense and I'm afraid I got myself into a spot of bother by refusing to sit on the bench. No, it wasn't a case of being difficult, just a matter of not being able to see the match from where I was sat.

The officials who make the rules never seem to take managers' problems into consideration. Other people, even press photographers, can walk up and down the line, but can managers? Can they hell! They're supposed to sit there rigidly, in a position in which they can see only the playing area directly in front of them. And that's an impossible situation from which to judge a game.

Some managers like to take themselves up to the stand to get an overview, but that was never on for me. I prefer to be in close proximity to my players at all times. I like to have a presence which can help the team.

Later in the game, I had a go at the referee when he booked Paul McGrath for a perfectly good tackle. But it merely produced a stern order to get back on the bench, and afterwards, a strongly worded letter of complaint from FIFA. Some things never change!

In extra time, neither side threatened to score, for the simple reason that they didn't have the energy to push on and look for a goal. Inevitably, it went to a penalty shoot-out, the first in the history of the competition. The idea was so novel that I hadn't even taken the precaution of nominating our penalty-takers in such an eventuality. That was laxness on my part – but in reality, we knew who our best penalty-takers were.

John Aldridge, our penalty specialist, was out of the game at that stage. I walked across to the players who were sat in the centre circle and asked, 'Who's going to take them?' Various hands went up, and the only one that surprised me was David O'Leary, who had replaced Stephen Staunton in extra time. He said he'd have one, providing he was allowed to go last. Fine.

I was quite relaxed at that stage. We'd done well to reach this far. Whatever happened now, nobody could say that we hadn't made our presence felt. My only instruction was, 'Make up your mind what you're going to do and don't change it!'

I was a bit annoyed – again – with the referee. The instruction was that as the players went to the penalty spot, they turned and showed him their number. But on three or four occasions after our lads had placed the ball, he beckoned them to him and made them turn around. He never did that with the Romanians.

Their keeper nearly got to Tony Cascarino's shot, but all kicks had been successful when Daniel Timofte put the ball down for Romania's last attempt. I've watched it on video a dozen times since, and it wasn't a good penalty. It was struck at a comfortable height, and the only chance he had of scoring was if Packie went the wrong way. But he didn't, and after going close to stopping the previous one, Packie read the line perfectly.

And so to O'Leary. I didn't know at that point that he had never previously taken a penalty and it was just as well I didn't!

I was now really uptight. I hadn't smoked for a couple of years, but now I desperately needed a fag. So I turned and cadged one from an Italian spectator, and then stuck my head through the wire for him to light it. In the next day's papers there was a picture of me looking the other way as David ran up to the ball, with the caption 'Jack couldn't bear to watch'. Nonsense! Of course Jack could bear to watch – except that with so many players stood in front of me, I thought it better to look at the big video screen at the other end of the stadium.

And then my nerve almost went. I put my hands over my face and said, 'No, I'm not watching this.' But I pulled them away just in time to see David send the goalkeeper the wrong way. Easy as winking! And all of a sudden, the lads are running, all determined to pile themselves on top of O'Leary and Bonner.

We're through! For the first time, Ireland are within touching distance of the World Cup. We're in the last eight, the last bloody eight! More than that, we're headed for the biggest stage of all, a quarter-final tie against Italy in the Olympic Stadium in Rome.

Within a few hours, I was made to realize that the win over Romania carried a price tag. Mick Byrne, the team physio, is a devout Catholic, all the players in the squad are Catholics – and when we first qualified for the finals, he came to me and said, 'Hey, boss, if we get to Rome, you've got to get us in to meet the Pope.' Sure, Mick, no problem!

Part of our entourage on all big occasions was Monsignor Liam Boyle, a fine man who paid all his own travelling expenses, but was otherwise a member of the official party. Any place I've ever been as a manager, I've encouraged the practice of having a padre around, not to preach but just to have a presence. If any players felt they needed to have a word with him, they could go and do so in private.

314

Mgr Boyle together with Bishop Tony Farquahar, who had travelled out to support us, were the key figures in getting us into the Vatican for an event which would rate as one of the lasting memories of our stay in Italy. To be honest, I wasn't much in favour of the idea when it was first put to me. No disrespect to the Pontiff, but somehow I was apprehensive about all the fuss in going there the day before a big game.

In my naïvety, I had this idea that we would be taken into a big room, the Pope would come in, say a prayer or something and leave. Not at all! We were ushered into a vast auditorium, with as many as six or seven thousand people present from all parts of the world. Fortunately, we were close to the side of the stage, just yards away from the papal throne.

Eventually, the Pope entered the chamber in his white robes, read a lesson for perhaps twenty minutes or so, and sat down. Then the bishops who were sat alongside him translated the lesson into various languages. It must have gone on for two or two and a half hours. I was hot and tired, and as we sat there, my eyes started to close. I was conscious of the battery of press photographers on the other side of the stage targeting us, and the last thing in the world I wanted was for Jack Charlton to nod off during his audience with the Pope! I could imagine the picture appearing on the front page of the *Sun* or the *Mirror* – and the caption which would go with it.

But I tell you, it was hard work staying awake. The Pope, apparently, has to do this three or four times a week, and from my brief experience, it takes some doing. Every so often, he'd cover his face with his hands, scratch behind his ear, or wipe his forehead, and at intervals of ten minutes or so, he'd make the sign of the cross to the audience, first to the left of the chamber, then the centre, and so on. I must have dozed off and he must have been on the third part of his blessing – but when I woke up, he was looking at me with his hand raised. And I swear to God, I thought he was waving at me. So I half stood up and waved back at him! The photographers didn't twig it, and hell, was I happy they didn't. Picture my embarrassment if they had!

Later we had our photograph taken with him, and one of the papal aides came and said the Pontiff wanted a word with me. I went across, half-falling over Mick Byrne, who was on his knees kissing the papal ring. 'Your Holiness, this is the team manager, Mr Charlton,' said the aide; and the Pope answered, 'Yes, I know who you are – you're The Boss.' He said a few other words to me which I don't remember.

We left soon afterwards, but it was an unbelievable experience, a sense of occasion I had never previously felt. Ninety per cent of what was happening that day was strange to me. I mean, Catholics to me have always been a bit strange. I think to all Protestants, Catholics are a bit strange. They go to mass, visit churches three times a week, ring bells, are there for hours and hours. I could never understand that, perhaps because I had never been brought up to understand it. But the feeling in the auditorium that day from the audience was one of total love for the guy. He is a very nice man.

I must confess that I am not that religious myself. I don't go to church regularly. But like most people, I do say the odd prayer.

One of the benefits of that visit to the Vatican was to distract my thoughts, briefly, from a matter which had lain heavily on my mind for the preceding twenty-four hours. Shortly after arriving in Rome, I discovered that our game was to be refereed by one Portuguese official – and that worried me no end.

I have always been wary of match officials from that region. I'm not saying they are out to stop you winning a game, but their interpretation of the laws, as I discovered on trips abroad with Leeds, England and Ireland, is vastly different to the rest of the world.

If you raise a boot five inches, they whistle. If you jump with an opponent, they whistle. If there is any kind of physical contact whatever, they whistle. And since our game plan was based in part on hustling and pressurizing opponents, it didn't augur well for our prospects in the Olympic Stadium.

And this was no ordinary Portuguese official. He was none other than Silva Valente, the man who had caused me to stand principle on its head and have a go at him, publicly, in that European championship game in Bulgaria a couple of years earlier.

Two diabolical decisions that day had cost us the game – and while he didn't do anything quite as drastic in Rome, he was certainly no help. Every time we got a bit of momentum going, he would stop the game for one reason or another. But they were always thirty or forty yards out. We had difficulty getting anywhere near their goal.

The Italian frees, it seemed to me, were always appreciably closer. At one point, the sequence of Italian frees was such that when he eventually gave us one, Kevin Moran clapped him – and promptly got booked.

Oddly enough, I agreed with the referee in that instance. You don't treat a match official with disrespect, and Kevin was out of order. So, too, was Mick McCarthy, who vented his frustration on a FIFA official as we were walking in at half-time. But if truth be known, I was more angry than the lot of them. We were simply not permitted to play our usual game, which is largely about giving and taking knocks and getting on with it. But now we were constantly stopped before a move could develop – and we suffered for it as a result.

Toto Schillaci's goal hurt in more ways than one. It was a bloody stupid score to concede, coming directly as a result of Kevin Sheedy playing a silly ball to John Aldridge. In our match plan, we gave the ball into the corner for the runner, but this time, strangely, John showed for it and Kevin played it to his feet.

That was inviting trouble, and sure enough, we got it. The Italians swept the ball three-quarters the length of the pitch in the twinkling of an eye, and when Packie could only parry Roberto Donadoni's shot, Schillaci stuck the rebound in the net.

We were out of the World Cup, the dream was over – and all because of one lapse of concentration. We had done better than anybody could reasonably have expected . . . and yet the thought persisted that it could have been even better. People have since asked if we could have won the championship. Who knows? But if I could have had two players from the England team of the period, I believe we would have gone very close to it.

John Aldridge, given a role which didn't fit his natural game, has been one of Ireland's finest players. But for all his qualities, he lacked a little bit of pace – the kind of pace which took Gary Lineker clear of defenders. Steve Staunton, too, was a great servant of Irish football, but he was essentially a full back who we converted into a midfield player after Tony Galvin was injured. How I would love to have had Chris Waddle running the left wing for us! Chris would have been a better player with Ireland than with England, because we would have deployed him wider and further up the pitch. And with Lineker and nine Irishmen playing alongside him, I reckon we would have been in with a shout of winning the World Cup in Italy.

In the pre-match talk, I had joked to the lads, 'Don't go winning this game today. I'm due on the Ridge Pool in Ballina on Monday and I aim to be there.' The Ridge Pool is one of the most coveted fishing waters anywhere, and two days' fishing there is not to be missed. And if there was a silver lining to being knocked out of the World Cup, it was that I was able to keep my appointment in Ballina.

Before that, of course, there was a tumultuous homecoming to Dublin. I'm told that half a million people turned out to welcome us. I'd never seen anything like it. There were masses and masses of people everywhere, clinging to window-ledges, hanging out of trees, doing anything for a glimpse of the squad on an open-topped coach in O'Connell Street.

I must confess that I was both embarrassed and frightened. Embarrassed that so many people had turned out when we hadn't won anything, frightened that some of the children along the way would fall under the wheels of the coach. England would go on to the semi-finals and lose only on a penalty shoot-out. But in their case, they came home to nothing. This was another example of the different levels of expectation in the two countries.

By eight o'clock the next morning, I was on a flight out of Dublin to Newcastle. I got to my house, grabbed my fishing gear, drove to Stranraer for the ferry and was back in the west of Ireland by five o'clock that afternoon. When we stopped at a pub in Sligo for a pint, the manager ushered me into a back room. 'This place has been heaving with people watching the football for the last three weeks. I've made a small fortune and this is your share of the profits.' And he handed me the biggest bottle of brandy that I'd ever seen!

After the pressures and the hype of the World Cup, fishing in the west of Ireland was a merciful relief. When you want to get away from it all, to get a few moments to unravel your thoughts, there's nothing to compare with being stood in the middle of a river with only fish on your mind. And I'm there, with only a gillie for company, when he starts shouting at me. But I can't for the life of me make out a word he's saying. Eventually, he points back up to a little bridge – and there must be a hundred or more people stood there watching me in the river!

In the middle of them, there's this red-faced policeman, ready to have kittens. There are so many people standing on the bridge that the traffic can't get through. He wants me out of there – quick. Now what did I say about the solitude of rivers?

22

DOWN AND UP AGAIN

Paul Mcgrath was one of the three best players I had in my time as Ireland manager. Together with Mick McCarthy and Andy Townsend, I would place him top of the list – at a time when I was privileged to work with some exceptional talent.

That assessment is not easy to make, for all of the regular first-team players had special qualities and a sense of commitment which put them apart from many of their contemporaries in Britain.

McCarthy was never the quickest defender and he could operate in only one position, on the right side of central defence. Move him a few yards across and he was never the same player. What made him extra special, however, were his competitive qualities and his ability to motivate others around him. I could say my piece in the dressing-room, but once they got on the park, it was down to the players themselves. And McCarthy made certain the instructions were carried out to the last detail.

Before the England game in Sardinia, I had warned our fellows to beware of Peter Beardsley. Once he was allowed to settle on the ball, he could destroy any defence. To minimize that threat, we had to get to him quickly, to force him to go in the direction we wanted him to go, not the other way round. And the game was only a couple of minutes in progress when I saw McCarthy charge through a forest of players, friend and foe alike, to light like a wasp on Peter. The casual onlooker may have missed it, but in that moment, Mick was laying down the benchmark for his team.

Townsend, too, is a great competitor who believes in leading from the front. And when you put that alongside the kind of engine he has, you end up with a player who would challenge for a place in any international team.

Yet in many respects, Paul McGrath was the most remarkable of them all. For twelve years or more, he has managed to stand football logic on its head.

That was down, in the first place, to the fact that he was a naturally gifted athlete. He has had so many problems with his knees that his clubs decided it was wiser to put him on the easy list in training to cut down the risk of further wear and tear on his joints. Basically, he trained through games, and that didn't augur well for a long career. Given all those circumstances, it is unbelievable that he has managed to keep going long after many of his age-group have finished.

One of the first pieces of advice I gave Paul when I took over the team concerned his attitude to opponents on the pitch. He was big and he was black, and I'd say to him, 'Don't go snarling at people. Just smile at them – that will intimidate the buggers even more.'

There was, of course, much more to Paul than mere physique. For one thing, his natural talent was such that he could play in any one of three or four positions. Originally he was a central defender, but I always thought he was too good a player to be put in there. So I played him in midfield, and, on occasions, at full back when we needed to improvise in that position.

But no matter where you posted him, he read the game perfectly, passed the ball well, and most important of all in those early days, he could always find that extra yard of pace when the situation demanded it. Put all those qualities together and you had one of the finest players in football at the time – but sadly, there was another side to Paul.

Down through the years, drink has been a problem for some of the biggest names in the game and, unfortunately, it was for him too. In time, his drinking became one of the biggest worries I had in my ten years with Ireland.

I wasn't long in the job when I first became aware of Paul's plight. We had gone to Poland for a game, and afterwards we visited a night-club in the team hotel for a social drink. Suddenly I noticed some of the players tittering and looking across the dance floor. Of course, they were watching Paul.

He was moving from table to table, clearly the worse for drink, joining people he didn't know. I remember one group getting right annoyed with him. I went across to Paul, but he obviously couldn't understand a word I was saying. So I said to the entire squad, 'That's it. We've had our drink, we've an early flight in the morning, everybody to bed.'

And they all left immediately and went to their rooms – that is, everybody except Paul and John Sheridan. I hadn't noticed them leave, so I went and stood behind a pillar in the foyer of the hotel. And sure enough, the two of them eventually emerged, jumped into a taxi and headed into town. I chose to avoid a confrontation, for with a lot of drink inside them, there could have been a nasty scene. Instead I went to see Mick Byrne and told him that if the two players weren't up and ready to leave with us at eight o'clock the next morning, we went without them. That, of course, was an empty threat, for I knew that Mick would break down the bloody door if necessary to get them on the coach.

I had a word with John the next morning, and it was some time before he was invited back to join us. Paul was different. At the time, he was on his way to becoming one of the best players in the world, the very heart of our team, and we simply couldn't afford to be without him.

The rest of the players, I have to say, were brilliant about Paul. They protected him, looked after him, and ensured that in those early years, the press never got to know about his problem. Whenever we travelled abroad, I would put one of the senior players next to him in the plane, to prevent him from taking any Jack. On one occasion, I discussed Paul's situation with Andy Townsend and I still recall his words to me. 'Don't worry, Boss, we'll take care of him, because we're a better team when he's with us.'

But, of course, it was impossible to look after him all the time. Paul would disappear from the hotel with his pockets full of money and come back with them empty. Most times, we knew where we were likely to find him – but on a few occasions, we had the police, and even the players themselves, out looking for him.

And the tragedy was that he was such a lovely, gentle person who sat by himself in his favourite seat at the back of the bus and who never said a wrong word to anybody. In time, I could tell at a range of twenty yards whether he had drink in him. Sober, he'd give you a little wave, a little smile and keep his head down. With a drink on board, it was always a big smile and his head was high. I tried to cajole him, to bully him, to warn him of the dangers but alas, to no avail.

To be fair, there were many, many occasions when he behaved himself perfectly and he resisted what must have been, for him, terrible temptations. We tried to help him as much as possible by insisting that the drinks cabinet in his room was always emptied before he arrived, and when we went to America for the World Cup finals, we even had people sleep outside his room to ensure that he didn't leave. It became standard practice for us to check on Paul's arrival times in Dublin when he came to join the squad, and we would arrange to go and meet him at the airport before he fell into the wrong company. It didn't always work, of course, and there was one occasion when, after attending a function in Cork, he went missing just twenty-four hours before we were to leave for Albania.

Then I get a phone call from him, telling me he is in Israel! By now, he's sobered up. 'Boss, I'm sorry for letting you down,' he says. 'Can I come back?' And without a moment's hesitation, I went, 'Of course you can come back. Get the next plane out of there and we'll try to keep it quiet.' But by this stage, I'm afraid, his binge-drinking was common knowledge.

His problems were getting worse by the year, and I had reason to curse them yet again when, in our first game in the qualifying rounds of the 1992 European championship, we played Turkey in Dublin in October 1990. I deliberately chose to start with a home game against the Turks, for I wanted to get early points in the bank. We had just done ourselves proud in the World Cup finals and, barring a miracle, there was no way they would beat us at Lansdowne Road. To that extent, there was no great pressure attached to the game, but for whatever reason, it seemed to get to Paul. Because of the fact that he chose to spend a lot of the time alone in his room, joining the rest of the lads for meals only occasionally, it wasn't always easy to keep tabs on him, but there didn't appear to be any problems when we set off for the ground.

I was one of the first off the coach and when I got inside, I did my usual things, like having a chat with my wife, talking to some of the people I'd invited to the game, dropping in to say hello to the referee. Then I went into our dressing-room to do my pre-match talk. Consternation – no Paul!

I asked where he was, and the lads told me that he was outside in the coach refusing to get off. Bloody hell! So I went back to the coach and there, sure enough, was Paul, sat in his usual seat at the back. He'd obviously been drinking. He told me he wasn't feeling well and demanded that he be taken back to the hotel immediately. I pointed out that we were about to play an important European game, there were 50,000 spectators out there waiting to see him perform, and that he had certain responsibilities. No go!

So I said, 'Paul, at least come into the ground, make an appearance in the dressing-room, and I'll tell the press that your knee has locked up on you and you're not playing. Then, when nobody's watching, we'll put you in a taxi and send you back to the hotel.'

I must have argued with him for ten or fifteen minutes, but would he budge off that coach? Would he hell! He just dug in his heels, and there was nothing I could do but leave him and get on with the game.

As it happened, we hammered the Turks 5–0, but I'm afraid those early signs proved deceptive. Our next two games were against England, home and away, and we twice let them off the hook, allowing them to escape with 1–1 draws when we should have won both matches easily. Ray Houghton missed a sitter in the Dublin game – and, incredibly, did the same thing again when we went to London, for a fixture which brought out Wembley's biggest crowd in years. We had started badly, with Steve Staunton deflecting Lee Dixon's shot past Packie Bonner, but then proceeded to give them a lesson in our pressure game. For the best part of ten minutes, we pinned them in the top third of the pitch. I heard Graham Taylor roar at his players, 'Get out, get out.' But we had them ringed so tight that they couldn't get out. In ten years, that was the single best illustration of our ability to pressurize opponents.

Eventually, Niall Quinn knocked in the equalizer from Paul's cross, but that was the very least we deserved to take out of the game. I mean, if we'd won 3–1 nobody, not even the most dyed-in-the-wool England supporter, could have complained about the scoreline.

But Kevin Sheedy on his wrong foot missed from no more than a couple of yards, before Houghton compounded it all in the last few minutes by shooting just past David Seaman's left-hand post when it looked so much easier to bury it in the net. That was typical of Ray, a brilliant player around the pitch, but not the most reliable when it came to finishing. And I remember saying to them at the end of the game, 'That's the chance which could cost us a place in the European finals.' Never did I speak truer words.

By the time we got to our last two games in Poland and Turkey, it was tight, desperately tight, as to whether England or ourselves would get the one qualifying place on offer in the group. For the Polish game in Poznan, I decided to change tack. Instead of going with two front players, I played a fifth midfielder. The plan was for Roy Keane and Andy Townsend to run at the Poles from deep positions and get on the end of crosses from our full backs.

For more than an hour it worked brilliantly. Time after time, we punched holes in their defence, and with twenty minutes to go, we led 3–1. But then came the miscalculation. Frankly, I hadn't reckoned on how much our new running game would take out of our players, and with our midfielders forced backwards to the point where they finished up on top of the defenders, the Poles got in for two late goals to save a point.

That was a lesson. It taught me that if you choose to play this kind of game with two people running from midfield, you need a couple of extra pairs of legs on the bench to utilize in the latter part of the game and prevent the opposition from getting at your defence.

Some people thought that we had blown our chances of qualifying in that late collapse, but I didn't agree. Mathematically, Poland still had a chance of going through – and that ensured they would be competitive when they met England in Poznan the following month.

To qualify, we needed to beat Turkey in Istanbul on the same night, and then depend on the Poles doing us a favour against Graham Taylor's team. And boy, did we give it a whirl! I had always found Turkey a difficult country to play in every time I went there. The spectators are very hostile. To win a game, you always had the impression that you had to beat the crowd as well as the Turkish team. This night, as it turned out, was no exception.

For a start, we had to fight our way off the bus to get into the ground. Once inside it, we were left in no doubt that we were in dangerous territory. For the unfortunate fans who had accompanied us, it was even worse. Many of them never even got into the stadium, and those who did discovered that their seats had already been taken.

It quickly became apparent that this would be a test of character as much as skill, and the lads responded magnificently. John Byrne, back in the side after a long absence, gave us an early lead, and while they equalized from a doubtful penalty, we quickly got back on top again to win with further goals from Byrne and Tony Cascarino. Great! And the word from Poland was even better. England are losing 1–0. If it stays like that, we're on our way to Sweden for the finals the following summer.

As I'm walking off the pitch at the end, the Turkish manager, Sepp Piontek, an old friend of mine, comes across to congratulate me. He says that Poland have won in Poznan, which means that we have qualified as first team in the group.

I can't wait to get inside to congratulate the lads, when suddenly, out of the corner of my eye, I catch a glimpse of Mick McCarthy. His face is about three foot long.

'What's wrong, Mick?' I ask.

'You haven't heard, then,' he says sadly. 'Gary Lineker has just gone and scored for England – we're out.'

In the space of perhaps no more than ninety seconds, I had gone from the summit all the way down to the valley, and the experience was awful. We haven't lost a game in the competition, we've squandered a hatful of chances along the way and now, we miss out on the finals by six or seven minutes!

Twenty-one years earlier, I had seen players numbed by disbelief after England had lost that World Cup quarter-final tie to West Germany. But if anything, this was even worse. For half an hour or so, nobody moved in the dressing-room. They refused to get showered, refused to dress, just sat there with their heads buried in their hands, trying to come to terms with it all. I tried to do the jollying bit, but deep down, I hurt as much as any of them. That was the time when the squad was at its strongest, when players were in their prime, when we could slot different people into different positions without sacrificing either power or skill. And that, unquestionably, was our best chance of winning a major championship.

But the reality of playing international football at the highest level is that you can't afford to spend too long thinking about what might have been. Almost before we knew it, we had to start preparing for the 1994 World Cup qualifying programme. One of our earliest fixtures was against the side that had won the European championship only a couple of months earlier. The Danes had produced perhaps the biggest upset in the history of international football when they beat Germany in the final. What made that achievement unique was that they had been eliminated in the qualifying rounds and only got back in when Yugoslavia were forced to withdraw. And rightly or wrongly, that merely deepened my conviction that we could have won the bloody thing had we not squandered what should have been a victory against England.

The remarkable thing about the Danes' success was that it was achieved on a method. They did have some good players, of course, but essentially they went right to the top by devising a system which caught the opposition cold. Their game plan was for Peter Schmeichel to hoof the ball as far as he could and for their centre forward to compete in the air for it with a couple of defenders. His prime responsibility was not to win it, but to put the opposition under so much pressure that they would be happy to knock it back anywhere in the general direction of midfield. By that stage, however, the Danes would have flooded the midfield area with players and when the ball came back out, they were able to run at the Germans in numbers.

It was different from anything they had ever done before – and it worked. A simple tactic, but good enough to win a European title. And to think that some people branded our game as too simplistic to be successful!

I was particularly interested in the Danes, for we had drawn them in a World Cup group which also included Spain, Northern Ireland, Latvia and Lithuania. I sent Maurice to watch them in their first game after the European final and I got right annoyed with him when he returned. No written report, no reference to their new style, just a bland statement that they were crap. And I couldn't believe that – until I went and watched a video of the game. Maurice was right! They had ditched the ploy which brought them the title and gone back to their old way of playing through the middle. That shocked me, but it also gave me heart that we could handle them in Copenhagen.

In the event, it bucketed down all through the game, but we were always comfortable in a scoreless draw. The scoreline was identical when we went to Seville the following month, and that was a hell of a result for us. Nobody had ever gone there and beaten Spain in a big game, but I tell you something, we came pretty close to it that night. Late in the game, John Aldridge chested the ball past their centre back, took it around the keeper and put it in the empty net. To everybody in the stadium, it was a perfectly good goal. I couldn't believe what I was seeing when a linesman stuck up his flag for offside.

At the end of the game, the Spanish manager, Javier Clemente, a nice little guy, came across and said, 'You won the game, Jackie. You won, for it was a bad decision in the end.' That was a nice gesture.

It was a disappointing result on the night, but with two vital away points to go with our win over Latvia in the first game, I was reasonably content on the journey home.

A 3–0 win over Northern Ireland in Dublin could have been doubled had we not stopped playing in the second half, and while a 1–1 draw in the return meeting with Denmark at Lansdowne Road was disappointing, I still thought we were in good shape facing up to our summer programme in eastern Europe.

Not too many people from the Western world have had the experience of travelling to Albania, and maybe that is just as well. I was there twice in 1993, and I can assure you it was pretty dreadful. One of the common complaints you hear from footballers who have been twice around the world is that they never get to see any of the cities in which they play. Apart from travelling to training and the match itself, most of the time is spent indoors, with socializing normally confined to a few drinks after the match. That's the way it was in my playing days – but in all my time in the game, I don't think I have ever seen a place quite as bad as Albania.

I first went there when Northern Ireland played in

Tirana in February. We had heard that it was desolate and since we were due to go back there three months later, I thought I had better go and check it out.

Albania was like a fortress. Nobody was encouraged to go into it, and the unfortunate people who lived there were not allowed out. The first things that struck you on the journey from the airport into the city were the bunkers, which the country's dictators apparently built to guard against invasion. They were like concrete mushrooms, rising just a couple of feet above the ground, and they were everywhere. Somebody told me that there were up to half a million of them, dotting the fields and the hills. When you consider that Albania is not a very big country, that adds up to security gone mad.

Shock number two was the hotel in which visiting teams were based. Presumably it was the biggest hotel in the place for it was situated on the city's main square, but without question, it was one of the worst places in which I've ever stayed. Panes of glass were missing from the windows, there was no electric light, the lifts didn't work, and we found ourselves hauling cases up five or six flights of stairs in pitch-dark. When we went outside the following morning, we discovered that things were even worse. The poverty was unbelievable. The traffic round the main square was nearly all horse-drawn, and the few cars we saw belonged to an era long gone in the West. I certainly wouldn't have fancied their chances of pulling up in a hurry and to make matters worse, they came at you from every direction. There were no traffic lights, and apparently no rules of the road.

It goes almost without saying that good food was in short supply. The Northern Ireland party had brought their own provisions with them and a chef to cook them, and that perhaps was the most important lesson I learned from the trip.

Subsequently, a letter of complaint was sent to FIFA and, whether by accident or design, things had improved considerably by the time we played there in May. The lights and the lifts worked, they had put some carpet on the floor, and there were even a few armchairs scattered here and there in the hotel foyer. It was scarcely luxury, but it was a damn sight better than what the Northern Ireland party had to endure.

Forewarned by Billy Bingham's experience, we took our own food and even our own utensils with us to Tirana, and thanks to Tony Cascarino's late strike, we got the win we needed after falling behind to a goal after only seven minutes.

Latvia and Lithuania were like paradise by contrast, and while the effects of a long hard season were by now catching up on the players, we banked six important points by winning 2–0 in Riga and beating Lithuania 1–0 in Vilnius the following week.

By the time we got to our second to last game, against Spain in Dublin, we knew exactly what we had to do to qualify. A win over the Spaniards would be enough to put us out of reach of the rest and spare us the need to get a good result against Northern Ireland in Belfast the following month. That was the doomsday situation I wanted to avoid at all costs. Local derbies are a great leveller in football, and while we had beaten Northern Ireland without too much hassle in Dublin, I sensed it would be a lot different when we got to Windsor Park. The Troubles were still claiming lives in Northern Ireland, and with no travelling support to help us, I didn't want to have to go there scrambling for points. To that extent, it was absolutely essential that we beat the Spaniards, and after handling them so comfortably in Seville, I was confident we would do just that.

The atmosphere in the ground on the day was something else. More than three years on, the excitement and the sense of national pride which made Italia '90 so special for us still lingered. Now it seemed the whole country wanted to be with us on the day we would book our place for the finals in America.

So much for expectation. Spain had never been the best of travellers in international football, but they caught fire in the rain that day and simply destroyed us. They were a goal up after just twelve minutes, scored a second time when Alan Kernaghan got himself into trouble by refusing to do the simple thing in a tussle with Julio Salinas – and when Salinas scored again before half-time, there was just no way back.

There was a numbed silence in our dressing-room at half-time. After a good start, we'd been taken apart at the back by the Spaniards. We didn't usually give goals away easily, particularly in Dublin, but now we were three down at half-time.

We did a bit better in the second half, pulling a goal back through John Sheridan. While it looked no more than a consolation score at the time, it would prove very important when it came to totting up the goal difference after an eventful night in Belfast four weeks later.

Because of that disaster against Spain, we now needed to beat Northern Ireland to make certain of going to America. A draw could still qualify us on goal difference – but only if Spain beat Denmark in the other game in the group, being played in Seville on the same night.

As I've said, I was deeply apprehensive about the trip to Belfast. Even by the worst standards of the Troubles, the weeks leading up to the game were disturbing, with a lot of shootings and killings. At one point, there was a lobby to have the match taken out of Belfast and played elsewhere. Far from solving anything, that kind of publicity merely aggravated the situation.

The football authorities, the security chiefs, and the people themselves wanted the game to be played in Windsor Park. And they said that even if it meant surrounding the stadium with a ring of steel, they would keep it there. That was precisely what they did, on a night which will forever live in the memory.

Then there was Billy Bingham. Bill was an old friend of mine, a man I respected both as a player and manager. He had earned himself a special place in the affection of his people by taking Northern Ireland to the final stage of two World Cups, but now, after a long spell in the job, he was quitting. Billy had been hurt by that 3–0 defeat in Dublin, not just by the scoreline but by the fact that his team didn't perform on the day. Now he wanted to wipe the slate clean and go out with a win which would satisfy the punters.

Fair enough. I could understand his feelings perfectly. But some of the things he said and did were over the top. For one thing, he was quoted in the papers describing our players as carpet-baggers. That hurt. I didn't mind him having a go at me, but for reasons which I have already stated, I would not have anybody disparage my players. Worse still was his attitude at the game. I didn't actually see the incident, but reports next day suggested that when he came out to take his place on the bench for the second half, he deliberately started to wind up the crowd. Not that they needed any encouragement. I have never seen a more hostile crowd anywhere – not even in Turkey – and they rained abuse on us from start to finish.

Still, we were never in trouble in a very competitive game, until out of the blue Jimmy Quinn volleyed a tremendous twenty-five-yard drive past Packie Bonner. The place erupts, and as we turn around in disbelief, Jimmy Nichol, Billy's assistant, gestures rudely at Maurice and shouts, 'Up yours!'.

Now things like that are not done in football. There is rivalry and rivalry, but insults are never traded between the benches. And Maurice, fuming, looks at me and says, 'Did you see what that prat has just done?'

I told him to forget it. There was bugger all we could do about it, anyway. We needed to get a goal back, and we did when Alan McLoughlin, who had come on as a replacement for Ray Houghton, fitted one in from just outside the box. It was a lovely goal, a lovely finish, made all the sweeter by the message I got at the end of the game that Spain had won 1–0 in Seville.

Smashing! After hugging my players, I was asked to do a piece for television on the pitch. The guy points to a monitor where they're showing pictures of the Spanish game. And my first question is, 'Why are they showing highlights when the match has just finished?'

And then he tells me that the game is still in progress. The Danes are chasing the equalizer that would put us out of the finals. Suddenly, my mind goes back to the European match in Istanbul, and from the elation I felt after being told we'd qualified, I'm now terrified that history will repeat itself. Fortunately, it didn't. Spain hung on, and we went through on goal difference.

I spotted Billy talking to his players and moved in his

direction to congratulate him on his retirement and compliment him on a good game. At least, that was my intention. Instead, in a moment I still find difficult to understand, I pointed a finger at him and blurted out, 'Up yours too, Billy.'

The words are no sooner out than I'm regretting them. For one thing, it wasn't him who uttered the original remark. And even if he had, I'd no right to act as I did. He just looked at me and turned away, dumbfounded. And I realized I'd gaffed, yet again.

Afterwards, I made it my business to seek him out, barging in on his press conference with the remark, intended to be jocular, 'It's all right, Billy, I've not come to flatten you.' And Billy, competitive to the last, says, 'It's OK, Jack, you wouldn't be able to manage it, anyway.' Cheeky bugger!

The incredible thing is that, minutes later, I'm hauled into a room to make a presentation. To whom? Yes, you've guessed it, to Billy Bingham, on his retirement. And some of the people who'd been abusing me all evening are stood there cheering. I think that said it all about a crazy, noisy night.

23

STEPPING WESTWARDS

One of the great blessings I've enjoyed in life is good health. Football injuries, yes, loads of them, but I've never had to spend a day in bed sick, never had to get a doctor out to look at me.

People who have been unlucky enough to get frequent illnesses probably know the score – but when you've been fit all your life and you suddenly feel unwell, you tend to panic. And that was my experience in Spain in January 1994.

I have a little house in Altea, just outside Benidorm – nothing fancy or elaborate, just a nice Spanish building set in a quiet village, with a couple of bars and restaurants around the corner. Pat and I like to go there to get away from the winter in Northumberland, but rarely, if ever, visit during the rest of the year. It's not the place to be in the summer when the weather gets very hot – but I tell you something, it can be a very attractive option when the wind is howling and the rain is belting down in Newcastle in January.

Dave McBeth, an old pal of mine, and his wife Maggie joined us in Altea that year, and the night before we were due to go home, we stayed indoors and watched a local game on the telly. Afterwards the talk stayed on football, and over a glass of whisky, we got to talking about different people in the game. I was trying to think of the name of a lad who had played for Arsenal for nine or ten years. I could visualize the player in my mind, but could I think of his name? Not a chance. I tried to ring home to check out some record books, but there was nobody there. Eventually, Dave said he'd call it a night – but for me, it was only just beginning.

I closed my eyes and tried to relax, to get it out of my mind, but I couldn't. It just kept coming back to me, coming back and tormenting me – a simple bloody matter of remembering a guy's name! It was near mid-night, and I decided to go for a walk along the pebble beach in the hope of finding inspiration. I must have walked for a mile or so, and then I got it. Brian . . . Brian Rix! No, not Brian Rix – Graham Rix. And I'm delighted, it's like a weight off my shoulders. Now I can get back to the house and sleep.

That, as it turned out, was easier said than done. All night long, my mind kept throwing up pictures and inviting me to put names to them. And in many instances, I couldn't. It was the same the next day, as if my brain was tuned in to a computer which kept say-ing, 'Get this one, now get this one.' And I think I'm cracking up.

The first thing I did when I got back to Newcastle the next day was to visit a local doctor. My ear had been giving me trouble and the doctor washed it out for me. But now my head hurt, my face hurt, and my throat felt horrible. I had to go to Dublin on FAI busi-ness shortly afterwards and decided to have a word with Dr Martin Walsh, medical consultant to the Irish team. I mentioned the fact that I was in some pain. Eventually, the diagnosis was that the wax in my ear had become compacted, and once it was removed, I certainly felt a lot more comfortable. But the messages in my mind still kept coming back. I booked myself into the Mater Hospital for a full check-up – blood tests, blood pressure, and even a brain scan. That was a bit frightening, but thankfully, everything was in order.

It was only after I had gone back for the specialist's report and talked things over with him for an hour that I got a handle on the problem. In his opinion, I was simply working too hard, and I was completely over-stressed. It was not the work I had done but rather the jobs that lay ahead which were the problem. We went through my diary – and between travelling to football meetings in Europe and America, preparing the team for games, after-dinner speaking engagements and tele-vision work, I didn't have a free day until after the World Cup finals four months ahead.

The specialist advised me to cancel everything for a month, but I told him I couldn't do that. Any job I'd ever accepted, I'd fulfilled, on the basis that if you give a commitment, you are duty bound to keep it. But he was adamant that unless I dropped everything, I was headed for even bigger trouble.

Among other things, that meant I had to cancel FIFA meetings in America and Zurich, where they were discussing the rules and regulations of the com-petition. They thought I was deliberately ignoring them – but hell, this was serious.

I contacted my agents and informed them that I was opting out of everything. For the next month, I did nothing but walk. I walked in the country, along rivers, in the hills, took my mother out for a bit of lunch – and suddenly I'm a new man. My mind is clear, no more messages, nothing except peace. And the feeling is wonderful.

I am not a nervous person, but that experience frightened me. Had I just stuck to football, it would have been fine. But I was travelling all over the country giving talks, sometimes at my wit's end trying to make plane and train arrangements that would get me from one venue to the next. And eventually, it took its toll.

That taught me a lesson which I'll never forget. There is only so much anybody, even the strongest, can do. And from that day, I've always insisted on keeping at least some free days in my diary.

It was a bad start to a year in which I had to prepare a team for the biggest competition of all. But within a couple of weeks of getting back into harness, I had pulled off something of a coup by adding players like Gary Kelly, Phil Babb, Tommy Coyne and Jason McAteer to my squad. I was acutely conscious that I needed more depth to get us through our programme in America. It was now obvious that the knee injury which Niall Quinn had sustained three months earlier would not heal in time, and in that situation I went to Celtic and persuaded Tommy Coyne to come and join us. One of my greatest regrets with the Irish team was that I never had a forward with pace. John Aldridge worked wonders for us in a role which was totally different to the one he filled for his club, but he'd be the first to admit that in his latter days, he lacked that little extra acceleration to get away from markers.

Coyne didn't have that kind of pace either, but he was excellent at holding the ball until the support arrived. And since I was now beginning to think in terms of going with a fifth midfielder and only one up front, that was an important asset.

Young Jason McAteer didn't know a lot about the game at the time, but I was impressed by his ability to run and run when I went to watch him at Bolton. That was the essence of our match plan and I reckoned he could fit into it. I remember the day I travelled to talk to him at Burnden Park – and I got the shock of my life when I discovered that my old pal, Jimmy Armfield, was there in front of me. Jimmy was now working for the FA, and obviously alerted to my interest in the player, he was trying to tie him to England by offering him an Under-21 cap. So I took McAteer aside and spelled out the facts of life to him. He could go and take his England Under-21 cap and, in a very competitive set-up, he might even get to making a couple of appearances in the senior team. If, on the other hand, he came to us, I could pretty well guarantee him an international career lasting anything up to ten years. That was an offer which was too good to turn down, and there and then, he said he'd throw in his lot with the Irish.

Unlike the days when I first took the job and struggled to get the right kind of fixture, we now had an attractive programme in place to ensure that when we arrived in America, we would be sharp and ready for action. In addition to home games against Russia, Bolivia and the Czech Republic, we were due to play in Holland and Germany. And if I needed proof that Ireland had now grown up among the big boys in international football, that was it.

The game against the Dutch was played in a little town called Tilburg, so small in fact that we'd a hell of a job getting the coach out of the place after the game. By that stage, however, we didn't really care, for we'd gone and won the match 1–0, a bloody good result when you considered the quality of the team the Dutch put out against us.

It was even better in Hanover the following month, when we played Germany in their last home game before they set off for America to defend the World Cup. There is always something special about games with the Germans. They have good players, a good system and anything you get out of a game with them, you earn. With a crowd of 54,000 jammed into the stadium to send them on their way to the States, I realized they would be more competitive than ever in this one.

Unfortunately, there were more problems with Paul McGrath. He'd missed a number of games for Aston Villa towards the end of the season through injury, but that wasn't my only worry. I felt Paul, for all his enormous talent, was already beginning to struggle, and I wondered if he'd make it through the finals. He had been our best player in Italy four years earlier, but the reports coming back to me from Villa Park weren't good. I needed to know the kind of shape he was in for America – and what better testing place than Hanover?

As it happened, Paul had a great game against the best the Germans could throw at him. The team played exceptionally well, and we came out with a great 2–0 win, thanks to goals from Tony Cascarino and young Gary Kelly. I have never placed too much importance on the results of friendly games, but we'd just gone and beaten two of the superpowers in Europe away from home. I wouldn't go as far as saying that we won with ease, but we showed that we could handle them. And it was deeply reassuring at that particular time.

It was unfortunate that I hadn't been well enough to go to the FIFA meeting in Zurich back in February, because they introduced a number of stupid changes there which would handicap us in America. If I'd been able to go, I could have said my piece against them – not that FIFA tend to listen to the views of managers or players anyway.

Within days of arriving in Orlando to start our acclimatization programme, I was bombarded with all kinds of fax messages from FIFA telling us what is and isn't permissible under the revised rules. Here I am, just a fortnight before our opening game against Italy, being lectured about 'the tackle'. And my first thoughts are – what tackle?

For years, they have been trying to eliminate the tackle from behind. Fair enough. We all know about that. But the impression you get from listening to the top brass these days is that they want to eliminate the tackle completely. And that's plain nonsense.

I remember Michel Platini suggesting something like this a few years ago. He said football should become a non-contact sport. It baffled me that a player of his stature could make a statement like that. The tackler is every bit as important to the game as the ball carrier. Bobby Charlton didn't become a great player by running through defences unopposed.

People often say to me, 'You were never as good a player as your kid.' I say, 'Well, no, I wasn't. I couldn't play like him. But I wasn't bad at stopping other people playing – which is just as much part of the game.' People tend to forget that defenders are entitled to try to win the ball, to tackle the players coming at them. These days if you're chasing somebody and you miss by a couple of inches, you get a yellow card. It's getting ridiculous when good, honest tackles get penalized like that. I mean, they're demeaning it. When I was a young lad, if we got a booking off the referee, we got a bollocking off the manager. He wanted to know what we'd done and why we'd done it. But it had to be a serious offence – not an honest mistake.

I'll tell you, I went to see a basketball game at Madison Square Garden, and I was amazed at what went on off the ball. I'd seen it on television many times, but I'd never been to see a live game. There were people jumping on each other, people having a go at each other – all this in a game that's supposed to be a non-contact sport! The television cameras just followed the ball, but never looked back to see what was going on at the other end.

The rules say that you can make a tackle, and providing you abide by them and the ball is there to be won, you can do it with as much physical contact as you like. Now FIFA seem to be standing the book on its head – and I, for one, am far from clear as to what is and isn't permitted.

More than that, they issued an ultimatum to referees that unless they implement the rules to the letter, they will be sent home on the next plane. What kind of legislation is that! If they think they're making it easier for the man in the middle, they're daft. Referees have to use their common sense to adjudicate, sometimes in a split-second, what's right and what's wrong. But cards are now being thrown about like confetti, just because match officials have to be seen to enforce the decisions of people who, in many instances, have never kicked a ball in their lives.

I went to see a game at Scarborough a couple of years ago, and I watched a winger send what we call a killer ball to his own full back. It was a ball that drew the full back into a tackle with someone running flat out towards him. The kid did his best, but it was a hell of a tackle and he went flying up in the air. When his head had cleared a bit, the lad got up and ran towards the winger who had dropped him in it. 'What kind of fucking ball is that?' he said. 'You nearly got me killed, you bastard' – or words to that effect. The linesman reported him to the referee for using foul and abusive language, and the referee waved a red card at him. I couldn't believe it – I mean, the boy was in shock. There's 'f' words used all the time now on television, there's 'f' words used in the movies – and yet if you use an 'f' word on the football field at somebody who's nearly got you killed, you get sent off!

Of course, if a player swears at a referee deliberately, then he's entitled to be punished. But not when you're involved in a game, not when you've got a lot of adrenalin going through your system and your mind is completely focused on a game of football. When somebody does something nasty to you then, you don't say, 'Oh, that was unlucky, you were tackling me a bit late.' If a player reacts in the heat of the moment, it's totally different from continuing when the whole thing has cooled down.

The players are the big losers in all of this, and I think it's high time that they were represented by some organization when the rules are being laid down for competitions like the World Cup. Back in the days of Jimmy Hill, the Professional Footballers' Association used its clout and got rid of the maximum wage in football. But because of the way the game has developed and the wages now being paid, it's lost its power. I mean, how do you tell guys earning crazy money in the Premiership that you are bringing them out on strike to make a point?

I've never been one for player power. But there are times when collective bargaining is needed, when new rules are being drafted to govern the way they do their job. There has to be a place at the table for players' representatives on those occasions – and that goes for referees as well. As things stand, if a ref has any sense and wants to improve his career prospects, he will bury his misgivings and toe the line. That is why I would appoint only referees in their last year before retiring to officiate in the big championships. That way, they could apply the rules as they saw them, without fear or favour.

The controversy over 'the tackle' was the biggest talking-point during that first week in Orlando preparing for the finals. But there was a second rule change around the same time – and, sadly, it had far greater implications for us.

The new rule banned the goalkeeper from handling the ball when it was played back to him by a team-mate. The effect on our game plan was profound. As I've said, our tactic when the ball was knocked forward was to condense the playing area as quickly as possible by pushing out from the back. Now, instead of taking the ball in his hands and waiting to see where he would place his clearance, thus giving us time to regroup, the opposing keeper was forced to hoof it back out as far as he could into the other half of the pitch. The ball could now be played in behind us – and from a situation in which we generally had that area all locked up, they suddenly began to run through us, and we had to give ground.

For the greater part of nine years, the opposition had struggled to find an answer to our method. Now, unwittingly, they found it in a bloody rule change. And we suffered accordingly.

Part of the reason for going to train in Orlando was to assess the effects of dehydration from playing in temperatures of 110 degrees plus. And it was frightening. I mean, a player could lose between four and five pounds in body weight in a forty-five-minute session. Given the fact that we were due to play Mexico there, that was, at best, disturbing.

Before travelling out, we had received a letter from FIFA's medical commission on the subject, advising managers that players should be allowed water at regular fifteen-minute intervals during a game. Otherwise, they said, there was a danger that they could slip into a coma. Imagine my astonishment, then, to discover on our arrival in America that we were forbidden to give players water, except in designated areas immediately in front of the dugout! That was fine for players on that side of the pitch, but what about those playing in the middle or on the opposite wing? How could we get a drink to them?

To make matters worse, a player taking a knock, no matter how slight, was obliged, on pain of a yellow card, to jump on a trolley and be treated off the pitch. This was supposed to save time, because some stupid statistician had worked out that we ought to have something like sixty-eight minutes' play in the course of a game! That's OK in a cooler country like England, but it doesn't make sense in the baking heat of Florida. Of course, they didn't really introduce this for the sake of the spectators or the players, they did it at the insistence of the television schedulers. It meant that we now couldn't get on even during normal stoppage times to hand out water.

I created hell about that, and at every press conference made the point that FIFA was putting players at unnecessary risk. The surprising thing was that I appeared to be the only manager challenging the situation. Now, whether that was because people like Berti Vogts, Arrigo Sacchi or Carlos Alberto Parreira had guys in their national federations who did those things for them, I don't know. But effectively, I ran the show in Ireland. I was responsible for the welfare of players who had been loaned to me by their clubs, and I was determined to honour that responsibility by ensuring they were not exposed to any unnecessary risks. I made a lot of headlines for standing up alone for what I thought was right, but it didn't ingratiate me with the power-brokers.

Five days before we were due to open our programme against Italy in the Giants Stadium in New Jersey, I went to see Northern Ireland play Mexico in a friendly in Miami. It was a nothing match, but the referee, incredibly, still insisted on refusing the players water in the boiling hot sunshine. And I tell you something, I was seething with rage. It was bloody ridiculous! Maybe, just maybe, the Latin teams could get away without an intake of liquid, but certainly not those from Northern Europe. There was never any great pace on in the game, but at the finish the Northern Ireland players were absolutely knackered. I looked down at Bryan Hamilton, their new manager, and I suspect that he was just as angry as I was. Surely, football was never meant to be like this?

The only silver lining was that we were playing our first game in New Jersey, and unless the barometer went through the roof, the temperature wouldn't be as high as we had experienced in Florida. Well . . . I was half right. On the day of the game, it was well into the nineties, and that made the job of beating the Italians even harder.

By any standard, it was a remarkable game. For one thing, the setting was like nothing else I'd ever experienced. It's not often that Italians are outnumbered in New York, but take it from me, this was one of them. I mean, there must have been 40,000 Irish people from all over the world in the stadium, and hell, did they make their presence felt! It was carnival time all the way, and, of course, we got the result we wanted. The game had only been on for ten or twelve minutes when Ray Houghton pulled down a bad clearance by Franco Baresi, and from the edge of the box chipped the goalkeeper, sweet as a nut. Six years earlier, I had seen Ray produce another crucial goal against England at roughly the same stage of the game, and I remembered how we had sat and suffered for the remainder of the match, minute by agonizing minute. But not this time.

From there on, we gave every bit as good as we got, and should have had a second goal when John Sheridan, taking a superb pass from Roy Keane, thumped the ball against the crossbar. Bloody great stuff. Out there playing us was one of the most respected teams in the world – and yet we handled them comfortably. Paul McGrath, the same Paul whom I fretted about for so long, was magnificent; Roy Keane and Andy Townsend got among the Italians in midfield; and up front, Tommy Coyne was bravery itself.

Within days of setting down in America, I had lost Tony Cascarino with a hamstring problem, and that, on top of the absence of Niall Quinn, was a terrible blow. I thought about playing John Aldridge in his place, but in the belief that Coyne was better equipped for the job of taking on the Italian defence on his own, I went for Tommy. And he was brilliant. He was the one who got under the high ball, knocked it back to the midfielders, and literally ran himself to a standstill in the process. Sadly, he would pay the price for those heroics.

We got through the remainder of the game safely, and the feeling of elation at the end was something else. Ireland had beaten Italy for the first time in eight meetings between the countries – more than that, we had outplayed one of the favourites for the competition. And did it feel good!

They still talk about the parties among the Irish in America that night, but I saw none of them. I stayed overnight in New Jersey to catch a flight to Washington where two other teams in the group, Mexico and Norway, were playing the following day. And with hindsight, that was probably just as well.

It was only after a phone call to the Irish team hotel the following morning that I discovered Tommy Coyne had been taken ill after the game. I nearly flipped. Tommy, as I've said, had run himself into the ground, and, unfortunately, his was the name which came out in the lottery to give a urine sample after the game. The lad was dehydrated to the point where he couldn't pee into the bottle. So they gave him water . . . and more water. So much water, in fact, that they apparently flooded his kidneys, and he was taken ill, very ill. That evening, he had to be wheeled onto the plane bringing the squad back to Florida, had to be given constant attention on the plane, and, not surprisingly, spent the next forty-eight hours in bed. And to think that those silly buggers who make the rules could get away with this!

My sense of outrage was even greater when I got to the stadium in Washington later in the day. I was seated in the VIP area, nicely shaded of course, with Dr Joao Havelange, FIFA's President, just two rows in front of me. He can't have been unaware of my presence for people were coming up and standing in front of him to take pictures of me. But never once did he turn around to acknowledge me. He obviously doesn't like people who speak their minds on his favourite game!

That didn't bother me one bit, but the general set-up in the place certainly did. As I've said, we were shaded from the sun, but from the moment we arrived, we were plied with bottles of all kinds of liquids. And then to compound matters, a girl brings around iced towels so that we can cool our heads. We're just sat there watching the game – and FIFA, in their wisdom, see fit to cool us off! But what about the poor buggers down on the pitch running their guts out? Are they not entitled to some consideration?

That trip cost me a night's sleep, for the plane out of Washington was cancelled because of thunderstorms. When I eventually got to Atlanta en route to Orlando, I discovered that there were no hotel beds available in the city. So I spent the night lying on a hard bench, afraid to go asleep in case somebody tried to pinch my bag.

Still, it was worth it. On my arrival at base, I discovered that my little crusade had not gone unnoticed. FIFA were now prepared to allow water bags to be thrown onto the pitch, and the players, if they were quick enough or lucky enough, could have a drink before the damn things burst. It was a ludicrous solution to a ludicrous problem, but I wasn't going to argue about it. We were due to play Mexico in Orlando in six days' time – and that scared the hell out of me. The Mexicans were used to the heat, lived and trained at altitude, and whatever chance they had of coping with a noon kick-off, we had precious little.

My first instinct on waking up on the morning of the game was to peep out through the curtains. The blood drained from my face at what I saw. Far from the cloud cover we were looking for to give us some protection from the sun, there wasn't a break in the blue sky. Now I knew for certain that we would struggle for a result.

When we got to the horseshoe-shaped stadium, they measured the ground temperature on the grass at 120 degrees. It was just appalling.

Officially, we were now allowed to throw water bags onto the pitch, but only from a designated area in front of the benches. And that still didn't address the problem of how we were to get them to players in the middle or on the other side of the pitch. Then somebody showed me a copy of the new rules where it said, quite specifically, that water bags could be thrown from behind the touchlines. Plural! I showed this to the FIFA guy and he said, 'No, no.' But I dug in, and eventually, by sheer persistence, got him to accept my point.

So I sent my son Peter and Larry Quinn, a member of the FAI staff, to the far side with hundreds of the bloody things. But still there were problems. In spite of the rule, the security people wouldn't let them anywhere near the line. Eventually, they ended up standing just in front of the crowd, having to throw the bags fifteen or twenty yards to the players. It was chaotic. Players were standing on them, grabbing them when they could. On one occasion, Houghton had one in his hand when the ball was played to him.

So what did the referee do? He blew for a free and gave Ray a yellow card into the bargain. It was that damn stupid!

My players were brave, but gradually, inevitably, the Mexicans got on top. They were leading 2–0 when I decided, well into the second half, to take off Tommy Coyne and Stephen Staunton and send on Jason McAteer and John Aldridge in a double substitution.

I'm following the play, and a good three or four minutes must have elapsed before I look around and see that Aldo is still on the touchline. He's trying to get on the pitch, but a guy has a hold of him, and John is shouting at him – 'You're a cheat, a fucking cheat!'

I honestly don't now what's happening, and as I walk to the edge of the rectangle in which I'm supposed to stay, this FIFA fellow in a blue coat and yellow hat comes towards me and shouts, 'You get back!'

'What's the problem?' I ask.

The answer is exactly the same, 'Get back, I'm going to report you to FIFA for this.' At that point he pushed me – but though I felt mad as hell by now, I buried my pride and retreated as ordered. The incident received worldwide coverage on television – and to this day, people still ask me what the real story was.

Well, this is it. If I wished to make a substitution, I would tell Charlie O'Leary, one of our technical staff. He would fill out a form with the name of the replacement and the player to be substituted, I would sign it, and then it would be handed to the fourth official. Only in cases of a dispute would the form be given to the fifth guy, the fellow in the yellow hat, and in that situation, he would pick up a phone beside the bench, call somebody back in the office and confirm that the player in question was properly registered.

The trouble in this instance arose because our friend in the yellow hat, an Egyptian, took the form from Charlie, and without reference to the fourth official, went directly to the phone to check. That was out of order. And the problem was compounded, apparently, by the fact that he couldn't pronounce the name Aldridge. The guy back in the office wasn't able to clear John because he couldn't find the name on the official list of players he'd been given. And so for three or four minutes, we were forced to play with only ten players – and I was once more in FIFA's bad books.

As it happened, we got a goal back through Aldridge. His goal meant that a draw in the next game against Norway would be good enough to see us through. We were denied a draw only by a flying save from the Mexican keeper, Jorge Campos, off a shot by Andy Townsend in the last minute.

I felt cheated by the fact that we were forced to play the Mexicans in conditions which gave them a huge advantage, and I felt even sorer the next day when I got back to the hotel and was informed by newsmen that I had been fined £7,000 by FIFA and banned from the bench for our next game against Norway. 'What for?' I asked. As far as I was concerned, I had done nothing wrong. The bloody Egyptian had been the culprit and was guilty of any violence there was, by pushing me.

After a meeting with some FAI officials, we decided to send a faxed message back to FIFA requesting clarification, on the basis that since they didn't specify my offence, I was liable to repeat it. And I'm still awaiting a reply!

What happened on the touchline that day was none of my making. I suspect that FIFA, in their petty way, were paying me back for the hassle I had caused them over the water. For that, I make no apologies. I acted solely in the best interests of my players – and others – and to hell with the consequences.

The interesting sequel to the fine was that as soon as it was announced publicly, supporters organized whip-rounds in the pubs back in Ireland to pay it for me. I was well capable of forking out the money myself, but it was still a lovely gesture of support by the Irish people. Whatever happened to that money? The answer is I don't know. I certainly never saw it, and I'm afraid it caused me a certain amount of grief. I happened to mention to a newsman that if there was a fund available, some of it should go to the family of the Colombian player who had been shot on his return home after conceding an own goal in the competition. That attracted one particularly nasty letter from an individual who asked if I was forgetting the people who had been shot in a bar in Northern Ireland while watching our game against Italy on television. I was getting into a situation which had been none of my making, and I didn't like it. As I said, I don't know who raised the money or where it went, but I tell you something – I never paid the bloody fine.

Watching the match against Norway from a television commentary box was a bit unnerving. Not that I was unused to commentary positions, but when you're directly involved with a team, the remoteness is terrible. In fact, we handled that game quite well, and a scoreless draw was good enough to get us into the last sixteen against Holland back in Orlando. The Mexican game had left me with painful memories of the place, but on this occasion we were at least playing another European team. And if the sun again got high in the sky, they would suffer just as much as us.

In spite of the fact that we had beaten them in Tilburg just a couple of months earlier, I was wary of the Dutch. They had a lot of good players who could turn it on, and we needed to be very careful about letting them get at our back four.

Still, they caused us no problems at all, until a silly mistake by Terry Phelan turned the whole competition sour for us. Terry had ample time to knock the ball away, but instead he let it bounce and then, from a distance of twenty-five yards or more, attempted to head it back in the direction of Packie Bonner. There was never enough pace on the ball to enable him to do that, and Marc Overmars, reading the situation perfectly, was away and running. Phil Babb and Paul McGrath had been caught square by Phelan's gaffe, and when Overmars crossed, Dennis Bergkamp had a simple job in sliding in the first goal.

Crass carelessness had cost us a vital score, but if that was bad, even worse was to follow. There were at least five Irish players between Wim Jonk and the goal when he let one go from all of thirty yards. Whether Packie misread the line of the shot, or whether the ball swerved in the air, I'll never know. But instead of making the straightforward save, he allowed the ball to clip the top of his fingers, and it dropped ever so gently over the line for a second and clinching goal.

Packie, the hero of Italy four years earlier, had gifted them a dolly goal – but could I really blame him? No less than the other players in the squad, he had given me 100 per cent commitment, and I couldn't ask for anything more than that.

Yes, we underachieved in America, and after the great days of Italia '90, that was hard to accept. But I took solace from the fact that there hadn't been one single unsavoury incident involving any of our players during the finals, and I was immensely proud of that.

Me? To be honest I didn't really enjoy it. There was too much pressure, too many conferences and not enough time for the fun which normally carries you through competitions like that. By the time it was through, I had already decided that there would be no more World Cup finals for me.

Again we were welcomed home by cheering crowds, and this time the Taoiseach himself, Albert Reynolds, was there to shake my hand at the foot of the plane steps. It was a great party and I'm glad I went, even though it meant I had to fly back again to Dallas the next day to work for ITV.

Just before the World Cup finals, I was made a freeman of the City of Dublin, the first Englishman to be given the honour this century. The last fellow was apparently a plumbing contractor, who had been brought over to install a new sanitary system in the city in 1854. And since there was a rule in operation at the time that only citizens of Dublin could undertake major schemes like that, they made him a freeman of the city. According to the records, that allowed him to drive his sheep and pigs across any bridge leading into the city. Since I had no animals to herd, I asked the Lord Mayor, Tomas MacGiolla, if this meant I could now park on double-yellow lines. 'Not a chance,' he told me.

Still, it was a great occasion. There were thousands of people on the square at College Green, and I got a bit of a chuckle when I saw that the name on the scroll was John Charlton. Now the only person who ever called me John, I told them, was the head teacher at Hirst Park School in Ashington, when he'd invariably say, 'Bend over, John . . .'

It wasn't the first honour I was proud to receive from the Irish people. An earlier Taoiseach, Charlie Haughey, had made me an honorary Irishman, in a little function over a few drinks in his office. I always found Charlie a charming man, but he had a bit of a reputation as a wheeler-dealer. I'm in an Irish club one night conducting a question-and-answer session, and this fellow is giving me a bit of stick because I'm English. So I promptly tell him that I'm more Irish than he is – and that I've a slip of paper, presented by the Taoiseach himself, to prove it.

'Yeah,' he says, 'but did you read the small print on the back?'

24

GOODBYE TO ALL THAT

One raw winter's morning a few days before Christmas 1995 I finally realized that even football fairy tales have a habit of ending painfully.

I was sat in the back of a car with a camera pointing at me and a microphone stuck in my face, on my way to catch a flight from Dublin home to Newcastle. Given the high media profile I had attracted as manager of the Republic of Ireland squad, there was nothing unusual in that – until the car pulled up in front of the airport complex.

Then a guy, obviously rushing for an earlier flight than mine, spots me getting out of the car, and runs across to say, 'Thanks for all the good times. You've given us some great memories – I'm sorry to see you go.'

'Go'? Bloody hell, I'd had a few beers the previous night, but suddenly the full implications of the day's decisions came into focus. I realized that this was no ordinary leaving. After some of the happiest times of my life, I'd quit as the manager of the Republic of Ireland team – and forty-five years of passionate involvement in the game were over.

I'd arrived in Dublin the previous morning in the full knowledge that this was it, that the parting of the ways had finally arrived. And yet . . .

For days, I'd been going around with a lump in my chest – and I didn't need any doctor to tell me what was causing it. I knew I had one of the most difficult decisions of my career to make and I kept backing away from it.

From a long way back, I'd made up my mind that my term in charge of the team would end with our last game in the 1996 European championship. Whether that happened at the end of the qualifying rounds or in the finals was largely irrelevant. I was on my way into retirement.

I'd always said that when the 'get out' signs showed, I'd be the first to recognize them. I'd quit before I was pushed. In my heart of hearts, I knew I'd wrung as much as I could out of the squad I'd got – that some of my older players had given me all they had to give.

Maybe, just maybe, a good performance by the Irish in the European finals might have persuaded me that, heck, I'll give it another go and ride my luck all the way to the 1998 World Cup finals. But when Holland put us out of the European championship that night at Anfield, I knew that it was time for me to say goodbye. The question was when, and because of the uncertainty – partly, I have to say, of my own making – I ended up in a situation in which for the first time in almost ten years, I had aggro with the Football Association of Ireland.

It should never have come to that. For one thing, we should have qualified for the European finals. Halfway through our qualifying programme, I was absolutely certain that we would. But then we lost a couple of key players at vital times, and for a small outfit like ours that was ruinous. Ever since I took the job, I'd staked my reputation on building a squad in which I had at least one viable option in all eleven positions in the team. I prided myself on the fact that despite limited resources, we had achieved that. But then we lost players like Roy Keane, Andy Townsend, John Sheridan and Steve Staunton. From a position in which we were coasting through our programme, the wheels suddenly came off. With each consecutive game, I watched the old confidence disappear before my eyes. After losing three of our last four matches, I sensed that the show was almost over as we got ready to go to Liverpool for the meeting with the Dutch.

With that in mind, I sought out Louis Kilcoyne, President of the FAI, before the game. I told him I had decided that if we lost I would announce my resignation at the post-match press conference. He advised that I should wait and think things over before making a decision.

To be honest, I was glad to hear that. We were just a few days away from Christmas, and without sounding big-headed, this wasn't the kind of Christmas present I wanted to give our supporters. To me, they were the only people who really mattered. The FAI might send on the pay cheques each month and the players, bless them, were the most dedicated, loyal group of men that it had been my privilege to manage. But my real love affair was with the Irish public. They had taken me to their hearts from day one – an Englishman who, apart from the odd football tour with Leeds United and more frequent visits with my fishing rod, had no real affinity with their country before 1986. In the ten years that followed, I had grown to love the people of Ireland – and the flood of goodwill which flowed in my direction told me that the feeling was mutual. One for all, all for one, we were pretty well unstoppable on our day, and together we would leave our imprint on football stadiums across the world.

Footballers, by definition, are high-profile figures, and in my time I'd got my fair share of publicity. I'd been born into one of the best-known footballing families in England. Over twenty-three seasons, I'd earned my living with Leeds United, a marvellous club which Don Revie had built into the envy of Europe, if not the world. And when a letter arrived from the Football Association telling me that I'd been chosen to follow my brother Bobby into the England team, I was set on a course which would bring the ultimate fulfilment of winning a World Cup winner's medal for my country at Wembley in 1966.

To that extent, I'd achieved enough for any man. I didn't need the affection of a people I had known only as our neighbours across the water. But when it came, it was warm and it was generous. And I prized it as much as anything in my life.

The FAI might, for whatever reason, want me to go. The media might turn turtle, but the doomsday scenario for me was when ordinary Irish men and women would turn their heads the other way as I walked up the street. That, for me, would be the wages of failure. I resolved that in so far as it lay in my hands, it would never happen.

Pat and I had arranged to go to Spain for a holiday early in the New Year. That would give me time to think my position through and, almost certainly, to announce my decision to go at a time of my choosing. In a matter of only six or seven weeks, I would have punched in ten years in the job. It seemed the ideal time for any manager to say 'enough is enough'.

Of course, I still hoped and prayed that we could

beat the Dutch and go on to play in the finals of Euro '96. But in my heart of hearts, I knew that I was only whistling in the dark. Holland had the kind of quality which we didn't possess at the time, and when you looked at the morale in both camps, there could only be one result.

Even by Anfield standards, the atmosphere in the stadium that night was remarkable – but for all the goodwill pouring down on us, we were never in control of a game in which the Dutch played some superb football. We did have a couple of chances, but not enough of them to give us a realistic chance of going through.

Paul, at the back, did his best, but he was no longer the quick, mobile player who had held us together in other times. It didn't take the Dutch long to realize that he had slipped a long way from the form he had shown in America, and they lost no opportunity to exploit it. Patrick Kluivert, at nineteen almost half Paul's age, was far too sharp for him, and after opening the scoring with a superb strike, he sealed our fate with a second goal late in the game. There were no more more miracles left in the locker.

Back in the dressing-room, we knew that we had thrown it all away, not that night at Anfield, but in those disastrous earlier games against Liechtenstein and Austria. It was all there for the taking, and we spurned it, not just once but three times.

And I'm sat there thinking of what might have been, when the police come into the dressing-room and ask me to go out and acknowledge the crowd. They're still out there singing, and they won't leave until I've put in an appearance. The last thing in the world that I want to do at that moment is to go back on the park. We've just been beaten, we're out of the European championship, and I'm depressed. But if they're good enough to hang around for me, who am I to refuse to go out and wave to them?

They were singing 'The Fields of Athenry'. And when they came to the line 'We had dreams and songs to sing', the sense of nostalgia was so real that you could almost reach out and touch it. And that, perhaps, was the saddest moment of all. Although I hadn't said so publicly, they knew that this was the end. We'd had some marvellous times together. But now the party was over. And I felt a little tear go down the side of my cheek.

As I sipped a drink back in the team hotel, Kilcoyne sought me out and told me that if I was in Dublin over the next few weeks, to come and talk things over. No problem, I'd do that. Imagine my surprise, then, when within a couple of days of arriving back in Newcastle, I get a phone call from Kilcoyne instructing me to come to Ireland to confirm that I'm packing it in! He tells me that he's informed the FAI that I'm through.

'Hold on a minute,' I go, 'I never said that I was definitely quitting now – you only asked me to come and talk it over.' And then he delivers the final indignity, 'If you don't come to us, we'll come and see you.'

So this was it. After all the good times, all the relative success we'd enjoyed, they can't wait until after Christmas to see me go. If this was the way they wanted it, however, I wouldn't overstay my welcome. I'd travel as requested to Dublin and tell them what they wanted to hear.

I walked out of the arrivals lounge at the airport that morning determined to say my piece. I'd paid my dues over and over again. I'd done the job I said I'd do, and given them the kind of success that they had only dreamed of in the past. In the process, we'd put a lot of money in their coffers. And, ironically, it was to a football complex which I and the players had helped to fund from the proceeds of a big game at Lansdowne Road, that they took me for the fateful farewell, away from the glare of the television cameras.

There were four of them sat across the table at the meeting: Kilcoyne and three of the Association's vice-presidents, Joe Delaney, Michael Hyland and Pat Quigley. Des Casey, another vice-president, wasn't at the meeting. The decision to pressurize me into going now had been taken sometime earlier.

Without beating about the bush, I asked them if they, collectively, wanted me to go now – and not a word came back. So I pointed my finger at them individually, and once Kilcoyne had nodded his head, the others followed suit. Pat Quigley couldn't look me in the eye as he nodded.

In that moment, the great days seemed a million miles away. We'd soldiered together in some beautiful places – and now it was all coming apart in a dank, uninviting room that smelled faintly of last night's revelries. But if that was the way they wanted it, they could have it. Trevor O'Rourke and John Givens, my agents, were with me, and together we informed the people on the other side of the table that as soon as a joint statement for the press was agreed, we'd be off.

In a sense, I was relieved, yet just a little bewildered. I'm the first to admit that I was in some respects responsible for what had happened; had I not planted the idea in their minds in the first instance, I'm sure that they would never have acted as they did.

And yet, I have to admit that I left the meeting with

a sour taste in my mouth. Throughout the hour-long talks, there hadn't been one word of appreciation for the job I'd done – much less a mention of a going-away present.

Now the last thing I wanted to do was to give the people of Ireland the impression that I was in some way holding out for a pay-off. And I bitterly resented suggestion afterwards that this was in fact the case.

Six months earlier, Michael Hyland had come to me and said that it was the Association's intention to stage a Jack Charlton testimonial game. It would be testimonial with a difference, however, inasmuch as I wouldn't get a penny from it. The proceeds would go into something like a Jack Charlton School of Excellence, for young boys coming into the game. I didn't say yes and I didn't say no. But had they decided to go ahead with it, I would almost certainly have fallen in with the idea.

People in the trade will tell you that I'm not short of a few quid. I've worked hard, bloody hard for my money. But with my hand on my heart, I can say that I've never, ever argued about money in all my time in football. I never fell out with Don Revie over money, nor with any of the three clubs I managed when I quit playing, Middlesbrough, Sheffield Wednesday or Newcastle United. And in 1986, I took the Ireland job for a salary which, in comparison with the going rate for other national team managers, was a pittance.

Unlike so many others, I wasn't paid a penny when I left the clubs I managed. Nor did I expect it. In all three instances, I left of my own volition, and in that situation, compensation is not normally forthcoming.

It was the same with the Irish. I was leaving of my own free will; though after all we'd achieved, I felt that a gesture of appreciation – and all I needed was a gesture – was in order. But it didn't happen.

But if I didn't push my own case particularly hard, I certainly did for my assistant, Maurice Setters. Unlike me, he wanted to keep his job. And I rejected their suggestion that he was my employee rather than theirs. Maurice could have done with a pay-off, for it was only in his later years in the job that he had goodish money. In his case, a severance settlement was definitely owing.

Newspaper reports the next day suggested that I'd been pushed – and that upset me a lot. I've never had the sack in my life – and the FAI most certainly didn't sack me. As I've said, I'd been planning to go for some time. And yet I felt let down by people whom I had regarded as friends. I simply couldn't believe that this was the way it would end – that the day would come when they would be glad to see the back of me.

There is no question, absolutely no question, that I had left home that morning determined to quit. After ten years in the job, it was time for new ideas. My successor – whoever he might be – would need time to settle into the job and get as many games as possible under his belt before venturing into the next World Cup campaign.

But even when you're bent on going, you somehow like to think that they'll try to persuade you to stay.

A couple of days earlier, I had talked to Des Casey on the phone. He told me that the Irish public thought it was time for me to go. With respect to Des, this turned out to be untrue. So why did they want to get rid of me now, why did they insist on dragging me to Dublin at a time when, contrary to their insistence, there was no immediate urgency attached to my resignation?

369

I don't know the answer to that. But a friend told me later – and perhaps he wasn't a million miles from the truth – that after all the popularity the players and I had enjoyed, the FAI wished to be seen to be in control at the end.

If I felt let down by my employers in the Football Association of Ireland, the reaction of the people in the street that day told me all I needed to know. It was common knowledge in Dublin that I was in town to discuss my retirement. On the journey into the city from the meeting, they left me in no doubt where their loyalties lay. I had made it clear that my greatest ambition was to enjoy the confidence of the public on the day of my departure. Now the evidence of that was everywhere to be seen. Motorists who had spotted the car in which I was travelling fell in behind, and for the last mile or so of the journey we formed a noisy motorcade that can only have mystified visitors to the city on that damp morning. At one point, even a policeman on point duty left his station and came across to tell me how sorry he was that I was going.

Coincidentally, John Major was in Dublin the same day for a meeting with the Irish Prime Minister, John Bruton. Streets had been closed off and barricades erected because of his visit. But I read in the paper next day that it hadn't occasioned half the interest of my little cameo. When it came right down to it, I could console myself with the thought that I was going as I always hoped I would, with the Irish people cheering me.

EPILOGUE: THICKER THAN WATER?

The phone rang as I sat in my hotel bedroom in Sardinia, just twenty-four hours before we opened our 1990 World Cup programme against England. It was our kid.

'What are you ringing for?' I asked.

'I just thought I'd give you a call and wish you all the best for the game,' was the reply.

'Wait a minute,' I said. 'You're an Englishman and we're playing England. You've never made contact to wish me well before. Why now?'

My reaction seemed to surprise him as much as his call had surprised me. It showed how distant the two of us had become, how we had grown apart and gone our different ways over the years.

It's a subject which has fascinated the press for a long time. Without being boastful, I think it's fair to say that we're the most famous brothers in English football, perhaps two of the best-known brothers in the entire country.

But we've rarely been seen together in public, even less when it came to socializing. And that has intrigued some of the media. There have been little hints here and there that all was not well in the family, but neither Robert nor I has ever gone public about it – until now.

I knew I would never be allowed to get away without alluding to my relationship with my brother in my autobiography, and I thought it was time to put the record straight. He, almost certainly, will have his version of the story, but I have tried to tell it as honestly and as openly as I can.

So, where do we stand after all these years, what is the relationship between the brothers who played alongside each other on the greatest day for English football? In a couple of words – not good. And that saddens me greatly!

It was all so very different when we were growing up. Sure, we had different interests, sure he was a lot more reserved than I was – but he was my kid brother. I was in charge of him, my mother wanted me to look after him. When his talent began to blossom no-one could have been prouder of him than his elder brother Jack. And as young pros making our way in the game, we remained very close, even though he was with a glamour club and I was with struggling Second Division Leeds United.

Jealousy? I never had a jealous thought about Robert in my life. He was an extremely gifted player, perhaps one of the five best in the history of the game. And me? I never had any illusions that I could be that good. There was never any doubt about where I stood in the pecking order.

I hugged him with delight when he won his first cap for England, I cheered for him when Manchester United beat Benfica in the European Cup final, I cried for him on that terrible day when a great team was almost wiped out in the Munich air disaster. In a way, Robert was never the same lad to me after Munich. How it affected him, how it coloured his thinking, I don't know. But I saw a big change in our kid from that day on. He stopped smiling, a trait which continues to this day. Friends occasionally come up to me and say, 'Your Bob goes around as if he has the weight of the world on his shoulders' – and I have to agree. He's had a great playing career, a good life and his business is doing well. I would say that he doesn't smile as much as somebody in his position should.

Before the disaster, he'd often come over to Leeds on Sunday mornings and we'd have a couple of pints together. Often he'd bring some of his team-mates with him. Afterwards he'd drive us – I didn't have a car at the time – up to see our parents in Ashington. He loved the place then, loved seeing his mother and father, enjoyed the sense of family. And then it all went sour.

Our Robert was the apple of my mother's eye. Like the rest of us, she was proud that her son had done so well in the game, proud that he carried himself so well, both on and off the pitch. And was she protective! On those occasions when we played Manchester United, she'd issue me with instructions: 'Now, don't you go kicking our Robert today.' And I never did. I do remember one occasion, though, when he nutmegged me and I chased him back towards our goal, yelling, 'Come back, you little bugger. Don't even think about putting that in our net!'

But gradually Robert withdrew more and more into himself. There was an incident in our house in Ashington one day when I sensed that he was beginning to drift away. The men in our family always had problems with losing hair. Robert lost his between the ages of twenty-four and twenty-eight, and my other brothers later went thin on top at roughly the same age. This incident I'm describing must have happened when Robert was still in his early twenties. We're all sat there having a meal when young Tom, who was only a boy at the time, remarked to Robert that he was going bald. Our Bob just put his head down and said, 'Yeah,' but I could see he was upset.

Not that a head of hair is all that important, but I suppose you're self-conscious at that age. Strangely enough, my mother was always highly sensitive about it too, and she once thumped a Scottish supporter who called Robert a 'baldy git'.

Perhaps that was the moment when our Bob began to distance himself from the family. The more significant thing by far, however, was his marriage in the early 1960s. Robert's wife, Norma, never really got on with our mother.

There was an incident at Old Trafford which didn't help matters. My parents had become good friends of Matt Busby and Jimmy Murphy after Robert had signed for Manchester United, and occasionally they'd get invitations to go and watch a game. Now, there wasn't a telephone in our house in Ashington – my father never used a telephone – and any communications between them and Manchester United would be conducted by letter. If they ever needed to contact either Robert or me by phone, they would use a public one. And that didn't happen very often.

Matt or Jimmy invited them to Old Trafford on this occasion and, out of the blue, they happened to bump into Robert. Instead of being pleased to see them, he went mad. 'What are you doing here?' he said. 'Don't ever come here again unless I tell you.' Now that was out of order, totally out of order. I've no idea why our Robert reacted the way he did, but it threw my mother. She couldn't understand it.

When my father and my uncle Tommy Skinner went to stay with Robert and Norma after going to watch a game at Old Trafford, Robert put them in a hotel, saying they had the decorators in. The story about the decorators might have been true – but neither my father nor my uncle Tommy Skinner wanted to go back after that.

I don't understand Norma. At one time I got on quite well with her. I'd occasionally drop a fish or a pheasant into the house at Knutsford and we'd have breakfast or a cup of tea. She was very pleasant when you spoke to her at home. On the odd occasion that I met her at Old Trafford or places like that, she was a different woman. I don't know why.

People who act one way in private and another in public tend to throw me off-balance. It became a situation in which I didn't feel comfortable and I never went back to their house after that.

My mother and father later moved into a house I had bought in the Dales. Then, after my father died in 1982, she moved back to Ashington.

For six or seven years before she died, my mother saw little if anything of our Robert. He'd be in the area, opening a supermarket or something, and the neighbours would say to her, 'I see Bobby was in Newcastle at the weekend, did he visit?' She'd have to admit that he didn't. And that must have hurt her no end. I'd get annoyed about it. Even when he came to Ashington itself, within hailing distance of the house, it seemed he never called round.

Now, I don't know what it was between Robert and my mother. Norma said she never influenced him, and I believed her. But the rift affected the family terribly. I couldn't understand it. I'd sometimes ask my mother,

375

but she was very, very loath to talk about it.

I can't be a reader of my brother's mind. Maybe he doesn't think about family the way that I do. Maybe as a bit of a mother's boy he needed to cut the apron strings. These are the questions I've posed again and again over the years . . .

Eventually, my mother went into a home. She was getting unsteady on her feet and on one occasion, she nearly burned herself. But still not a word from our Robert. I tried to get him to go and see her, even phone her, send a card. And he just said, 'I'll do it when I think the time is right. I'll run my life the way I see it, and I'll do what I want to.'

But of course I still hoped I could persuade him to go and see our mother. I caught hold of him finally at a hotel one night in London, took him to one side and tried to lay it on the line as urgently as I could. 'Listen,' I said, 'I'm sick of bloody arguing with you about going to see our mother. I don't want to mention it again. It's down to your conscience.'

She desperately wanted him to go and see her. But he never did.

He did turn up on the day of her funeral, and I was pleased about that. I thanked Norma, too, for I didn't want anything to happen that would take away from our mother's funeral. By this time, the press were aware that something was wrong, and they were only too ready to make a meal of it.

Apart from the way he treated our mother, I don't hold any bad feelings towards him, even though I thought he could have been more supportive when I was being vilified over the black book episode. He knew that I was never a dirty player, and he could have spoken publicly in my defence. But he chose to hold his peace. He's always been loath to say anything which will upset anybody.

It wasn't always like that, as I've said, and there was one incident, well publicized, in the infamous World Cup game against Argentina at Wembley which proved it. I was knocked down after going for a corner kick and the Argies are standing on me and kicking me to bits. Suddenly, the kicking stops. I look up to see our kid standing guard over me. When it comes right down to it, I suppose, blood is thicker than water. That was in 1966.

After we finished playing, Robert went his way and I went mine. He once told me that he wanted to be part of the governing body in football, to have a say in the decisions which affected the game and, generally, to have an input at the top level. Although he managed Preston North End for a while, Robert was never a coach, always sharing the Manchester United philosophy that they didn't need Lilleshall, they would play the game the way they wanted to play it. I, of course, was different. I valued my coaching badges, and I felt they made the vital difference when it came to management.

When you're striving for the things Robert is aiming for, it's probably right to be diplomatic. For many people, that is probably the biggest difference between us. I tend to say things without thinking them through. If it feels right, I'll say it. But our kid will invariably take two steps backwards and have a little think about it before responding. And that makes him a better diplomat than I'll ever be.

It's funny, but people sometimes mix us up. Occasionally I'll be greeted at functions with the words 'Hello, Bobby,' and I smile. I used to wonder if people

called him Jack – and if they did, how he reacted.
Recently I found out that it happens to him, too.
Strange, really. So alike on the outside, and yet so
different inside . . .

JACK CHARLTON – THE PLAYER

Leeds United Debut: 25 April 1953 at Elland Road v Doncaster Rovers in Division Two. The match finished 1–1 and Jack wore number five. He finished the season with just this one appearance.

1953/54: no appearances for Leeds.

1954/55: he played just one game on the 28 August 1954 at Elland Road v Lincoln City and again wore number five, the match finished 3–2 to Lincoln City.

1955/56: he played 34 League games – no goals.

1956/57: he played in 21 League games – no goals. Jack also played in the FA Cup at Elland Road v Cardiff City, which City won 2–1.

1957/58: he played in 40 of the 42 League games plus the club's only FA Cup game against Cardiff City.

1958/59: he played in 39 of the 42 League games and scored his first goal for the club – v Blackburn Rovers at Elland Road on 11 April in a 2–1 win. Jack also played in the FA Cup match at Luton which Leeds lost 5–1.

1959/60: he played 41 of the 42 League games, scoring three goals, plus the FA Cup game against Aston Villa.

1960/61: he played in 41 of the 42 League games scoring seven goals. Jack managed two goals in successive matches: 3 April at Scunthorpe (one a penalty) and five days later at home to Swansea in the 2–2 draw. He played in all four FA

Cup games and scored at Southampton in the 5–4 defeat in the Fourth Round. Jack wore the number nine shirt six times in this season.

1961/62: Jack scored nine goals in his 34 League appearances – two goals coming against Walsall on 25 November in a 4–1 win. A further five domestic cup appearances (three goals).

1962/63: he made 38 League appearances (two goals – one a penalty v Derby County on 2 March) plus four domestic cup appearances (two goals).

1963/64: he made 25 League appearances (three goals) plus two domestic cup appearances.

1964/65: he made 39 League appearances (nine goals) including two against Burnley on 15 March in a 5–1 win. Jack also played in all eight FA Cup games (including the Wembley final v Liverpool) and scored one goal v Everton in the Fourth Round replay. Two further appearances were made in the League Cup.

1965/66: he made 40 League appearances scoring six goals, including two against Leicester City on 12 March in a 3–2 win. He made a further three appearances in domestic cup games plus eleven games in the Inter-Cities Fairs Cup (scored two goals). Jack's first club game in Europe was against Torino at Elland Road; Leeds won 2–1.

1966/67: he played in 28 League games (five goals) plus a further ten domestic cup games (two goals). Jack played in seven Inter-Cities Fairs Cup games including both legs of the final, which Leeds lost 2–0 on aggregate to Dinamo Zagreb.

1967/68: he played 34 League games (five goals) plus a further nine domestic cup games (two goals). He also played in eleven of the twelve Inter-Cities Fairs games – including both legs of the final, which Leeds won 1–0 on aggregate over Ferencvaros. He scored against Hibernian in the away match on 10 January.

1968/69: he played in 41 League games (three goals) plus four domestic cup games. He played in a further seven Inter-Cities Fairs Cup games (four goals, including both of the goals in a 2–0 win at Elland Road v Napoli).

1969/70: he played 32 League games (three goals) plus a further eleven domestic cup games (two goals). In the FA Cup this season, Jack played in the Cup final and the Cup final replay v Chelsea. He actually scored in the match at Wembley Stadium.

1970/71: he played 41 League games (six goals) plus a further five domestic cup games. In the Inter-Cities Fairs Cup, Jack played ten games (three goals) including the two-legged final against Juventus which Leeds won on the 'away goal' rule.

1971/72: he played 41 League games (five goals). Jack played in nine domestic cup games – including the FA Cup final against Arsenal at Wembley, he scored in the Sixth Round tie against Tottenham Hotspur at Elland Road.

1972/73: he played 18 League games (three goals) plus five domestic cup appearances (one goal). He also played in two European Cup Winners Cup matches. On 28 April 1973 at Southampton, Leeds lost 3–1; Jack pulled off his Leeds United shirt for the last time.

SUMMARY

LEAGUE APPEARANCES	GOALS	DOMESTIC CUP APPEARANCES	GOALS	EUROPEAN APPEARANCES	GOALS	LEEDS UNITED SEASO
1952/53	1	-				
1953/54	-					
1954/55	1	-				
1955/56	34	-				Promoted
1956/57	21	-	1	-		
1957/58	40	-	1	-		
1958/59	39	1	1	-		
1959/60	41	3	1	-		Relegated
1960/61	41	7	4	1		
1961/62	34	9	5	3		
1962/63	38	2	4	2		
1963/64	25	3	2	-		Promoted
1964/65	39	9	10	1		FA Cup Finalists League Runners-up
1965/66	40	6	3	-	11	2	League Runners-up
1966/67	28	5	10	2	7	-	Inter-Cities Fairs Cup Finalists
1967/68	34	5	9	2	11	1	League Cup Winners Inter-Cities Fairs Cup Winners
1968/69	41	3	4	-	7	4	League Champions
1969/70	32	3	11	2			League Runners-up FA Cup Finalists
1970/71	41	6	5	-	10	3	League Runners-up Inter-Cities Fair Cup Winners
1971/72	41	5	9	1			League Runners-up FA Cup Winners
1972/73	18	3	5	1	2	-	FA Cup Finalists E C W Cup Finalists

JACK CHARLTON'S AFFAIR WITH ENGLAND

10 April 1965	v	Scotland	Wembley	2-2		
5 May 1965	v	Hungary	Wembley	1-0		
9 May 1965	v	Yugoslavia	Belgrade	1-1		
12 May 1965	v	West Germany	Nuremberg	1-0		
16 May 1965	v	Sweden	Gothenberg	2-1		
2 October 1965	v	Wales	Cardiff	0-0		
20 October 1965	v	Austria	Wembley	2-3		
10 November 1965	v	Northern Ireland	Wembley	2-1		
8 December 1965	v	Spain	Madrid	2-0		
5 January 1966	v	Poland	Everton	1-1		
23 February 1966	v	West Germany	Wembley	1-0		
2 April 1966	v	Scotland	Glasgow	4-3		
4 May 1966	v	Yugoslavia	Wembley	2-0		
26 June 1966	v	Finland	Helsinki	3-0	1 goal	
3 July 1966	v	Denmark	Copenhagen	2-0	1 goal	
5 July 1966	v	Poland	Chorzow	1-0		
11 July 1966	v	Uruguay	Wembley	0-0	World Cu	
16 July 1966	v	Mexico	Wembley	2-0	World Cu	
20 July 1966	v	France	Wembley	2-0	World Cu	
23 July 1966	v	Argentina	Wembley	1-0	World Cu	
26 July 1966	v	Portugal	Wembley	2-1	World Cu	
30 July 1966	v	West Germany	Wembley	4-2	World Cu	
22 October 1966	v	Northern Ireland	Belfast	2-0	ECq	
2 November 1966	v	Czechoslovakia	Wembley	0-0		
16 November 1966	v	Wales	Wembley	5-1	ECq 1 goal	
15 April 1967	v	Scotland	Wembley	2-3	ECq 1 goal	
21 October 1967	v	Wales	Cardiff	3-0	ECq	
3 April 1968	v	Spain	Wembley	1-0	ECq	
15 January 1969	v	Romania	Wembley	1-1	1 goal	
12 March 1969	v	France	Wembley	5-0		
7 May 1969	v	Wales	Wembley	2-1		
5 November 1969	v	Holland	Amsterdam	1-0		
10 December 1969	v	Portugal	Wembley	1-0	1 goal	
14 January 1970	v	Holland	Wembley	0-0		
11 June 1970	v	Czechoslovakia	Guadalajara	1-0	World Cu	

(ECq – European Championship qualifier)

383

JACK CHARLTON IN THE MANAGER'S CHAIR

MIDDLESBROUGH
Appointed 7 May 1973. Resigned 21 April 1977

	LEAGUE GAMES	WON	DRAWN	LOST	HONOURS
1973/74	42	27	11	4	Promotion
1974/75	42	18	12	12	-
1975/76	42	15	10	17	-
1976/77	42	14	13	15	-

SHEFFIELD WEDNESDAY
Appointed 8 October 1977. Resigned 27 May 1983

	LEAGUE GAMES	WON	DRAWN	LOST	HONOURS
1977/78	36	15	11	10	-
1978/79	46	13	19	14	-
1979/80	46	21	16	9	Promotion
1980/81	42	17	8	17	-
1981/82	42	20	10	12	-
1982/83	42	16	15	11	-

MIDDLESBROUGH
Appointed 28 March 1984. Resigned 2 June 1984

	LEAGUE GAMES	WON	DRAWN	LOST	HONOURS
1983/84	9	3	3	3	-

NEWCASTLE UNITED
Appointed 14 June 1984. Resigned 13 August 1985

	LEAGUE GAMES	WON	DRAWN	LOST	HONOUR
1984/85	42	13	13	16	-

REPUBLIC OF IRELAND
Appointed 7 February 1986. Resigned 21 January 1996

		GAMES	WON	DRAWN	LOST
World Cup		29	13	11	5
European Championship		28	12	10	6
Friendly		36	21	9	6
Total		93	46	30	17

World Cup

14 September 1988	v	Northern Ireland	Belfast	0–0	
16 November 1988	v	Spain	Seville	0–2	
8 March 1989	v	Hungary	Budapest	0–0	
26 April 1989	v	Spain	Dublin	1–0	
28 May 1989	v	Malta	Dublin	2–0	
4 June 1989	v	Hungary	Dublin	2–0	
11 October 1989	v	Northern Ireland	Dublin	3–0	
15 November 1989	v	Malta	Valetta	2–0	
11 June 1990	v	England	Cagliari	1–1	Finals
17 June 1990	v	Egypt	Palermo	0–0	Finals
21 June 1990	v	Holland	Palermo	1–1	Finals
25 June 1990	v	Romania	Genoa	0–0	Finals
				Won 5–4 on Penalties	
30 June 1990	v	Italy	Rome	0–1	Finals
26 May 1992	v	Albania	Dublin	2–0	
9 September 1992	v	Latvia	Dublin	4–0	
14 October 1992	v	Denmark	Copenhagen	0–0	
18 November 1992	v	Spain	Seville	0–0	
31 March 1993	v	Northern Ireland	Dublin	3–0	
28 April 1993	v	Denmark	Dublin	1–1	
26 May 1993	v	Albania	Tirana	2–1	
9 June 1993	v	Latvia	Riga	2–0	
16 June 1993	v	Lithuania	Vilnius	1–0	
8 September 1993	v	Lithuania	Dublin	2–0	
13 October 1993	v	Spain	Dublin	1–3	
17 November 1993	v	Northern Ireland	Belfast	1–1	
18 June 1994	v	Italy	New York	1–0	Finals
24 June 1994	v	Mexico	Orlando	1–2	Finals
28 June 1994	v	Norway	New York	0–0	Finals
1 July 1994	v	Holland	Orlando	0–2	Finals

European Championship

Date		Opponent	Venue	Score	
10 September 1986	v	Belgium	Brussels	2–2	
15 October 1986	v	Scotland	Dublin	0–0	
18 February 1987	v	Scotland	Glasgow	1–0	
1 April 1987	v	Bulgaria	Sofia	1–2	
29 April 1987	v	Belgium	Dublin	0–0	
28 May 1987	v	Luxembourg	Luxembourg	2–0	
9 September 1987	v	Luxembourg	Dublin	2–1	
14 October 1987	v	Bulgaria	Dublin	2–0	
12 June 1988	v	England	Stuttgart	1–0	Final
15 June 1988	v	USSR	Hanover	1–1	Fina
18 June 1988	v	Holland	Gelsenkirchen	0–1	Fina
17 October 1990	v	Turkey	Dublin	5–0	
14 November 1990	v	England	Dublin	1–1	
27 March 1991	v	England	Wembley	1–1	
1 May 1991	v	Poland	Dublin	0–0	
16 October 1991	v	Poland	Poznan	3–3	
13 November 1991	v	Turkey	Istanbul	3–1	
7 September 1994	v	Latvia	Riga	3–0	
12 October 1994	v	Liechtenstein	Dublin	4–0	
16 November 1994	v	Northern Ireland	Belfast	4–0	
29 March 1995	v	Northern Ireland	Dublin	1–1	
26 April 1995	v	Portugal	Dublin	1–0	
3 June 1995	v	Liechtenstein	Eschen	0–0	
11 June 1995	v	Austria	Dublin	1–3	
6 September 1995	v	Austria	Vienna	1–3	
11 October 1995	v	Latvia	Dublin	2–1	
15 November 1995	v	Portugal	Lisbon	0–3	
13 December 1995	v	Holland	Liverpool	0–2	

INDEX

343, 358, 365
Horn, Leo 92
Hornsby, Brian 204, 210
Houghton, Ray 247, 249,
   253, 264, 272, 280, 289,
   293, 298, 327, 351, 354
Hughes, John 137
Hungary 101–2, 288, 294–5
Hunt, Roger 91, 107
   World Cup final 118
   World Cup matches 110,
      114
   World Cup warm-up tour
      108
Hunter, Norman 81–2, 85,
   90, 96, 134, 159
Hurst, Geoff 107, 125, 126
   1966 World Cup final
      116–19
   1966 World Cup matches
      112, 114
   1970 World Cup 154,
      157
Hutchinson, Ian 137, 138
Hyland, Michael 367–8

Iceland 252, 254
Ipswich 98, 204
Ireland
   1988 European
      championship 270–84
   1990 World Cup 288,
      302–20
   game plan 251–4
   Italia '90 304
   partying 265
   Sean South story 286–7
   supporters 278, 298, 304,
      351, 357, 363, 370

v Albania 332–4
v Austria 365
v Belgium 262–3, 266
v Bulgaria 266, 267
v Czechoslovakia 255
v Denmark 241
v Egypt 307
v England 224, 279–81,
   304–7, 326
v Germany 344
v Holland 283, 309, 343,
   358, 365
v Hungary 290, 294–5
v Iceland 252, 254
v Italy 317, 351–2
v Latvia 331, 334
v Lichtenstein 365
v Lithuania 334
v Luxembourg 266–7
v Malta 294–5, 298–9
v Mexico 253–6
v Northern Ireland
   287–9, 297–8, 331,
   335–6
v Norway 357
v Poland 327–8
v Romania 311
v Scotland 264–5
v Soviet Union 282
v Spain 288–93, 331,
   334–5
v Turkey 303, 326, 328
v Uruguay 249
v Wales 247
v West Germany 295–7
v Yugoslavia 275
Vatican visit 315–16
Italia '90 300–20
Italy 317, 351–2

393

397

A SELECTION OF SPORTS TITLES AVAILABLE FROM TRANSWORLD

THE PRICES SHOWN BELOW WERE CORRECT AT THE TIME OF GOING TO PRESS. HOWEVER TRANSWORLD PUBLISHERS RESERVE THE RIGHT TO SHOW NEW RETAIL PRICES ON COVERS WHICH MAY DIFFER FROM THOSE PREVIOUSLY ADVERTISED IN THE TEXT OR ELSEWHERE.

☐ 25267 7 **CHRIS BOARDMAN'S COMPLETE**
BOOK OF CYCLING (Hardback) *Chris Boardman* **£17.99**
☐ 14519 X **JACK CHARLTON:**
THE AUTOBIOGRAPHY *Jack Charlton* **£6.99**
☐ 14003 1 **CLOUGH: THE AUTOBIOGRAPHY** *Brian Clough* **£5.99**
☐ 04747 8 **AT THE MERCY OF**
THE WINDS (Hardback) *David Hempleman-Adams* **£17.99**
☐ 14688 9 **THE GREAT NUMBER TENS** *Frank Keating* **£7.99**
☐ 14758 3 **BOYCS: THE TRUE STORY** *Leo McKinstry* **£7.99**
☐ 99631 9 **SUMMERS WILL NEVER**
BE THE SAME *Christopher Martin-Jenkins & Pat Gibson* **£6.99**
☐ 04901 2 **BRADMAN'S BEST (Hardback)** *Roland Perry* **£18.99**
☐ 25230 8 **STEVEN REDGRAVE'S COMPLETE**
BOOK OF ROWING (Hardback) *Steven Redgrave* **£20.00**
☐ 99787 0 **GREG NORMAN: THE BIOGRAPHY** *Lauren St John* **£6.99**
☐ 14552 1 **DICKIE: A TRIBUTE**
TO UMPIRE HAROLD BIRD *ed. Brian Scovell* **£6.99**

All Transworld titles are available by post from:

Bookpost, P.O. Box 29, Douglas, Isle of Man IM99 1BQ

Credit cards accepted. Please telephone 01624 836000,
fax 01624 837033, Internet http://www.bookpost.co.uk or
e-mail: bookshop@enterprise.net for details.

Free postage and packing in the UK. Overseas customers allow
£1 per book (paperbacks) and £3 per book (hardbacks).